D1277574

Conversations With Visionary Leaders

With contributing authors

Barbara Corcoran

Gary & Carolyn Norris

Mark Morrell

McKay Matheson

David Nahm

Mike Driggers

Sharon Wahlig

Susan Bond Ross

Teresa R. Martin

Wylene Benson

Kevin Wallace & Carolyn Johnson

Tracy & LaVieve Roberts

Dean Demos

Sam Prentice

Kevin Clayson

Helen verDuin Palit

Jonathan Jaussi

Marci Lock

Mykola Latansky

Paul Novin

D.U. Publishing
www.dupublishing.com

Warning—Disclaimer

ISBN: 978-0-9785802-2-3

Contents

Introduction

What does it take to succeed as an entrepreneur? Over the years I have come to the conclusion that the best way to get an answer to that question is to ask someone who knows. While it sounds simple, that is exactly what we did with this book. *Entrepreneur on Fire: Conversations with Visionary Leaders* is a compilation of real conversations where entrepreneurs were asked about their journeys in business and life. While each of these individuals shares a love for entrepreneurship, they come from all walks of life and have diverse business backgrounds. Some are *New York Times* best-selling authors or television celebrities, while others are just like you and me. Each has experienced success and has a message to share. If you pay close attention you will discover similar patterns and principles, within each conversation, that you can apply to achieve results in your own ventures. So, please join me as I interview these inspiring individuals.

Sincerely,

Levi McPherson

Inspiring Millions

Barbara Corcoran

Barbara Corcoran's credentials include straight D's in high school and college and twenty jobs by the time she turned twenty-three. It was her next job that would make her one of the most successful entrepreneurs in the country when she took a $1000 loan to start The Corcoran Group. As one of the "Sharks" on ABC's hit TV show, *SHARK TANK*, Barbara has ponied up her own money and invested in twenty-two businesses, competing to make those deals for all to see, then shepherding them to success. Her newest book, *SHARK TALES*, takes you behind the scenes of her life and business and her 'seen on TV' venture capitalism. Barbara is famously brash and blunt, bold and courageous, and a brilliant identifier of opportunity and talent (often invisible to others).

Visit her website at:
www.barbaracorcoran.com

John Lee Dumas:

At the age of 23, Barbara took a $1,000 loan to start The Corcoran Group. She parlayed that loan into a $5 billion real estate business, which she sold in 2001 for $66 million.

I've given Fire Nation a little overview, but could you tell us more about your business and what you have going on right now.

Barbara Corcoran:

Well, I got that very lucky break that started me on the road to riches, so to speak, although it didn't come so quickly, I must say. But, I did get a $1,000 loan from a boyfriend. I know that you're not supposed to do that, but I did. That's how I actually got started in the real estate business.

John Lee Dumas:

That is just a great start to any entrepreneurial journey. Barbara, before we delve more into that, and we're definitely going to, we like to start every show off at Entrepreneur On Fire with a success quote. It gets that motivational ball rolling.

Barbara Corcoran:

Okay. So, the best thing that I have ever read is "You don't have to get it right, you just have to get it going." I like that quote because it really moves you off the box, and I'm like, "Oh, okay, let me just pick up the phone and get it going." That's usually the hardest part. After that, it takes on a life of its own, as you know.

John Lee Dumas:

That is so true. So, Barbara, we'd like to take this down to the ground level because this is about you. You're our spotlighted entrepreneur today. So, please share with us how you've actually applied this quote or this mentality to your life at some point.

Barbara Corcoran:

Well, when I sold Corcoran Group for $66 million, you would think that I should have been the happiest gal in town, and I was for about a week, particularly the day after the closing. However, the experience forced me to reinvent myself because even though I had the money in the bank, it seemed somehow that it didn't replace all the things that the business had brought to me personally. So, I decided that I'd go into the TV world as a TV talent and become an expert on real estate. I knew a bit more about it than most people out there did. I had great notoriety. But, no one returned my phone calls. I found out that my old rolodex was only good for the real estate brokerage business. It sure didn't help me in the TV business. Once in a while, someone would agree to meet with me. I'd pitch them my ideas, such as what I wanted to do for their network, their station, and the kind of segments that I had in mind. And, they would ask me, "What do you think my apartment is worth?" And, that's really why they invited me in.

John Lee Dumas:
[Laughs]

Barbara Corcoran:
So, it got very, very discouraging. And, for someone who had worked so hard to create such a clear success—I mean I couldn't argue with my own success—I found that I was feeling depressed, and I had a very hard time picking up the phone, getting ready for a presentation, and asking for the job. I found it mortifying, frankly. Then, I realized that I just wanted to have everything come out right. So that, I think, was the first time that I started practicing that quote. I picked up the phone, and I did something. I realized that you don't have to get it right. And, I do that still every day. I had a rough week last week. A number of the entrepreneurs that I had invested in were going through rough patches. But, then I decided to make a list of the projects and the problems. And, I just picked up the phone, not knowing the solutions, and talked to them.

So, if I have a list of say 15 things on my to do list, then I always do something different. I go through the whole list and rate them as A's, B's and C's based on which ones are likely to produce the biggest effect on my business. So, the A's are obviously the ones that have the biggest net on it if you attend to those first. But, let me tell you, I will often sit down and do two C's, and then I'll attack the A's that I don't want to do.

3

John Lee Dumas:
That's a perfect insight, Barbara. Thank you for clarifying that. It is a good idea to do something kind of fun at first in order to get that ball rolling…

That's a perfect lead in to our next topic, Barbara, and that is failure, or challenges, or obstacles.

Barbara Corcoran:
Oh, that I'm good at. You're with the expert here on failure. I'm really good at that one.

John Lee Dumas:
Well, you and every entrepreneur, Barbara, because as entrepreneurs, part of our journey is failure, and if we're not failing on some level, then we're really not being honest with ourselves as entrepreneurs. We're not pushing the envelope, and we're not stretching our limits. So, we need to be failing and making mistakes.

Barbara Corcoran:
I would walk a mile to avoid a failure and embarrassment, but they come anyway. They come and find you.

John Lee Dumas:
Have you learned from your failures, Barbara? If so, could you pick out one that would really be a valuable lesson to Fire Nation?

Barbara Corcoran:
Oh, I could give you a thousand. Every single great thing that happened to me in building my career was immediately on the heels of a terrible, embarrassing failure, every single time. I never got a big, whopping success unless I had gone through some trial of hell. It's not one way or the other. So, let me give you a few examples.

I had the idea to take all of the apartments and homes that we had for sale in New York City and put them on videotape. This was before the Internet.

I wanted to offer an alternative to a little spot ad in The New York Times or The Wall Street Journal. I spent my $77,000 in profit—the first year that I ever had a profit—and I blew it on my "HOT Homes on Tape." Well, of course, no one handed out the tapes, and you know why? My agents didn't want potential clients to see the next agent and how pretty she looked, and then decide to go with her instead. So, they sabotaged my efforts by doing nothing. And so, my "HOT Homes on Tape" venture was a dismal failure.

Then, when there was an Internet, I registered the Corcoran Group URL that next morning. We had the sales meeting that weekend and I announced, "We're now taking all of these listings into cyberspace." I didn't even know what that word meant, and I still can't state it, as you can hear. However, we told it to the salespeople as though it was part of the plan. Everybody thought that I was a genius all over again. I wasn't a genius. I was just covering up for my mistake. I never thought that I would do anything with this thing called the Internet. However, we had two sales out of London within that week. Well, all I did was take all my units that I had from "HOT Homes on Tape" and put them onto the Internet. Then, I registered all the URLs of my competitors in New York City, and they had to call me to ask for them back. But, that would have never happened if I wasn't trying to cover up an embarrassment. It just wouldn't happen. And, every single great thing that pushed my business ahead happened on the heels of failure.

I was lucky, and I was industrious enough to try to cover up my pain. However, I had no idea that that was going to be the best thing. So, I was lucky and persistent, but smart wasn't part of it.

John Lee Dumas:
What is the major lesson that you really pulled out of that failure?

Barbara Corcoran:
That there's great power in moving forward, whether you're moving in the right direction or not. I also learned the sense of making the right calls in business, as well as how to hire the right people, and how to put your right priorities forward. All these judgment calls are key to building a business, as you know. You have to be fairly savvy to make decent judgments. But, I think that it's so much more important to just make a judgment and move on with it.

John Lee Dumas:

You've already shared with us a light bulb that went off in your head with the Internet. But, you've had so many aha moments and light bulbs that have gone off. Can you share with Fire Nation one or two aha moments, and how you turned those moments into success?

Barbara Corcoran:

I remember sitting around feeling ready to take a gun and shoot one of my sales agents. Salespeople are not so easy to manage. They're a pain in the ass, and that also gives them their tremendous success as a salesperson. So, they're hard to live with, but they're great to the outside. They often have two personalities. They were whining because I wasn't advertising for them. Of course, I knew that I wasn't advertising for them because I had no money. I would have advertised for them if I had the money, but it was a terrible real estate market. Interest rates were at 18%.

I'm sitting around and thinking, okay, what else could I do? And, I decided to take the 11 sales that we had had for the year. We had 11 sales for the 12-month period among 14 agents. I added them all up, I divided by 11, and I decided that I would write a sales report. The Corcoran Report listed an average New York City apartment price of $54,400.

John Lee Dumas:
Right.

Barbara Corcoran:

Two weeks later, I open up The New York Times, and on the front page of the real estate section the title reads "New York City Prices Hit All Time Low." Carter Horsley, the reporter, wrote, "According to Barbara Corcoran, the President of The Corcoran Group, New York City prices have hit an all-time low at $54,400." I couldn't believe my eyes. It was like a miracle.

That was my aha moment because when I went to the office that afternoon, for the first time in my life, I heard one of our salespeople say to whoever was on the other end of the phone, "Oh, you've heard of us?" Awestruck was the salesman, John Beckman, and I realized that I had a new partner and it was called The New York Times. I started churning out so many reports, anything that I could think of. I churned out one report after another for the rest of my life, and the reason that I was paid $66 million for my business was because $44 million of it was in the brand, while $22 million was on production. If they had paid for my business based on how we were producing, then I was really entitled to a third of what I was paid. However, I was paid that hefty sum because I had discovered the magic of producing a statistical report, churning it out day in and day out to the press, and stealing the limelight from my competitors, which built my brand. That's how I did it. So, that was beyond an aha moment. That was like having God himself come down and bless me.

John Lee Dumas:
Such a powerful aha moment, and how you just used that to turn it into success is just inspiring, Barbara.

Barbara Corcoran:
The press never needs a story idea. What they need are statistics. No matter what industry you're in, what seems boring to you, if turned into statistics, makes you an expert and gives you notoriety. And, that's the name and game changer of building a brand.

John Lee Dumas:
It totally proves the point. It's extremely valuable advice. Barbara, have you had an I've made it moment?

Barbara Corcoran:
It was one year when I just couldn't believe it. I had over $60,000 in profits in one year, which was a lot. The business was medium-sized. And, I didn't expect it. I always spent the money about a mile before it even landed on my desk. But, when I realized that I had this wind-fall, I immediately went and got my mother and father a brand new car. They had never had a new car. To this day, that is still the most satisfying moment because I could actually pay somebody back.

John Lee Dumas:

Barbara, you have so many exciting things going on in your world right now. Can you just pull out one or two things that are just really exciting right now in what you're doing with your business?

Barbara Corcoran:

Well, what excites me the most is when I meet entrepreneurs that have tremendous potential. They typically become my new partners.

There's nothing more contagious than rubbing shoulders with someone who's dreaming, but also has the will and capacity as well as the ability to jump over problems to actually get there and to really make their dream come true. Being around people like that makes you smarter, makes your energy higher, and makes you feel satisfied.

John Lee Dumas:

Awesome! So, Barbara, before we launch into the last segment of the show, which is the Lightning Round, I just want to ask for my listeners because they are all such Shark Tank fans. I mean they crowd around their televisions at 8:00 PM every single Friday night. They refuse to go out. They are just eyes glued to the television. Can you just tell us something about Shark Tank that you think that fans might find really interesting or really appealing?

Barbara Corcoran:

Yes. Actually, what you don't see at home, and you should be aware that it happens, is that when the production staff sends the entrepreneur into the tank walking through that shark tunnel, they're always given the same marching orders. They're wired, and they have earpieces in so they could hear everything. But anyway, they're standing there and that's a lonely spot to sit in, but right before they enter they say, "Don't start your pitch until one of the sharks talks to you." They are pumped. They've been practicing their pitch, and they really want to do a good job. They're like ready to burst out so they run through that tank. They always have a cocky look. They are looking you straight in the eye, and they're feeling really good about themselves. They're dying to pitch. Then, nobody talks to them for a full five minutes.

John Lee Dumas:
Five minutes?!

Barbara Corcoran:
Yes, it's five minutes. Now, at home, you see them walking to the tank and someone asks a question.

John Lee Dumas:
Right away.

Barbara Corcoran:
Yes. But, what I see is somebody who's terrible under pressure or someone who's great under pressure, and what a great test that is. Do you know before they even open their mouth, I know who I'm out on. I just sort of come up with a reason why I can say on camera, "I'm out because..." Okay? But, the truth is that I know when I'm out right away because the guy takes his hand out of his pocket, then he's shifting, and he's no longer making eye contact. His eyes are going crossed, he's sweating the bullets, and his knees are juggling. I mean this is a guy that I'm going to give my money to. Is he going to make it to the finish line? I don't think so. Alright. So, that is like a dirty, nasty trick, but it works like a dream, and you know what it does for the production staff? It lets them have these giant cameras. They have these giant cameras that are like the size of an elephant that come within inches of the person's face. They try to record the sweat beads on the face. They're making TV after all. So, it's a lot of pressure for those poor entrepreneurs, and it is no wonder when they start talking that sometimes they don't have a voice right away, or that it takes them a while to get their ego back up, but it's a great trick. It is mean, but it works really well.

John Lee Dumas:
Barbara, that is so fascinating. Thank you so much for sharing that with us. That is just something that people are going to take to the bank that's going to change the way that they watch Shark Tank from this point forward.

Barbara Corcoran:
You're going to feel sorry for every entrepreneur.

John Lee Dumas:
Every single one.

Barbara Corcoran:
Yes. Every pitch that you hear at home, we're usually listening to the pitch for 45 minutes to an hour-and-a-half, which is of course slimmed down to what? Five to eight minutes, I think.

John Lee Dumas:
Yes.

Barbara Corcoran:
Don't go on Shark Tank.

John Lee Dumas:
So, Barbara, I want to be incredibly respectful of your time because you're being so generous with Fire Nation. So, we're going to move on, unfortunately, to the last segment. We're going to enter the Lightning Round.

This is where I get to ask you a series of questions, and you can come back at us, Fire Nation, with amazing and mind-blowing answers. Does that sound like a plan?

Barbara Corcoran:
Okay.

John Lee Dumas:
What was holding you back from becoming an entrepreneur?

Barbara Corcoran:
Nothing at all, I have to say. My dad was fired every six months from his job as a printing press foreman, and he had 10 kids to feed. I mean that he'd come home from work early, and we knew that he was fired. He was like our John Wayne. We'd tell him, "Hey, Dad, were

you fired?" and he'd tell us all the story. We loved it. But, my mother didn't. She had to feed the kids, right? So, we were raised by a guy who should've been an entrepreneur.

John Lee Dumas:
Absolutely!

Barbara Corcoran:
He was arrogant. Talented, but arrogant, and he had to feed 10 kids. So, that wasn't an option. But you know? Everyone in my family grew up to be an entrepreneur. Every single one of us started our own business, I think because he was a perfect walking and talking example of insubordination. You know what's great about coming from a poor family? You're not trying to please your parents. You have no pressure. You didn't have to go to college if you don't want to or whatever. You have nothing to lose and nowhere to go but up.

John Lee Dumas:
I hear you. What is the best business advice that you ever received?

Barbara Corcoran:
Well, all of my business advice came from my mother who never worked a day in her life. She knew nothing about business, but what she had is enormous common sense, and she raised 10 kids on a shoestring budget. She was the most organized and motivating person that you will ever meet.

Once, I was complaining about competing against a Dolly Parton type waitress at the Fort Lee Diner. My mother suggested that I braid my hair. She said, "If you don't have big breasts, then why don't you put ribbons on your pigtails or braids or something?" I braided my hair and put on red ribbons, and that's what got Ramon Simone to sit at my counter. That was the best advice because if I hadn't met him that night, then he may not have given me a ride home, and he may not have given me the $1,000 to start my business. So, that was great marketing advice. You should always play up the assets that you have, and forget about what you don't have. I think that I've used that successfully with all of my entrepreneurs, and of course with my own business by trying to make the most of what I've got there with a marketing gimmick.

John Lee Dumas:
What do you regret doing or not doing at some point in your journey? And, what lessons did you learn from that?

Barbara Corcoran:
I would say that my only regret was when my boyfriend left me. My boyfriend and business partner, Ramon Simone, with accents on both names, left me and married my secretary. I just couldn't believe it. I was raising his three kids. I thought that we were the item. We had been together seven years, I guess.

John Lee Dumas:
Yes.

Barbara Corcoran:
It was the seven-year itch. But, when he left to marry Tina, I stayed in the business. He owned a 51% share, and he told me that I couldn't fire Tina. He was the controlling partner. He was right. But, it was a heartbreaker for me to work every day with someone who just used to be my secretary. Now, she's Mrs. Simone, and at the time, I felt ashamed of myself. Rejection is not an easy thing in love.

John Lee Dumas:
Of course.

Barbara Corcoran:
But, I stayed with that for over a year, and I accepted that situation, until one day I walked in and said, "We're ending this business. Now let me tell you how we're going to do it." We divvied it up just like a football draw. He picked the best salesperson, and I picked the next. It was fair. I moved out, and he stayed. But, I'm embarrassed that I took so long to wake up on that when I should've said, "No, this is

not acceptable." But, I didn't have the confidence. He had found me in my little town. He had discovered me. He had told me that I was smart. He had given me the $1,000. So, a lot of my confidence rode on that card. So, that's my excuse, but it is not an excuse really because I should've just said, "Oh, really? I'm out of here, baby!" But, I didn't know that the salespeople would follow me. I didn't know that I had the power that I had. You tend to undermine that if you're self-effacing, and it can be very dangerous if you let it get in your way of making needed changes. Sadly, for me, I was a slow changer on that one, and I should not have been.

John Lee Dumas:
Powerful! Barbara, besides the two phenomenal entrepreneurs that you've mentioned, which entrepreneur that you've invested in excites you the most right now?

Barbara Corcoran:
This is like asking a mother who her favorite child is, and they're all like my children. I don't want to tell you. So, why don't I add to your list so that I won't get in trouble because I love any entrepreneur who has the energy and the desire. But, I have Daisy Cakes. She is an amazing human being. She is a terrific promoter. She deserves her success.

I have to say that I admire Tiffany Krumins, who is the inventor of Eva the Elephant, because it's a medicine dispenser that she invented to make kids who have AIDS take their medicines 18 times a day. I admire her because after she did that, she came down with cancer and pulled that business out from under a tent in a hospital room where she was in bed for over 14 months.

John Lee Dumas:
So, I'm going to change it up just a little bit here. If you could recommend one book to Fire Nation, what would it be?

Barbara Corcoran:
I would say *"How to Win Friends and Influence People."*

John Lee Dumas:
Yes, Dale Carnegie.

Barbara Corcoran:
Can I tell you, it doesn't get old somehow. It's such common sense. It's all about people skills. A business really has everything to do with people. How well you work with people, what kind of teams you build, how you get people on your side, how to persuade people, and how to really care about the quality because you don't want to disappoint your customers. It's all about the people, and that book is a great one about telling you how to influence people.

John Lee Dumas:
You're so right. It's so great to reread. For three months after you read that, you are going to act differently because you see how your actions are mirrored by the people that you're talking to.

Barbara Corcoran:
Yes. Do you know what the second best business book in the entire world is after that one? It would have to be my book, *"Shark Tales"* [Laughs].

John Lee Dumas:
I love it!

Barbara Corcoran:
Of course, I'm a self-promoter. I don't know if it's the second best book, but that one I've read 500 times because I had to write the damn thing and edit it 5 million times, okay? But, I do get phenomenal feedback on it. I think honestly that I get more feedback on that than I do on Shark Tank because I think that it touches people in a certain way.

John Lee Dumas:
Wonderful! Well, I'm going to link that up in the show notes front and center.

Barbara Corcoran:
Don't bother! I only make 50¢ a copy. It's not worth it.

John Lee Dumas:
Oh, you need to publish that on Amazon. You'll make $7 a copy.

Barbara Corcoran:
Really? Then, why did I go to Penguin and Putnam?

John Lee Dumas:
We'll talk.

Barbara Corcoran:
Is that true? That's upsetting me. You're too late on that advice.

John Lee Dumas:
You get 70% of every sale that you make on Amazon Publishing. That's why Tim Ferriss just came out with "The 4-Hour Chef" solely on Amazon Publishing. He's selling for $9.99, and he makes $6.99 on every sale.

Barbara Corcoran:
Well, guess what, honey, I love you now.

John Lee Dumas:
We're going to move on to the last question of the interview. It's my favorite. It's kind of difficult. So, you should take your time, digest it, and then come back at Fire Nation with an amazing answer.

Barbara Corcoran:
Oh God, the pressure!

John Lee Dumas:
Imagine that you woke up tomorrow morning, Barbara, in a brand new world, identical to earth, but you knew nobody. You still have all the experience and knowledge that you currently have right now. Your food and shelter is taken care of, but all you have is a laptop and $500. What do you do in the next seven days?

Barbara Corcoran:
500 bucks and a laptop, and you don't know anyone? Well, I would work

on the missing piece, which isn't the money. $500 is still $500. It isn't the access, which would be the laptop. You have access. I would work on finding new people. I'd start a blog on anything. If there were people who wanted to do real estate, then I could do that. If I wanted to do small business, then I'd do that. I'd just start writing a blog with the sole purpose of trying to find followers. Now, that might not sound like a business plan, but once I had enough people reading my blog, then I'd figure out what to do so that they would be willing to follow me [Laughs].

John Lee Dumas:
[Laughs]

Barbara Corcoran:
If you have the people who are listening to you, then it's really like a question of filling in the blank, and then you also can talk back again. Like, "Hey, what do you need help with?" You're going to find probably an embarrassment of 12 different new businesses within that communication, but you're not going to find anything or even think of anything good if you don't have the people. So, yes, I would do this definitely. And, with the 500 bucks, I'd probably go out and buy myself a new outfit so I'd feel really nice.

John Lee Dumas:
Barbara, you've just given us some great, actionable advice. You've given us great, actionable advice this entire interview, and we are all the better for it. Please give Fire Nation one parting piece of guidance, and then share with us how we can connect with you.

Barbara Corcoran:
I'm a workaholic, no doubt, and I love it. I don't know why they call it work for me. But, you should go to your calendar right now and cross out the days that you're going on vacation, even if you have nowhere to go.

I vacation every fifth week like clockwork. You can't find me, and you can't reach me. You know why? Because I come back a better leader, a better businessperson, a better person, a better mom, and a better wife. And, it makes a big difference, believe me.

John Lee Dumas:
Barbara, how can we connect with you?

Barbara Corcoran:
You can connect with me on Facebook, and through email, Barbara@barbaracorcoran.com.

John Lee Dumas:
Barbara, thank you for being so generous with your time. I know that you don't like to play favorites, but I'm going to play a favorite. This is my 123rd interview, 123.

Barbara Corcoran:
Wow!

John Lee Dumas:
And, you are my favorite interviewee.

Barbara Corcoran:
John, I'm going to check your other tapes and see how many times you said that. I don't believe you.

John Lee Dumas:
Zero times, Barbara.

Barbara Corcoran:
[Laughs]

John Lee Dumas:
123 interviews, and zero other times. You are my favorite.

Barbara Corcoran:
You had better get better interviews then. That's all I have to say.

John Lee Dumas:
Thank you so much for sharing your journey with Fire Nation.

Gary & Carolyn Norris

Gary and Carolyn know what it's like to face challenges as entrepreneurs. They have experienced both success and failure more than once, including a business partnership going south, laying off employees, closing the doors of a once successful endeavor, losing three homes to foreclosure and finding themselves with over $200,000 in debt while refusing to declare bankruptcy. As a result of their financial reset, their marriage hung on by a thread and their precious daughter tried to "check out" of life, but they knew they had to "Get Their Rebel On" and create something different; that's just what they did! Those were trying times, but against all odds, they rebuilt their family, their marriage, their business, and their brand, "Rebel Entrepreneur." They have learned how to survive and then thrive... Now, they spend their time helping others do the same!

Gary is the author of *The ABC's of Success* and owner and host of "*The Rebel Entrepreneur Radio Show*" at RebelBizRadio.com, which is a powerful real estate investing podcast which encompasses a mix of mindset, humor and empowered entrepreneurship! Gary has had the pleasure of featuring well known entrepreneurs such as the

CEO of the Og Mandino company and Dave Ramsey's business partner to the lesser known, but wildly successful and inspiring Rebel Entrepreneur's who are making a difference and moving the universe! A favorite guest that Gary would love to have on his podcast one day is the legendary Rebel Entrepreneur, Mr. Glenn Beck!

Carolyn is the President of Mindset Cashflow Solutions, Inc. and the author of From Victim to Victor. She is passionate about helping others successfully navigate through their challenges to create an EXTRAORDINARY life. Carolyn is a certified Life Success Consultant through Bob Proctor and has personally trained with him. She is also a Conscious Creator Facilitator for Strongbrook University. Carolyn has mentored and consulted groups—and individuals—ranging from small business owners to multi-millionaires. She founded the Strongbrook Women's Empowerment Group which provides a powerful environment to develop and share entrepreneurial skills and ideas. Additionally, Carolyn loves singing and is a skilled song writer. She recently released her first recorded song written by her and arranged by her brother Ted Baker.

Gary and Carolyn are highly sought after speakers. In addition to speaking at real estate investing and educational seminars, they speak to businesses, networking groups and schools on the power of proper mindset, motivation and of course, Rebel Entrepreneurship. Their passion is doing whatever it takes to help connect people to their purpose, to awaken the rebel within so that they can show up in life and make an incredible positive difference in the world.

They live in Orem, Utah and love spending time with their three children, including their happily married and very much alive daughter. When they aren't working or with family, they are most likely enjoying one of Utah's many mountain trails.

Contact: *reicwithgary@gmail.com*
             CarolynNorris1@gmail.com

Websites: *www.GetYourRebelOn.com*
             www.RebelBizRadio.com
             www.Victim-to-Victor.com
             www.TheRealEstateRebels.com

Levi:

All right, Gary and Carolyn. I know you promote breaking the status quo and you're definitely doing that going into business as a married couple and using your entrepreneurial skills to make a difference. You like to say that you're rebel entrepreneurs, and to start out, go ahead and just tell us what that means. What does it mean to be a rebel entrepreneur?

Gary:

We love that question. You know, it used to be bad to be called a rebel, like you were a menace to society, a rebel without a cause. Now, things are very different. Being a rebel means that you are willing to take a stand in the same way our Founding Fathers did for this great country. We urge Americans everywhere to recognize that if they are sick and tired of being sick and tired they can rise up, take responsibility and do something about it! Rebel entrepreneurism is all about having the courage to make your dreams actually happen instead of just waiting and wishing that they would. Being a rebel entrepreneur means continual dedication to being your very best self. It means being the incredible person you were meant to be, and in that process, blessing and enhancing many, many lives. In that journey, you will find an absolutely extraordinary life for yourself.

Levi:
Wonderful.

Carolyn:

This country is still an amazing land of opportunity. Americans need to stand firm in the belief that they create and control their own financial freedom and destiny. A rebel entrepreneur takes responsibility for that by going against the grain, not settling for mediocrity, being incredibly solution-oriented and thinking outside of the box. Gary and I educate people to recognize that trading dollars for hours will never create the exponential growth necessary for generating true wealth. A rebel entrepreneur differs from other entrepreneurs in that they don't just start a business on a whim to get away from a job. They are dedicated to taking the appropriate steps to insure success. They take time to effectively plan, create duplicable systems, take intelligent calculated risks, and persist through challenges. They are dedicated to providing others something of great value, thus enhancing many lives.

Being a rebel entrepreneur is an exciting adventure. It is a life fully lived. I think a lot of people settle for boring and mediocrity because they are afraid of the unknown. They are unwilling to embrace fear and risk. They are willing to sacrifice all for the sake of perceived security. The paradox is that once the decision is made to embrace fear and risk, what is left behind is one of the biggest risks of all – the risk of having the fantastic person you are on the inside never actually show up on the outside. I tell people, "If you're sick and tired of what the universe is dishing out to you, if it feels like it's you versus the universe when it comes to achieving your goals, you just need to rise up and make the universe move!!!"

Levi:

Absolutely. I believe that success leaves clues, and those clues are often embedded in personal stories. You are successful and your business is successful and you are doing it in a different way as a couple. I'd love to find out how you got started in business and working together.

Gary:

I've always had an entrepreneurial bug in me. I was 11 years old when I had my first paper route. I worked that for four years. When I was 14 years old, my dad opened my eyes to the wonderful world of old cars. We started buying and selling classic cars together. I was a child of the 80s and I would buy 1950s cars, as well as some 60s and some 40s. I would drive them for a while, fix them up a little, and sell them. I'd always make money doing it, and by the time I had graduated high school, I had flipped 25 cars. When Carolyn and I were first married, I even sold cars on the Internet, long before eBay existed. I loved it!

As an entrepreneur, I was always looking for an opportunity to hit a home run. Everyone wants to hit a home run in life. The problem is, sometimes while we go off on our quest to hit home runs, life actually passes you by and you miss out on all the singles, the doubles; all the good stuff.

That's what I was doing. I was doing my business ventures without my wife. I was doing them without my family. I was out trying to be entrepreneurial while life was passing me by. I was seldom engaged with my family along the way. Without realizing it, I was hurting my family, hurting my marriage, hurting my wife. Many people do that.

Fortunately for us, in 2008 we lost everything in a total financial reset. As part of that, we experienced embezzling business partners, losing homes to foreclosure, and even a kid that wanted to check out of life through suicide. I call these experiences fortunate because they caused us to wake up as a family. They were a powerful reminder that we wanted to create something different, something so much better.

We hunkered down deep and started digging ourselves out of the mess we were in. We took a stand. We said enough of this mediocre life, let's together create something great. My wife and I were finally on the same page. We were working as a team. Together, we were determined to conquer circumstances we would no longer put up with. It has been a powerful journey and that is why we love to help wake other people up to their own rebel opportunities.

Carolyn:

So many fabulous changes in our marriage occurred when we chose to be an entrepreneurial couple together. I'm so grateful that Gary had this spirit within him because I was not raised that way. My family taught me many great things, but they were not an entrepreneurial family. I did not get those kinds of ideas growing up.

Like many of us, I was taught to do well in school so that I could go to college and get a good job. I thought having a good job was where financial security in life came from. Now don't get me wrong, I think education is very important, but I would now challenge the idea that a good job is where financial security comes from. I think so many Americans are duped by that belief and yet, if you ask them how many people they know that have recently been fired or laid off, they could give you quite a lengthy list.

I think more and more people are waking up to the fact that when you're an entrepreneur you are probably not going to fire yourself. You don't have to worry about being downsized or laid off and you aren't waiting around for someone else to dictate your destiny. There are obviously some serious advantages to that, but it still took me a long time to really get onboard with what Gary was doing. There was a lot of friction and conflict in our marriage along the way, but once we figured out how to be entrepreneurs together as a team, that all changed. Since that time, we have experienced such amazing synergy between us, excitement in our work, and incredible healing in our marriage. That's one of the things that we love to share with people, because it's been such a phenomenal change for us.

Levi:

That's interesting that you put it that way, because usually in business, when we think about working with family, it's usually just an ongoing conflict instead of a healthy, positive experience like you're describing. It sounds to me like not only have you figured out a formula for succeeding in business, but you've also figured out a formula to move forward successfully in the most important relationship in your life. I would love to hear a little bit more about that discovery process and how that can benefit others.

Gary:

Sure. I'll touch on the formula that works for us in helping others in business and then perhaps Carolyn can address the formula that we have discovered works for us as a couple. Our mission, our goal, the reason we're even in this book and the reason we've branded ourselves the Rebel Entrepreneur, is that we want to help others find a system that works for them. A big part of our formula for success in business is matching people to opportunities that powerfully fit their needs. Zig Ziglar said, "You can have everything in life you want, if you will just help enough other people get what they want." I believe that is true. I believe that in business, when you focus on helping others get connected to opportunities that will truly serve them, you will find yourself being successful along the way. For people that don't know what it is they want in life, they just know they are looking for something different, we're here to help them reach their greatest potential. We help people get connected to moneymaking opportunities that create true, meaningful incomes and empowerment through financial wealth and financial wellness. One avenue that we use to do this is by connecting people to the best, tip of the spear, "done for you" real estate investment opportunities. We also connect people with estate planning, with setting up their business properly, with self-directing IRAs and 401Ks, with insurance plans, etc. To sum up our formula for business, we connect people to the best opportunities that help them create, manage, maintain and build their wealth.

Carolyn:
Our formula for working together as a couple in business involves both of us engaging in our work with a high level of passion, commitment, and respect for each other. This formula had its beginnings at the Strongbrook National Convention, the primary company we're affiliated with, about a year and a half ago. At that Convention, Gary received a $35,000 bonus check for his efforts in referring clients to the company. Gary is amazing! He's an amazing connector with people and I had been watching him build our business. I was kind of off and on with my support, not really sure if this entrepreneurial venture was going to be better than getting a "real job." Obviously, after experiencing a serious financial reset, $35,000 made a big impact on me. It really opened my mind to the possibility that there might be hope of getting back on our feet again financially. It was that hope that reignited a fire within me. Something seriously shifted in my mindset, and I realized that if our business and affiliation with this company had created an avenue of hope for me, perhaps as I engaged fully in our business, I could create that same kind of hope for others.

One of the thoughts that came to me as I was pondering the decision to become fully engaged in our business had to do with one of the main functions of our company. Strongbrook is expert at taking non-performing and underperforming assets and turning them into high-performing assets. For some reason, thoughts about that particular part of what our company does was really on my mind. Then, it hit me like a ton of bricks! Up to that point in our business, I had been participating like an underperforming asset. I realized that there was so much more inside of me to give. It was like I just woke up to the fact that I had the power to make a huge difference in the lives of so many for good. I made a huge decision right then that I was going to become a powerful asset, not only to my family and my country, but also to the company that had really helped get us back on our feet. From that day forward, I have joined Gary in our mutual passion for being financial liberators that deliver tangible hope and practical solutions to people. We have a passion for what we do, we are committed to serving and enhancing the lives of others, and we maintain mutual respect for each other as we work together; that is our formula.

Levi:
You talk about getting back on your feet and you mentioned earlier that at one point you both had lost everything. Yet, you were able to turn it around and generate a massive income for yourself. Then, turn around and do that for others. The question I have is for entrepreneurs that are reading this book, whether or not they're entrepreneurs that are trying to make it out there, they're already doing something or they're just entrepreneurs in their heart, but they haven't tasted success. Where do they start?

Gary:
That is an awesome question. One of my favorite quotes is, "You don't have to get it right; you just have to get it going." That's where you start. You start by taking action. If you have an idea, whatever that idea is, act on your idea. Keep in mind, you don't even need to have a business idea to be a rebel entrepreneur. In fact, I don't even recommend it! That's a bold statement, I know, but here's where I'm going with it. Many people we work with have no idea how or where to start their entrepreneurial journey, they just know that they are done living a life of mediocrity, they want to create change, and create it fast.

The quickest and best way to get started is by tapping into and leveraging an already existing business. A business that already has products and/or services, already has fulfillment, already has systems in place – your part is to market the system and let the system deliver your profit. This is exactly what we have done and what we have helped hundreds of other rebel entrepreneurs do as well. Our primary business is with Strongbrook, an 8-year-old, multi-million dollar company with integrity and with an entrepreneurial system already in place. Strongbrook is 100% in alignment with our goals, our dreams, and our vision as rebel entrepreneurs. It brings in hundreds of thousands of dollars in profit to us each year. The amazing thing is that our cost to "tap into the business" is only $240 per year.

Strongbrook works for us! We resonate with the company's ethics and their product line. Strongbrook is empowering people all over the country. Just last year alone, our efforts with Strongbrook had a $35 million dollar impact on the American economy. We plug people into systems like this, when they don't have something of their own to go do. But by all means, if you are reading this book and you want to go open up a business of your own or start your own entrepreneurial dream; do it. Again, remember, you don't have to get it right, you just have to get it going. What we love about that saying in regards to Strongbrook, is they've already got it going, we're just plugging people in and helping them create their own success. It works for us; it may work for you as well!

So here's our answer to people that say, "Where do I begin?" Begin today by taking action on your very first thought that would move you a step closer to your goals and continue moving in that direction and don't stop. Learn as you go. Every single person that's created anything of value has learned as they've gone along. I would dare say that the biggest mistake to a plan or an idea is waiting for that plan or idea to be a perfect. It will never happen. You don't reach perfection until you've gone through the trials and errors.

Carolyn:
Additionally, when you are in a financial reset like we were, and are in a bad spot financially, sometimes it feels like you've got so much debt over your head that you can't breathe. You feel trapped. Your problems seem so huge that it is hard to focus on anything else. When we lost everything, every moment of my life seemed to revolve around our debt and our disastrous finances and the pain and the struggle. It is easy to not know how to get out of that space when it feels so all consuming.

Fortunately, there is a way out. It may not be the most obvious way, but there is a way. When I really got passionately engaged in the idea of serving others and of making a huge positive difference in their lives it was amazing how, even though I still had so much financial debt over my head, the change in my thoughts was like night and day. My thoughts started being completely about how can I serve more? How can I be a better example? How can I get up earlier, so I can inspire my team? How can I lead them better? How can I think bigger? What ideas will help them to be successful in their life so they can feel empowered and have a fantastic year this year?

It was one of the biggest blessings in my life to have that mindset shift so that I could stop focusing on our negative situation and start focusing on creating something incredibly positive. My recommendation to anybody that wants to start tasting success is to put yourself and your troubles aside and just get out there and start figuring out an amazing solution for other people. If you'll do that, your troubles are going to go away pretty darn fast.

Levi:

That's awesome. I've actually encountered on more than one occasion the economic benefit of doing exactly, Carolyn, what you just described, which is instead of taking a self-centered approach, taking a social-centered approach. Looking outside of yourself and trying to create value. My experience is that the value always follows back.

A question that I always like to ask is about how no one succeeds in a vacuum and there are always individuals that you come along, that you have come across in your path to greatness, your path to success. Tell us a little bit about some of those individuals and the importance of those individuals in turning it around for yourself and then also for others that are trying to succeed in life.

Gary:

Okay, good question, by the way. I feel super strongly that everybody needs a coach. Everybody. Coaches have coaches. I look at Tiger Woods. Tiger Woods had a coach, yet he was the best in the world. He had a coach that helped him learn that he could be better if he changed his golf swing. He totally revamped his entire golf swing, and for a year went off the circuit while he relearned a new swing. He came back stronger than ever.

Every time I've had my greatest success in my business, I've also noticed that it's right when I've been putting myself through coaching and mentoring. Now, coaching and mentoring could be reading good books, right?

Levi:
Right.

Gary:
It also could be going out and hiring a business coach or a life coach or mentor, but surround yourself with them regardless of what you do, whether it's by reading their books, listening to their audios or paying them for actual mentorship. That has been a big key to our success. It's what I found has helped us reach peaks that we otherwise thought we could not reach. Carolyn, do you have anything you'd like to add to that?

Carolyn:
I think one of the greatest advantages of having a mentor or coach is that they can, like Gary was saying, take you places that you've never been. You've never thought in certain ways, you've never taken action in certain ways, you've never known how to lead in certain ways. They can open your mind to whole new possibilities and solutions. I appreciate the bigger thinking that I've been able to gain from all the mentors in our life.

One of Gary's first business coaches was Dave Blanchard. He's the CEO of the Og Mandino Company. He is an amazing man and taught us so much about giving, serving, love, and leadership. The inspiration and positive examples that you experience by surrounding yourself with the best people can have an incredible impact on your life.

Levi:
I definitely agree with the concept of finding inspiring individuals and then also, Gary you said something interesting, you said even books can

be mentors. I think the recurring theme in actually all the success conver-
sations that I've ever had is that change begins first as a mindset change.

There's a different process of thinking, and then, Carolyn what you
brought up on several points, actually leads into belief. You get new
knowledge, then you get new belief, and that redirects the path of your
actions. I believe that's really central to what I've been hearing from each
of you is that there is a way to change things, but you have to start with
your mindset.

You have to change your beliefs, then you have to change your pro-
cess of action, which is interesting, because I always teach people that if
you change your process you will change your outcome. I'm certain that
you've seen that over and over in your own experience and then in the
experience of the lives of those that you've been helping.

Could you share perhaps even an example from some people, an in-
dividual that really stands out that you knew through this process that
you're talking about?

Carolyn:
I had the opportunity to coach a lady a couple of years ago that had
lost her husband and her two sons in an airplane accident where one
of her sons was the pilot. Working with someone that had dealt with
so much pain and loss was an incredible experience for me and a
tender blessing in my life. It was a neat journey for us together. I was
able to help and mentor her because, although our struggles were
different, the challenges I had faced in my life had prepared me with
a deep empathy for what she was going through. My training as a life
coach helped me keep her focused on solutions for now and in the
future, so that she felt hope in her life regardless of the past.

I remember her asking me one time, "How do you get this? How
do you even understand the kind of emotional pain that I'm talking
about?" I have always had the gift of being very intuitive and she appreciated that. I think it is important as you work with people in any
situation to seek to understand where they're coming from. Not so
they continue to stay stuck where they are, but so you will know how
to best lead them to a better place in their life. Life is challenging, we
each have our own stories and as we conquer and rise above them

we are able to serve each other from a better perspective. It is the beautiful miracle of how we can each be a gift in each others' lives.

Levi:

We live in an achievement-based society, meaning that there's tons of information out there. It's usually directed toward making a change. We have access to all these things, but if you were to take someone and just give them a call to action, something they actually need to do and do right now if they want to turn their life around, what would that one call to action be?

Carolyn:

If you are a person that is serious about getting your life moving forward in a successful direction, one of the most important things you can do is get really connected with your why; figure out why you want to do whatever it is you want to do – the reason being that when you have an idea and you want to go out there and act on it, if you're not strongly connected with why you're even doing it, you will easily give up. The first obstacle that comes along is going to squelch you, because there's nothing emotionally driving you to keep you going. The rewards of being an entrepreneur are vast and many, but the challenges are vast and many as well. If you spend some time building a solid foundation of your why and your purpose and what really drives you, many obstacles will feel like small bumps in the road instead of huge road blocks. My biggest call to action would be to find out the real reason you even want to go on this journey.

Levi:

Gary, do you have anything to add to that?

Gary:

No, that's perfect, I love it.

Levi:

Right, I have to agree with you. In conclusion, I always like to find out that you're obviously doing something that you're very passionate about.

It's very fulfilling to you, but looking to the future, looking to what's on the next horizon, what type of legacy, at the end of the day, do you want to leave? What do you want to be written about what you're doing now? What do you want to be spoken about what you're doing now?

Carolyn:

I recently spoke at our National Convention about our journey from financial devastation, marital discord, severe issues with our kids, etc., to the extraordinary life that Gary and I are blessed with now. I titled my speech, "From Victim to Victor; a Strongbrook Fairytale." Ever since I made the determined decision to create the life of my dreams, it has truly felt like a fairytale. So many days since then have been filled with something amazing, something surreal, something absolutely fantastic occurring. My life now is such a huge contrast to what it was for so many years that I am deeply passionate about inspiring others. I want to motivate people that are in challenging situations to take their life back, to create the life they always wanted, and my platform, fairytalephenom.com and our couple platform getyourrebelon.com, are serving those needs. I love teaching people that they can create their own "happily ever after" as soon as they start showing up for themselves.

I went from having PTSD and severe depression to jumping out of bed so early one morning freed from those maladies. What made the difference is that I finally realized that I could make a difference. I could make a difference in my own life, my family's life, and the lives of so many others. I wake up now full of a driving passion to love, serve, create, and inspire the biggest tribe that I possibly can so that when I leave this life I will know that I gave it my all. I will know that I blessed as many as I could. I will know that making the effort to rise above my challenges was worth it because it gave me the beautiful opportunity to inspire others to reclaim their life and their destiny as well.

Gary:

Too bad you can't put her voice in the book, huh? You can tell from her passion that she speaks from her heart.

Levi:

Agreed.

Gary:

What kind of legacy do you want to leave is an interesting question. To me, the legacy someone wants to leave is often directly connected to their why. Your why does not need to be anything magnanimous. It doesn't need to be "feed the hungry in a poor third world country." It doesn't need to be "save all the children." Those are great why's, but your why needs to be something very personal to you. It needs to be something that emotionally moves you to do something great.

Your legacy can be as big or as small as you want it to be. My grandmother's entire goal when she died was to be able to leave $1,000 to each of her remaining children that were alive. That's all she had and she left it. She was so proud that she left this world with no debt to her children and they all had $1,000. Then there's other people who leave a legacy of feeding millions around the world. Whatever your legacy is, it's your legacy. You get to choose what it is, what you want it to be.

For me, I want to leave a legacy that includes impacting millions of people for the better. That is why we created getyourrebelon.com as a hub for rebel entrepreneurism. I want to know that we helped wake up America. I want to know that we helped many, many families get back on their feet financially. I want to know that we inspired entrepreneurs everywhere to rise up and get their rebel on; to take responsibility for their financial destinies. I want people to remember me as someone that lived with purpose and passion and that Carolyn and I together, made an incredibly positive impact on this world. To me, that is legacy.

Mark Morrell

Mark Morrell grew up in Orem, Utah. He and his wife, Kaylinn, work as Independent Business Developers for Strongbrook REIC and as the Diz Daddy. Mark currently lives in Salt Lake City with his wonderful family and they are always awaiting their next trip to the Magic Kingdom. For more information about Mark and the magical work that he is a part of, please visit *www.marklmorrell.com*

Levi:
You're kind of a Disney nut, which has translated into the way that you do business. As part of that, you hold to the mantra of pursuing big dreams. Just to start out: why don't you tell us a little bit about having big dreams and how it has impacted your journey of entrepreneurship.

Mark:
First of all, thank you so much for this opportunity. A Disney Nut is putting it lightly. I think I have a borderline unhealthy obsession or even an illness for which I do not want a cure. Ever since I was a little kid, I have absolutely loved going to Disneyland. Not that we went much, I grew up in Utah, but we went a few times. I just loved

the feeling I had when I was there—the sights, the sounds, and those incredible smells. I loved watching other people taking it all in. When I started college, I set a goal for myself—a dream—that I would some-day work for the place that I loved so much and help others experience it the way I always did. That was my ultimate dream.

After college, I entered into Walt Disney World's College Program. I spent about four months there and grew to love it almost as much as I loved Disneyland. However, I still had my dream of working for Disneyland. About two months into my experience, I had some fantastic leaders who came up to me and suggested I apply for the professional internship program there at Disney World.

I decided to give it a try. When I went to apply, I noticed that they actually had the same position open at Disneyland, so I applied for both and interviewed for both, was accepted to both, but my dream was my dream and I agreed to work for Disneyland. I was disappointed that I would not be able to work inside of the Park, but the Disneyland Hotel proved to be exactly what I needed. I went out there in January of 2007 and completed my management training and a month later, they hired me in full time.

I don't know how many people get to experience what I did. I was actually working for the place that I had dreamed about my entire life! However, I learned something rather quickly, dreams can change. 10 months after I moved there, I met the girl of my dreams who, soon after, became my wife and we kind of noticed that both of our dreams began to change. A situation arose with my father-in-law passing away and my mother-in-law needed help to maintain the family pool maintenance business. She came down to visit and asked us if we'd be willing to come up and run the business for her. It was an opportunity I never thought I would have—to be a business owner. We pondered and conversed and ultimately decided it was the right opportunity for us. We dropped everything and moved up to Northern California and I literally jumped right into a pool business. Not wanting to use an annoying pun or anything, but that's really what happened is we just jumped right in. It didn't take long for me to realize how unprepared I was to run a business and I learned through trial by fire. It was the best experience I could have had as an entrepreneur. There was a lot of mistakes made and lessons learned, but it was incredible.

What we noticed is that our new dream became that of freedom, of being in control of our own lives and destiny. That's what began to drive us. Every little pathway or step that we've taken has led us in the right direction and it has been really fun and exciting to be on this journey.

Levi:

I think most entrepreneurs will say that they discover their path at least as much as they pursue it. In your journey you had this dream to work for Disney, and then you started tasting a little bit of entrepreneurship. Talk to us just a little bit about finding your dreams.

Mark:

When my wife and I met, I was working for one of the biggest corporations in the world and she was teaching at a high school. I worked nights, weekends, holidays; she worked mornings. We didn't get to see each other very much and it was getting difficult to be excited to go to work. We wanted to start a family and I realized how much I wanted to be a father. Not only a father, but a father that was available at all times. I realized I couldn't be working with Disney and be that kind of father. It just kind of all fell into place with my mother-in-law coming to me and offering us that position. I was now able to focus on being self-employed, which allowed me some freedom.

As I worked with the pool business and we got it to the point where we were ready to sell it, we also had the option to keep it. My passion wasn't in cleaning and repairing pools and I knew I didn't want to do it just for the sake of doing it. So, once again, our dreams kind of changed again with the situation. My dream was to not only be self-employed but to be an entrepreneur, because even if you're self-employed, you can still be technically "employed."

We sold the business and ended up moving to Utah for me to jump again into another business I knew little about. I wanted to build a real estate business. I learned very quickly that you have to be able to drum up your own business, which for some reason was very difficult for me. It didn't take long to see why; it wasn't what I was passionate about. Struggling to make ends meet, a friend introduced me to a company. Strongbrook became a vehicle for us to pursue our ultimate dreams and goals. Dreams can be situational, but that's what makes chasing them so fun! If we lived our lives only chasing one dream, then life would get pretty boring once you reach that dream. The best part about being an entrepreneur or somebody that has that mindset, is you're able to have multiple dreams and make the most of the opportunities to chase them.

Levi:

I think at the heart of being an entrepreneur is recognizing opportunities when they come up and knowing when the best time is to take the leap, when is the best time to sell a business, when the best time to buy a business is, when is the best time to start a business, along with when is the best time to invest in a business. It sounds like, although you're a little bit younger in the game, you're definitely playing it and playing it well.

You said something very interesting. You said that you felt like you had been self-employed, and you wanted to jump into being an entrepreneur versus being self-employed. Can you talk to us just a little bit about that?

Mark:

I was at a convention not too long ago and one of the speakers talked about this principle, and it struck me to the core. He talked about that, even though you're self-employed, you can still be "employed." That's one thing that we noticed about the pool business, and in the real estate business, is even though technically you're "self-employed" you're still tied down to all of the wants and needs of your clientele. Anytime they need anything, you are expected to drop everything and attend to them. That's what they pay you for. So I couldn't see the difference between being employed by a major corporation or by 150 individuals. It was basically the same thing to me.

Now, I didn't want to be lazy and complacent. I simply wanted to be able to be in a position, with an opportunity that I could not only do what I wanted to and how I wanted to, but that I wouldn't have to answer to anybody. That's the kind of the concept that my wife and I have really embraced when it came to entrepreneurship. You're not technically employed by other people when you are an entrepreneur because you're the one that runs your own show and you run your own business. You call the shots. That's the freedom that we really were searching for.

Levi:
Do you believe that anybody can be an entrepreneur?

Mark:
Yeah. Yes, I do. The funny thing is, if you would have asked me six months ago when my real estate business wasn't taking off or my wife and I were living off of our savings for about three or four months, I would have told you, "No, not everybody can be an entrepreneur." Even with this current opportunity, about two or three months ago we kind of were in that same type of rut of not knowing if we would be able to pay our bills. It was an extremely scary time for us and the old confidence had once again been shaken.

One of my favorite quotes from Walt Disney is, "All of our dreams can come true if we have the courage to pursue them."

That is why I think anyone can be an entrepreneur. Everyone, to some degree, has a dream or an ambition. The biggest roadblock to achieving your dream is yourself. The most debilitating thought anyone can have is the fear of failure, and even more so is the fear of success. If you can find what your true passion, ability, and potential is, and have the courage to do something about it, you can be successful.

All it really took for us was to have the courage to put our own debilitating thoughts aside and trust in ourselves. I really had to take a long look in the mirror everyday and tell myself that I could do this, especially during our moments of failure. But we did it and if I can be an entrepreneur, then, anybody can be.

Levi:
Not to steal your earlier pun, but is the best approach to just jump in with both feet?

Mark:
I think it depends on the individual. For me, I had the opportunity

to go and take over an already established business. I knew there would be income every month and I knew that my family would be taken care of, so it made sense for me. For others, the thought of taking the plunge and jumping right in might not be the smartest move. I think that providing for your family's needs is the most important thing that you can do, and should be your first priority. However, if the right opportunity comes along for you and you are able to support your family while still taking the plunge, I would highly recommend that.

I also know a lot of successful entrepreneurs who started their business part-time and it got to the point where they no longer could perform those responsibilities part-time and it was lucrative enough for them to quit their full-time job and focus on their business. It takes a lot of work and dedication, but if you can stick with it in the short term, it will definitely pay off in the long run.

Levi:
You mentioned that when you took the plunge, you had gone through some challenges. Talk to us just briefly about how you overcame those challenges, because I'm sure there were times when you thought, "What in the world are we doing?"

Mark:
With the pool business, doubt and failure was almost a daily occurrence for me—at least, in the beginning. I had no engineering background, no chemistry background, and I had to learn how to, without any training, fix pool equipment, and to plumb pool equipment, and learn chemistry, etc. It got pretty sticky there for a while and a few minor injuries to show for it. I learned something very quickly though: If I put my mind to something, I can do anything.

I reassure myself about this mindset every day. My wife and I have a board posted on our wall that we call our vision board. Many successful people that I know do something like this. You place your biggest goals and aspirations in a place where you can see it every single day. Then, you place smaller goals which help you get to the bigger goals just below it. When you achieve one of your smaller goals, you replace it with the next step and so on. This little activity helps remind me that our goals and dreams are worth fighting for. Those little steps are what create the biggest victories. I also keep a journal of my completed goals, so that when failure does present itself I can go back and look at all the things I have accomplished. It is hard to doubt yourself when you have a continual reminder of how many successes you have had. We also anticipated some failure. You kind of have to as an entrepreneur. It helps to prepare yourself to get through it. We didn't expect failure but we have prepared for it.

Levi:
You have brought up your wife a few times. I'm curious how that journey has gone with your wife. In your mind, how important it is to be on the same page with your wife?

Mark:
For us it was never a question of whether or not she would be a partner with me in the decision process. Every decision that we have made, we have made together. Our most recent opportunity has been our most successful opportunity. I pretty much forced her to go into that meeting with me to hear the presentation. She didn't want anything to do with it. We had already been struggling with building up our real estate business and the last thing she wanted for me was to get distracted and lose focus from that. She was very quiet on the drive there, let's just say that. She was reluctant to go.

After that meeting, I think she and I probably had the best conversation we've ever had, by just re-establishing what our ultimate dreams and goals are, and how we're going to get there. We discovered that this was our opportunity. That's one of the things I love most about her, is not only is she able to recognize an opportunity but she is so good at supporting me and pushing me forward in those opportunities. And it was no surprise to me that she has had more success with what we have been doing then I have, because she is amazing like that.

After having some success with our business, I was able to do what I thought I wanted. I was able to be home with my family, determine when I worked, and control my own schedule.

A few months into this routine she had a sit down with me, and she said "Mark, what are you going to do with your life?"

I said, "Well, I think we're doing it. I'm here at home with the family; we're enjoying our time together. Isn't that enough?"

In not so many words and in the most loving way possible, she pretty much told me that there's more that I can do with my life than what I'm currently doing.

Once again, that put us on the same page. It isn't easy to do. You have to be willing to swallow your pride and to take a look at yourself from the one person who has the best outside perspective of you. My wife has been the best thing that could have happened to me; especially as an entrepreneur and we will continue to move forward together.

Levi:
So basically, she's been there for you, she's supported you, you've been able to be on the same page, which allows you to succeed, yet at the same time there she is pushing you. It's interesting, in the conversations that I have with entrepreneurs throughout the world, that the common thread or a common thread that I encounter on a regular basis is relationships. Individuals, whether or not they're within your own family circle, or whether or not they're mentors, but people that push you to the next level. It sounds like your wife has done that for you. Have there been others that have helped you in your journey?

Mark:
Definitely. I grew up with an amazing family that taught me amazing practices and principles about how to lead my life. I look up to my parents and have listened to their advice all my life and I still do. The same goes with my siblings, they have always been there for me and even when my ideas seem out of whack, they have always supported me.

My wife's family has been the same. Completely supportive and encouraging us onward, even when I am sure our families have looked at us and said, "What in the world have they gotten themselves into?"

I also knew that, for me, it was essential to find somebody that was willing to push me outside of my comfort zone, and to put me in front of the proverbial mirror, and told me to take a look at myself. I found mentors that were willing to do that. They were my critical eye and were able to not only point me in the right direction, but to also be a wealth of knowledge and experience for me to draw on.

Even my wife has benefited from that mentoring. As we associate and communicate with our mentors and their wives, we have learned we can work as a power couple to accelerate our success. I think it's crucial for any entrepreneur with a desire to be successful, to find that person that they can go to. Not only look up to, but to emulate. The greatest thing about this world of entrepreneurship is that it kind of becomes a fraternity of like-minded people, and they are usually willing to help and mentor others. I hope to be counted among those who are willing to help others achieve their dreams, too.

Levi:

I'd have to agree with you more than 100% there. It seems to be just a trend of every successful person that I've talked to, that the relationships are the core of the direction of their path, supporting them through that, helping give them the knowledge and insight that they need. Your wife kind of called you on it. I'm just curious what she, you know, she must know something about your future, your horizon. Talk to us about legacy. What is on your horizon? What are your goals and dreams that you're aiming for next?

Mark:

Our goals and dreams have, like we had talked about, kind of evolved. One thing that we did know is that with whatever success that we had, we didn't want to just keep it for ourselves.

Recently, our family motto has become, "Elevate yourself so that you can lift others."

That all derived from a quote that I heard from a seminar I attended while I was at college. The man who spoke, who I admire deeply, encouraged teachers to reach a little lower so that they can lift a little higher.

When my wife and I were talking about doing more, becoming more, we realized you can't lift somebody else if you're on the same playing field that they are at. It's hard to push somebody up to higher ground. It's a lot easier to bring yourself up to a point where you can reach down and lift them up to where you're at. That has become our driving force.

Knowing our ultimate goal, we had to think of a way to get us to that point. We sat down with our great friend and mentor, Kevin Clayson, who was in an earlier edition of this book and I also believe is in this book, and he told us of a dream that he always had. In that moment, I realized that his dream was my life's calling. I had no idea that is what I wanted to do with my life until that moment. One of my favorite things in the world is going to Disneyland with a family that has never been and help them have the best experience that I possibly could. To help people experience Disney in a way they have never done before. His dream was essentially to do what I love, to send a deserving family to Disneyland every Christmas, like a Disney "Secret Santa." We started to talk more and more about it and it has evolved. I knew that we had to take certain steps to get there, so we talked about me and my personal brand. Also, I knew that I have a wealth of Disney Parks' knowledge that I have shared with friends to help them have the best experience that they could have.

I have always been a "Disney Nerd" and I thought it would be so fun to create a website that is just a place where I could share all of my Disney love and knowledge. If you think about it, families save up for years to go and experience the magic of Disney, and once they are there, they don't necessarily get the most out of the money they have spent. Essentially I wanted to become a resource to help families get the most bang for their buck at Disneyland, like a Disney personal trainer! I wanted it to be more than that as well, I wanted it to be a place where Disney nerds like me could go and share their thoughts, ideas, and experiences with everyone else. We call it TheDizDaddy.com. It has been so much fun! I get excited everyday to wake up and see what I can add to it.

In addition, a few of us, Kevin and his wife included, are in the process of creating a non-profit organization called The SayChEARS Foundation. We believe that every family deserves an opportunity to experience the magic of Disney. We focus on helping deserving families have the best Disney Experience they possibly could. We help families that have worked their whole life to get their families on a Disney vacation, but just couldn't make ends meet. We also have desires to partner with the Wounded Warriors and other various organizations to help make this possible. Essentially, I will get to live out my passion every single day by helping these families, and I am so excited for it. It feels more like play-time for me than work-time.

Essentially, I want my legacy to be helping people experience the Disney Parks the way I have, and helping them to love it as much as I do. I think that every successful entrepreneur gets to this point where we are at. They find a place where their professional life and their passion merge onto the same road. For us, that's really what this has turned out to be, theDizDaddy.com and TheSayChEARS.org have become our playground. We're really excited to not only give us a reason to go to the parks more and to be as nerdy as possible, but to help other people have the same kind of joy and experiences that we've had visiting those parks.

Levi:

That's awesome. Yeah, I agree with you that you hit a point where your entrepreneurship, your business skills and experiences, there is a crossover. I've talked to a lot of entrepreneurs that they ... a lot of times you run across people that, usually due to a fear of money; they make the declaration that you don't have to have money to experience life or live your dreams. Which to some degree is definitely true, but if you want to do something more, like what you're talking about, this "Diz Daddy thing" where you want to help fund people experiencing a dream that every kid has the dream to experience Disney, you have to succeed at a new level. You have to take things to new heights.

First of all, I just admire the cause. Tell us just a little bit how you see that transpiring. Is it going to be part of your current venture that funds that, or just something that you want to develop out?

Mark:

A little bit of both. I think that my current venture is going to help kind of be the financial vehicle to get us going in that direction. Our first step is to build up a strong following on our website and Facebook page. Once I start to build up a solid following, I expect for our website to be the go to source not only for first-time visitors to

Disney Parks, but to those who have been before and are looking to get more out of their experience.

Basically, I want it to become the hub of Disney nerd-dom, I guess you could say.

I would then like to open myself up to doing corporate trainings, or just speeches and seminars; to kind of spread what I feel is the biggest detriment to corporate America right now. There are a lot of things I have learned through my professional career, as well with the amazing training I received through Disney. Corporations that focus too much on the numbers and not enough on the people who they serve, the employees and clientele, are the corporations that are struggling. I hope to be a resource for them in the future.

All of that will help in the funding of our foundation along with fundraisers and donations. We have already determined that we will dedicate a certain percentage of our income to it every month, and that gives me more of a drive to go out there and work hard.

It's just kind of funny. Once you find that point where your passions cross over with your business, it doesn't matter what you will need to do to take make that happen. Now it just becomes fun. It just becomes one of those daily challenges you wake up being excited to do.

Levi:

Sure. Just switching gears just a little bit, maybe it actually applies to what you're talking about, now, having gone from working at Disney and then jumping into entrepreneurship, you're now in your second venture. Do you define success any differently than you used to?

Mark:

I think that by working with Disney, I defined my success on my rank. When you're in corporate America, you kind of determine your success by your position. If you're getting promoted, that means you're having success.

For me, something felt wrong about that system. I didn't like the fact that what I was doing to get myself positioned to be promoted was what was considered successful, because I found myself in doing those things kind of neglecting some of the things that were more important. That's not to say anything negative about corporate America, that's just the nature of it. When people want to get promoted they have to do certain things, and they have to network, and they have to be able to get themselves into a position where a promotion makes sense.

When I jumped in and started with the pool business, I ranked my success on having our numbers be in the black every month. That was really important; especially since we had had a few months there at the beginning that were quite the struggle. Once again, I kind of looked at that and said, "Well, is that really success? I don't know. I still feel like my life is incomplete."

With jumping into the real estate business, it's not that I hadn't seen some success, because we had helped some clients sell and we'd had some homes move, but once again, we were kind of at that position, that cross point when we were introduced to our current opportunity where we knew that whatever it is we were going to do we wanted to be able to serve other people while we were doing it. Not just serve our bank account, but be able to utilize our funds and our ability to help serve other people.

That's where I rank success now. I kind of look around and I see how many people have we helped to a better way of life than we did before? That's how I rate success today, and I feel like we are well on our way to making that happen.

Levi:
That's actually another common thread that I hear from entrepreneurs. It really falls into the component of legacy, but the desire to elevate beyond profit, beyond whatever other recognitions occur in the industry or marketplace, towards making an impact. Making a difference. Knowing that what we do matters and it doesn't just matter to me, but it matters to someone else.

We've talked a lot about living the dream, which we've talked about Disney, we've talked about your journey. For a budding entrepreneur, somebody that maybe they haven't taken the leap yet, they haven't jumped in with both feet, what's the first step you recommend for someone that wants to live that dream, so that maybe they can skip past some

*of the frustrations and struggles and jump right into a legacy-style busi-
ness opportunity?*

Mark:
That's a great question. I think everyone's journey is just very unique.
I think one of the biggest problems that somebody who has that desire to make that leap, one of the biggest mistakes they can make is
waiting for the "right opportunity." I think that the right opportunity manifests itself after you've put in some legwork to get yourself
in the position that you'll be able to recognize the right opportunity
when it comes.

I told my wife from the beginning that I didn't feel like the pool
business was the end game. It was just going to be a means to an
end. I didn't know what end that was going to be, but I knew it was
going to be that, a means to an end. Instead of trying to find a way to
skip past those frustrations, is to experience them and let them mold
you and your business. The truly successful use their differences and
struggles they have been through to their advantage.

One step I would advise though, is do not make the mistake of making money your main ambition. Your clientele can see right through
that. Set a goal for yourself or a dream, an ambition that involves
your ability to serve other people. Yes there are those companies that
have success without doing that, but I guarantee that their employees and clientele aren't as happy as they would be otherwise. I think
that's just the biggest first step you can make, choose now to create
your business with the intention to serve. I think that's what will get
people moving in the right direction.

Levi:
*Great advice, and a great challenge for all of us no matter where we're
at in our entrepreneurial journey. In conclusion, if there was one parting
piece of advice, if there was only one thing that you could tell somebody
who wants to be successful what would that one thing be?*

Mark:
I think it would be kind of a collaboration of things that I've learned

through my successes and my failures, which is: dream big, work smart, lift others and spread the magic.

Dream Big.

If you set your dreams and ambitions too low, then when you achieve them you're not going to feel like you've accomplished much. Even though there are little dreams that are along the way, and little ambitions and goals to help you get there, just make sure that you're shooting for the stars. Because if you're not shooting for the stars; you're not going to get where you want to be. I think Walt Disney is the perfect example of that. There is no reason in the world why Walt Disney should have arrived at where he did. He started as a somewhat poor child in a family where he was delivering newspapers in snow that was taller than him. He had a dream that went from wanting to be a cartoonist, to animate moving pictures, to opening his own animation studio. All the steps that he took were little dreams that led to his biggest dream, which I feel was to leave this world a better place than it was when he came into it.

Work Smart.

I don't intend this to mean you don't have to work hard, but rather learn from those who have failed before you. Surround yourself with people who are smarter than you in their areas of expertise. Save yourself from the aches and pains that come from not trusting other people.

Another one of my mentors, Kris Krohn, always says, "If you want something done right, don't do it yourself."

Trust those you work with to do their job and you will find that not only will your work load be less, but your employees will perform better and will ultimately be happier.

Lift Others:

I already spoke about this in great detail earlier, but make this your driving force. I truly believe that a business cannot fail if their clientele feels that you are there for them, and not for their payment. My father-in-law was the perfect example of this and his client's were loyal to him even after he was gone.

Spread the Magic:

What I mean by "spread the magic" is just be as happy and optimistic as you can possibly be. Optimism and happiness is just as contagious as pessimism. If you go into your business everyday dreading what you need to do, then get out! The culture and attitude of your business trickles from the top down. If you are wondering why your business is struggling, the first thing to look at is yourself and change your attitude into that of optimism.

If you can just figure out how to integrate all of four of those things into your business, there is no way you can't succeed, because your focus and goal is going to be on lifting those around you. When you create the culture of service, the money will follow.

McKay Matheson

McKay has experience in many different types of business. He has years of experience in the sales and airline industries as well as years of experience working with residential treatment facilities where he helped troubled youth. He has spent time as a financial planner. In addition, he has been employed as a Spanish translator and interpreter. He has a Bachelor of Arts degree in Spanish Translation.

McKay currently works with a client-based real estate investment company. He has spent several years and thousands of dollars studying real estate investing. He is passionate about helping people to invest in real estate that do not have the time, money, or knowledge to do so.

Contact: mckay.matheson@strongbrook.com
Website: *www.mckay.strongbrook.com*

Levi:
All right, McKay, now you've been involved in, on some level or another, over 40 ventures. You've seen a lot of what works and a lot of what doesn't work. You've been able to develop your own formula that you're now use to implement in your own business and it produces success for

you, but beyond that, you've talked before about the objective of creating generational wealth. Which I think is a wonderful topic that really doesn't get discussed much in American culture and so, to start out why don't you share a little bit about generational wealth, what that means, and what you're doing with it.

McKay:
Well, to me, it started back with me growing up and seeing the status of my parents and the struggles that they had while I was growing up. They didn't talk about money much out in the open, but I could see in their faces the difficulties that they were having… not being able to cover many of expenses that needed to be covered. At a young age, I realized that I did not want that for me. I began researching different areas of business and just thinking to myself, what is it about what my parents are doing versus what more financially successful people in the world are doing. What's the difference there? Why are these people financially successful and why aren't my parents?

My dad did everything right; what society taught him. He went to school got a Bachelor's degree, Master's degree, and went on and got a Doctorate degree. He got a job as a professor. He did everything right, he is very smart, but he's lived pay check to pay check. My parents taught me the best they could with the knowledge that they received. They taught me to go to school, get good grades, because then I'll get a little piece of paper that says I'm smart. Then I'd be able to use that piece of paper to get a great job which would make me wealthy and help me save to have plenty of money for retirement. I've met many people over the years that are proof that this system that we've been taught doesn't work. At a very young age I realized that there had to be something more to it than that.

I realized at that it wasn't working out as I was being taught by society. I asked myself, "What else can I do, what else needs to be done? What can I do to change that?" I started searching for and researching successful people and looking up their stories, what did they do differently, what are their current businesses, what their mindsets are. I found that these successful people are not only successful in their business lives, but one of the major reasons why they are having that success is, they think differently than most people. They're different in the way that they think about life. There's a lot more to them than just their businesses. I started researching that and tried to find out exactly what it was they were thinking.

After much research, I found that many successful people were not employees, they were business owners. So I decided that I wanted to own my own business, though I didn't know what business. I researched hundreds of different types of businesses. I have been involved in, on some level or another, approximately 40 different ventures in different areas of business. I've become very familiar with different types of businesses and what it takes to be successful.

I've paid thousands and thousands of dollars and traveled around the country learning from experts on how to be successful in business. I've put in the time and money to learn this information. The problem is that this information is not taught in our schools or anywhere that's easily accessible to the general population. My goal is to get this information out there in order to make it accessible to people so that they can learn and apply it if they choose. People don't know what they don't know. They're blinded by what society has taught them their whole lives.

There is so much more information out there to help us get what we really want in life, and I believe that deep down, it's not money. Money is just a means to an end to really get us in a position that we can accomplish what we're really passionate about; blessing the lives of those around us. My goal is to make this information accessible to the masses to help them get what they want. Make it accessible to them, and I'm starting with my very own family, so generational wealth, making it accessible to the families and creating a legacy for my own family. Starting with my parents, me, my kids, my grandkids, on and on, so this information is there and taught inside of my family forever. It's more than just having the money there forever for generations to come. It's about having that knowledge taught inside of my family. I want them to all be able to have what I didn't have growing up, and be taught the truth about how money works, the truth about how to be successful in business.

Levi:

It's very admirable in my mind. It's a very captivating story, you basically tried a lot of stuff and you kept what worked. What you're proposing is that, hey instead of making everyone else go through the experience that I went through, part of generational wealth it sounds like is a knowledge treasury that is full of timeless principles that anyone can access regardless of their age. Does that sound about right?

McKay:

It does, yeah, it's more than the money; it's knowledge. Knowledge breeds empowerment. It comes with that confidence to be able to take those steps forward that are necessary to be successful. To do that requires a lot of leaps of faith and in some cases, knowing when to take them in the right moments and having that confidence to do so. I think you're right. All those principles are hand-in-hand I believe.

Levi:

How do you define success?

McKay:

My favorite definition of success comes from Earl Nightingale.

He says, "Success is the progressive realization of a worthy ideal."

As long as you are continually moving forward and progressing towards your goals, you are successful; never quitting. I'll even take it one step further. Success, for me, is more than just having a goal, moving forward and achieving it. Success, I believe, really comes down to how are you changing and blessing the world, how are you blessing the lives of others. I can take myself, I can set a goal to make a million dollars in a year and I can achieve that goal and maybe call myself successful, but I believe there's a lot more to it than that. In my opinion, it's what are you doing with that million dollars. It's what are you doing once you've made your money. It's who are blessing, who you are, and which lives are you changing with that. What type of service—and how—are you going to serve mankind with the success that you achieve? What you do with the money that you've earned is your real success.

Levi:

I absolutely agree with you on that. Now, on the next level, there are obviously different medians that lead to success. With your background in exploring so many different business types, so many different ventures. Are there certain sets of tools or different market area that you have found that produce more success than others? You've obviously experienced quite a bit of success in real estate. Also, is there a common pattern or a common trait there that people should be looking for?

McKay:

In all the different businesses that I have been involved with, I've seen a lot of semi-successful people who have achieved mediocre success. I've also seen a lot of people who have gone above and beyond and been extremely successful and they've not only gained a lot of money, but they've created the culture that they are passing onto other people. Looking at the difference in them, I believe that the difference between the two different types of people is who they are, the mindset of them. The extremely successful people are people that have taken the time to develop themselves.

As far as what they're doing with their business, most of the people that I come across that are extremely successful, to some degree, have their hands in the real estate industry. They either do quite a bit of investing themselves or find people who will do that investing for them. To some degree most of the successful people spend quite a bit of their time in the real estate industry. That's why at one point in my career, I turned my head in that direction realizing that and started to study that industry trying to soak in as much as I could.

Levi:

Real estate, anyway, certainly in my own experience for diversifying wealth is definitely an advantageous tool. I think you also pointed out that there are multiple medians that cause success. I think that, you had acknowledged that there are principles that regardless of the platform that you've chosen you could apply. Those are the types of things that you're trying to teach your children and the generations that you're trying to impact. Can you share a little bit what some of those principles are that are universal across all mechanisms?

McKay:

The most successful people have a different outlook on life. They think differently, they have a different confidence about themselves. They're people who serve other people. Every successful person whom I've met in my life has had a huge focus on service to others and charity work. I believe that to be a huge part of it, whether you're religious or not, just service in general, finding ways to give back to the community, give back to the world. I believe that to be one of the most common traits in extremely successful people.

Levi:

We've talked a lot about success, so, I am just curious, how do you define failure?

McKay:

In my opinion, there is no failure, there are only results. Basically, failure for me is stopping to try, you've given up, you are striving for something and you stop; that is failure. If you are trying and don't give up then you're moving forward. In my opinion, the fact that you are moving forward you're not failing. Thomas Edison failed however many thousands of times before he finally invented the light bulb and succeeded. Had he stopped at any point, history would have been written differently. He just kept eliminating all the different ways that it didn't work. Just because you aren't achieving the goals immediately that you are shooting for, doesn't mean you should give up. Keep trying and moving forward.

Levi:

I think it's brilliant that you chose Thomas Edison because I really feel that he highlights actually the process that you went through. This is, you did try a lot of things, but you never quit. I think that's essential in success in any area of life, is the willingness to move forward, the willingness to recognize that hey I got a bad result, but I still have a dream, I'm still moving forward, I still want to achieve this. Absolutely love that you chose Thomas Edison. On another level, you're obviously working to build a foundation for your own family and then also to use it as a template for others so they can basically tap into this knowledge trea-

sury. At the end of your life, what do you want your legacy to be? What do you want people to talk about?

McKay:
I'd like to be remembered by the generational wealth concept. I'd like to have the lives of thousands of families blessed because of increased knowledge. Like I mentioned before, the money that I hope to be leaving for generations to come is not what is truly important. It's what I have taught those generations, the knowledge I have left with them, and how I have changed the outlook on life and improved it for my family and those that I love. Hopefully, even more than that. I'd like to expand it and make this knowledge very accessible to as many people as I can. I have had to work very hard, travel around the country, pay thousands of dollars and put in thousands of hours to gain the knowledge and experience I have. I'd love to look back on my life and see that the knowledge that I had to search so hard for has changed the lives of families all over the world.

Levi:
McKay, you're certainly a very inspiring individual, and I believe you have discovered knowledge that others would want to have access to. In conclusion, if someone, perhaps further down, the road, maybe even where you were when you started needs to know how to get started, I am sure they would like to know what the first step that they need to take is. If you could give a piece of advice to them so that they don't have to go through trying so many things before they land on that gem that's going to truly give them leverage? What piece of advice could you give them as far as where do they start? What actions do they need to take now?

McKay:
Figure out what you want in life. Decide what your dream is, what you want to accomplish, and then start moving in that direction. You might not know what it is completely, but that's ok. I believe as you start moving in that direction it will start to become clearer to you the further you go. What you want to accomplish will possibly even change a little bit as you move forward and as you learn more.

You don't know what you don't know. That's the most dangerous information. You've got to just start moving forward in that direction and your why will come to you.

Friedrich Nietzsche said "He who has a why to live for can bear almost any how."

The how will work itself out. Just start moving in the direction and don't listen to what others say. There are going to be a lot of people that are going to want to pull you down. People who aren't successful and aren't making it in life, I have found, really enjoy trying to pull you down and shoot your dreams down. So, plow through it, ignore those people. A lot of people just don't know what to do first, don't know what direction even to go or what to do, they have no clue. I found that if you just start taking steps, even if you don't know what direction to go in, just start taking steps, it will come. Your why will come, you will find what you want out of life, you will find the success that you want in life. If you just start taking those steps, even if they're blind at first.

I'd like to end by quoting neurologist, psychiatrist and Holocaust survivor Viktor Frankl.

He said, "Everything can be taken from a man but one thing: the last of the human freedoms—to choose one's attitude in any given set of circumstances, to choose one's own way."

David Nahm

David Nahm has worked in the financial services industry since 2001. His primary focus is helping affluent families grow, manage, and protect their wealth; while also providing services that solve client priorities, such as, wealth transfer and charitable giving. David helps manage over $500 million in AUM (Assets under Management), while assisting corporate executives and top employees in several industries, as well as, entrepreneurs and business owners.

David has a strong passion for helping others, both professionally and personally. This includes volunteering his time to assist the homeless and less fortunate with clothing drives. David has also focused a lot of his spare time in helping the local chapter of his Fraternity, and the collegiate, as the President of their Alumni Board of Trustees. David believes in serving others and takes pride in giving of himself to make a difference in someone else's life.

David graduated from California State University Hayward. He has a wife and young daughter. He enjoys barbecuing for family and friends, reading and traveling, playing sports and is especially grateful for the time spent at home with his family.

Website: *www.planyourlastinglegacy.com*

Levi:

David, you've spent your career building not only personal wealth, but helping others to create and manage wealth. In your experience, you've actually honed in on this concept that's quite actually provocative that work is optional. To start out, I want you to just talk to us about what "making work optional" means and how you came across that concept and your experience there.

David:

In the Financial Services industry, it all starts with understanding each client's current financial situation, then getting them to expand on the finer details of their lives, including their family dynamics, career goals, passions and hobbies. It's about finding out what makes them tick, because retirement might not be something they feel is important at that particular time. The concept of making work optional is a marketing idea, which I learned early in my career from two top producers in our firm whom I worked closely with for the first 11–12 years. It's a way of expressing to our clients that our purpose is to make sure we've thought through their financial life, so they can feel comfortable leaving the workforce when they want to pursue other chapters of their life.

Ironically, not many of our clients actually retire early, even though they could afford to. The majority of our clients are ultra-high net worth individuals, with backgrounds ranging from engineers and scientists to corporate executives and medical professionals to business owners and entrepreneurs. For the most part, they love to be challenged and have no intention of retiring until normal retirement age. There are only a select few who have successfully transitioned into early retirement, mostly in pursuit of philanthropic or personal growth.

Levi:

For you, the objective is to, either through the use of principals, mechanisms, or financial tools, help a client get to a point where they literally are free to do whatever they want?

David:

Absolutely. It's always been our premise that we want to make their financial lives as simple as possible so that they don't have to worry about their future financial well-being. They can focus on what is most important to them; ideally, a healthy balance between work and family.

Levi:

How did you get started in this line of business?

David:

Only a few years out of college, I was self-employed and working independently to help others with their financial well-being and debt consolidation. As fate would have it, that path led to an introduction and opportunity to work with a leading wealth management team at a large brokerage firm. After a couple of years doing the basic review planning and implementation, I advanced into a unique role within the team which allowed me to help our team and business grow.

Interestingly, I didn't have a background in finance when I started out, but I was hungry and wanted to learn. I knew that focusing on growth and helping others would give me opportunities that I wouldn't normally achieve if I focused solely on making money.

Levi:

What I love about that is it highlights that at the core of entrepreneurship your background doesn't really matter, what matters is that you can recognize an opportunity and that you can take advantage of it by either qualifying yourself or aligning the proper resources in order to achieve it. It also brings up a question for me.

Now, you mentioned that you work with ultra-high wealth individuals to put themselves in a position where work truly is optional; however, it's an aspiration, I think, for all entrepreneurs to get to that point. Is there a point in an entrepreneur's career where they can start taking advantage of the principals you teach, if there's something they should start sooner rather than later? Talk to us a little bit about that.

David:

Entrepreneurs can experience the greatest gains due to their higher earning potential, but they can also endure bigger losses if they aren't careful, due to their comfort in taking risks. It's important for those who are still creating wealth, and not just entrepreneurs, to learn how to live within their means and to not spend their money before they've earned it. It's such a basic concept, to spend less than you earn, but peoples' shortsightedness has handcuffed many Americans, including myself early on. To help stay focused on their financial future, an entrepreneur should prepare a financial strategy, or game plan, to make sure they know what they'll need at retirement to support their future lifestyle. Then, it's a matter of getting a retirement account started and contributing regularly so the investments have time to grow. It's just unfortunate that most people just don't take the time to seek guidance to learn how to budget, save or invest regularly to achieve that goal.

Levi:

For sure. So basically, the principle there is that not only do you have to create wealth through cash flow/income stream, you also need to incorporate the principal of reinvesting so you can take advantage of the tools that are out there in the marketplace to create perpetual wealth.

David:

Correct.

Levi:

In your line of work, is there a secret combination for success?

David:

I think our success can be attributed to two things: service and reputation. We strive to provide a level of service and attention to our clients' needs that goes above and beyond their expectations. We consider ourselves their Chief Financial Officer, so it's our goal to try and assist with anything that could affect their life financially. It's our mission to help clients grow, manage and protect their wealth, so that covers everything from life insurance and estate planning to charitable giving and tax efficient investing.

Our reputation comes from execution and the client experience. It's not just a matter of doing, but doing it well, in a timely manner, and with a personal touch that eases the client so they feel comfortable and understand the value of what we're doing for them.

Levi:

I would definitely agree with those concepts. What you're describing also is the importance of building relationships, so talk to us a little bit about the relationships that are necessary to succeed in business in your mind.

David:

There's certainly the network of professionals you need to have in order to succeed in our industry. You need to have professionals that you can trust, that you understand, are like-minded, who have the necessary skills to deliver the service for each client's goals, whether it be with estate planning, insurance or taxes.

Client relationships aren't solely about the primary contact. It's important to remember familial relationships are also worth building. You need to understand the dynamics of the family, not just the spouse and children, because siblings and/or parents might need to rely on you in the future, or else they can easily leave and take their assets with them.

Lastly, I think that anyone looking to build a successful business, whether small or large, should build personal relationships within their team. It requires open communication, respect for one another, trust and patience. The relationships you build will suffer long-term if you don't keep those ideals in mind.

Levi:

This question is for aspiring entrepreneurs. In your experience, is there a way to preempt some of the problems that are often associated with partnerships? Maybe a way to identify quality partnerships and align with the right people earlier in your career?

David:

Oh, absolutely. Obviously, you don't want to put all your eggs in one basket. If you're looking at partnering with one person in particular, I would try and find out as much about the potential prospect or partner as possible. It might be as easy as going to dinner or meeting their family, kind of an interviewing process, to see how that person's thought processes might align with your own. Don't expect to have similar views on everything, either. Having a conflicting approach or ideology could be positive, as they would complement each other in managing a business.

Levi:

That's excellent advice. What I would absolutely concur with is the concept of having differing opinions. And what it does is it allows you to eliminate confirmation bias, where you think it's a great idea, but a lot of people, entrepreneurs specifically, especially when starting out, due to insecurity try and align ourselves with a bunch of people that agree with us. And as a result, we miss the potential pitfalls in our concepts. So, excellent advice. A topic that perhaps is not so popular in the investing world, but I would like to ask on a personal level, what's the biggest risk that you have personally ever taken, was it worth it and how did it turn out?

David:

The biggest risk that I have taken financially? Well, there are two things to mention here. My first big risk was investing in my primary residence, perhaps a little bit earlier than when I should have. I alluded to this earlier, as I overextended myself by buying based on an income I expected to have in the future (back when mortgage lending was lax). I let emotions get in the way of what traditional investment practices might suggest because I wanted to own a home. For a time there, it didn't work out well, but the long-term financial strain of owning a primary residence lifted when my income grew.

My second big risk was purchasing investment properties while still having debt to pay off. It seems counterintuitive to incur new debt, but not all debt is bad debt when done correctly. Those investments have been financially sound, and have certainly helped me more than hindered me.

Levi:

How important is risk in order to achieve success, in your opinion?

David:

Risk is very important in that if you don't take any risk, you're likely to never see an outcome that you would hope for. Everything has risk associated with it; even if you sit in cash, you will lose to inflation. It's just the matter of managing risk and what your comfort levels are.

Levi:

In making decisions about risk, you brought up earlier that you had made an emotional decision, and as hard as we try, it's human nature for us to default to our emotions. How do you calculate emotions into the decision-making process in your line of business?

David:

With respect to clients, we sometimes have clients who want to make a decision based on their gut instinct. Since most of our clients can afford to take higher risks relative to their net worth, we don't typically intervene unless it's out of their tolerance levels. Clients need to understand that we have their best interest in mind, but we do try to understand their need to make an emotional decision. Still, depending on how much it might affect their overall financial situation, we realize we hold a fiduciary role to intervene if necessary.

Levi:

Your firm has been effective at coaching and mentoring people through these types of issues in order to achieve wealth in their own space. How important have coaches and mentors been in your own career?

David:

Very helpful in the financial services industry. As I mentioned earlier, I worked with two partners that helped me focus on what I enjoy most about the business, and to grow myself within the industry. They've certainly helped guide me to understand the importance of doing what's best for the client at all times and do it to the best of my abilities.

In addition to mentors within my work environment, I also participated in an outside mentoring program, which had a profound effect
on me. It helped me refocus myself, to give me the confidence to pursue more personal career goals, as well as to find an inner purpose
that I ignored for a long time. The mentoring program also helped me
consciously battle some inner doubts and create a vision of prosperity and fulfillment that I had been missing for a long time. Mentoring
is vital to the growth of one's self.

Levi:
*I would definitely agree with you, in fact, it's interesting. I've interviewed
so many entrepreneurs over the years, and that tends to be a recurring
theme over and over. When I ask about formulas for success, without
fail, they always bring that up. In talking about game plans and your
entrepreneurial journey, would you say that you have a greatest "A-ha"
moment where things suddenly just switched for you?*

David:
Someone recently made a comment that really resonated with me,
and the gist of the message was, "In order to receive more, you must
give more." So, the idea behind it is if you're trying to provide a service, you need to focus on providing the best quality service possible.
If you're doing it because you love it, then your financial or personal
gains, will come without question.

Levi:
*That perfectly aligns with the principle that I teach, which is the love
exchange, that in order for us to give up something that we have of
value, it always has to be that for the intention that we're going to get
something greater in return; so flip that on its head, what you just
said, your greatest "A-ha" was that in order to get the value that you
want out in the market space, you have to put more value out there.
You have to put a greater level of value in order for people to want to
exchange. If I understood what you said correctly, would that align
with your message?*

David:

Yes, that's a great assessment.

Levi:

Again, this question is for budding entrepreneurs or those that are early in the game, what advice would give them that could help them in their entrepreneurial journey?

David:

First is the importance of perseverance. The most successful entrepreneurs have failed more than anyone and heard "NO" more times than you could ever imagine. Think of this world without telephones, light bulbs, airplanes and the Internet. It's perseverance that will make you successful. Another way to think of it is each "NO" brings you closer to the next "YES," based on the odds, so thank them for their time and move on.

Second is passion. If you are not passionate about what you're doing and the service you're providing, then it will reflect in the results.

Finally, I would recommend creating a specific vision of your ideal business to build towards. Imagine what you want to be doing in that business, how much income you want to be generating, how much time you want to be spending on the business each day, and the clientele you're working with. Create a vision that encompasses your daily life and figure out what it takes to achieve that, because if you're not working towards it, then you're working against it.

Levi:

Great advice, especially on the topic of holding a vision, or creating a vision, of what you're trying to achieve. That actually leads to me a question that I like to ask entrepreneurs as well. In creating your own vision for the future, you're already at success with the level you are, but for all of us there's always the next level. What inspires you? What is that next level for you?

David:

My next level is ultimately getting myself to the point where work is optional. It's funny that I deal with it so often, but a lot of times when you're in this industry, you often overlook your own personal situation. Ideally, I want my business to grow to the point where either I can make my work optional or my wife's work optional. And my greatest motivation for that is my family. I have a young daughter, she's a toddler, and since I spend 12+ hours away from home, I don't get much time to be with her except on the weekends. That's my motivation, to be a family man, to be a father and work on my own time.

Levi:

A follow up question to that, what legacy do you want to leave?

David:

There are a couple things that I'm working on. I work in a large metropolitan area, and there is homelessness throughout the area. I have started to reach out to friends and family, to gather articles of clothing and blankets to hand out and donate to the homeless. With the help of many, we made a good impact during the cold winter months and holiday season. That is one legacy that I'm really working on, to set up a foundation to assist those who need help more than ourselves.

My family legacy would be to have a financial backing to support my family, my children and future generations so they can focus on what makes an impact, as well as what makes them happy.

Levi:

In conclusion, I always like to bring it back to action steps. For anyone out there that wants to achieve a work optional scenario, if you could give them one first step that they need to take right now, what would that first step be?

David:

I think the biggest step that anyone can take in being successful, whether it be an entrepreneur, or just a business person, is find out what you love most about what you're doing and learn how to master it, because if you don't love it, you're going to have a harder time being successful in it. I think that most successful people learn how to monetize what they love to do most!

Levi:

Excellent advice. I concur with that. In fact, that is advice that is a recurring theme among all successful individuals that I've ever encountered, and so I would issue the same challenge to any entrepreneur to first find their passion, and then follow the principles of wealth. Thank you very much.

David:

You're welcome.

Mike Driggers

Mike is an in-demand international success coach, consultant, and trainer. He speaks on subjects like entrepreneurship, mindset, leadership, marketing, high performance, and motivation. His clientele is a who's who in the areas of Sports, Business, Entertainment, and Politics. His passion, desire, and willingness to be a self-servant leader have helped thousands of people to achieve greatness within their personal and professional lives.

Mike is a successful author. He is the author of *"Mastering the Mindset-The Power of Affirmations."* He has also recently written *"The 1099 vs The W2 Attitude—Learn How To Break The Barrier From Being an Employee to Being Self Employed."*

Mike has owned and operated several successful businesses, including a marketing and advertising agency called Unleashed Media in the San Francisco Bay Area. In 2004, he was voted Entrepreneur of the Year by President Bush. For over 26 years, he has been in the top 10% of producers for the direct sales industry. Mike currently owns IME Publishing, AMG Investments, and Expert Innovations Inc.

In addition, Mike is the co-founder of the syndicated radio show *"Get The You Factor."* Episodes and information about the show are available at GetTheYouFactor.com.

Contact: *Mike@SuccessWithMikeDriggers.com*
Website: *www.SuccessWithMikeDriggers.com*

Levi:
Mike, you have been in the entrepreneurial world for a very long time. You've experienced a lot of success and I know that you're a big advocate of entrepreneurship itself. You've written books on the topic and just to lead in, I got to ask the question, how did you first become an entrepreneur? How did you know that was something that you wanted to do in your life?

Mike:
I come from a family that has an entrepreneurial spirit. At an early age, I really didn't know what that meant. My mom, dad, sister and I lived in Wichita Falls, Texas. My father was in the military and my mother worked at a dry cleaner. They did not make a lot of money between the both of them. There were certain things that I wanted such as, a special bike to do tricks and things of that nature. However, they just didn't have the money to afford a lot of luxuries. I knew that if I wanted these things, I would need to figure out how to go out and make the money myself. When you have a goal to get something at an early age, you'll find a way to get it. No choice. No problem.

If you desire it and want it, you'll reach out and do whatever it takes to get it. That's where I was at the age of 12. I created my first business without even really understanding what business truly was. We had moved into a trailer park near the Air Force base. There were all these lawns that needed to be mowed. There were military and elderly folk that needed their lawns fixed and mowed. I would go in and create a contract to where I would mow their lawn on a bi weekly basis and based on the size of the lawn I would charge anywhere from $5, $7 or $10. However I quickly discovered that I was only one person and I needed to leverage others, so I brought my friends in and would pay them $3, $5, and $7 to mow the lawns for me.

I was able to manage the process and make money. I was able to have several lawns mowed at the same time. At an early age, that's where it started for me. I was always trying to figure out ways to make money outside of the typical lemonade stand that most kids would do. Usually that's the first stage of entrepreneurship that most people start with which I tried as well. I did all kinds of things. I'd take toothpicks and put them in water and then dip them in cinnamon. I would then put them into little baggies and sell them at the schools. The kids would just buy them up like crazy. I was always creative in ways to earn money.

Levi:

It's interesting; just hearing you tell that story reminds me of my own background. I did a lot of the same kind of things. What's interesting to me, as well, was that the concept of entrepreneurship wasn't as popular as it is now. You probably noticed the shift as well that as we've gone through like this technology revolution and it really is easier to become an entrepreneur that the identity actually has become a lot more popular. Would you agree with that?

Mike:

Absolutely. What people don't realize is our founding fathers came to this country and everything that they did was based on entrepreneurship. If you think about it their survival was based on it. They would typically claim their land and they would have a farm, cattle and harvest the crops for their families. They would also sale to others cattle, vegetables, or hay. It started with that. When the pilgrims came and landed on lands, they didn't look into the local newspaper for the want ads. The Indians were not hiring and there was no place to get a job. They reached out and developed their land and cultivated and produced their own products and devices to create money or trade at the time.

That's the true environment of what was entrepreneurship. Over time, we've lost that. We've been enticed with 401K's and health benefits and the golden carrot that the possibilities of being rich off some stocks. All to be controlled buy a boss, or you're told what you're worth when you know you're not getting really what you think your worth. We know you're worth a lot more. They control when you go on vacations or when you can take breaks. They control what time you have to start work and when you end. You pretty much have given up freedom for this illusion called "security."

I still believe that there are a very small percentage of people out there that have actually stepped into entrepreneurship compared to the percentages that have not. However, you're right about one thing, which is that technology has made it a lot better and a lot easier for people to become entrepreneurs. There's a lot more resources. There's a lot more education and the possibilities to learn from others or even to find out what the latest trends are in the world than when I was growing up. I'm amazed with the technology.

For example, my son once asked me, "Dad, can you help me solve this Rubik's cube?"

I said, "Son, I had a hard time when I was your age trying to solve this and I never could really figure it out. I would bust it apart and put it back together to make it look like I did it."

Next thing I know, he is on YouTube and he researched on how to solve it. He learned about a mathematical algorithm and now he can solve the Rubik's Cube in less than two minutes. I still can't do it!

He used technology to learn how to do something. There's so much information out there to learn about and there are so many people like myself that provide information on how to do certain things. Folks like to film just about anything just for the heck of it, then post it to the web and they make money from everybody viewing the videos to see how they did something. It has become allot easier to be an entrepreneur. Even personal development is a lot easier to get to now on entrepreneurship like my new book that is coming out on how to change the mindset to be an entrepreneur is called *"The 1099 vs. The W2 Attitude—Learn How To Break The Barrier From Being an Employee to Being Self Employed."*

Levi:
Talk to us a little bit more about that, what is the 1099 Vs. W2 attitude?

Mike:
Among the hardest transitions for individuals is to move from the employee to the entrepreneur mentality. The idea of getting on your own, getting your own business is fantastic. It's the desire of a lot of individuals to leave their jobs and to be successful business owners.

However, there is a transition that has to be made from the employee mentality (W2 Attitude) to the entrepreneur mentality (The 1099 Attitude) (which is the tax codes for reporting taxes at the end of the year)? It is exceedingly crucial that you bear this entrepreneur mentality to succeed in business on your own because most of the principles you'll need to succeed are based off of being a true entrepreneur. There are gigantic differences between that and an employee mentality, I'm not pulling your leg; let's take a look at it here.

Many small business owners and enterprisers got their beginning as an employee. They worked for somebody else. The issue is that if you've been an employee for years, it may be difficult to shake off the bonds of the employee mentality. What does this mean? If you have an employee mentality, you're more likely to look to other people to tell you what to do. You'll find it difficult to take responsibility for the success and failure of your endeavor. You just work hard to prove your value so that you can stay employed.

Let's take a look and talk about some of the differences. First, let's examine the *"Monday mentality."* Employees fear Monday (or, whatever the beginning day of their work week is). Entrepreneurs are not bolted into a specific work week. They approach each day as a different chance to go after their dreams. The Employees have *"It's not my problem mentality."* This mentality they view everything on the job by whether or not it's their problem. Entrepreneurs view everything as their duty as they have ownership of what is happening in their business. Then, there is the *"T. G. I. F. (Thank Goodness It's Friday) mentality."* Employees are constantly looking forward to their off days. Entrepreneurs are forever seeking ways to extend their business even when they're not "working" they're considering ways to extend their entrepreneurial talents. They look forward to each day! How about the *"When am I going to receive a raise?"* mentality. Employees think that raises ought to come according to the calendar, instead of according to their work habits. Entrepreneurs seldom consider when they'll receive an increase. They realize that the more they work towards helping other people the greater their reward will be. The *"Oh no, what now?" mentality*. Employees set about meetings with an *"oh no"* mentality. Entrepreneurs set about meetings with a mastermind mentality. They realize that excellent ideas come out of these meetings.

Like most employees that are under a W2 environment, they don't care about if the lights are left on. They don't care if the copier is left open or there's no paper and inks ran out. They don't care. They don't want to replace it. They don't want to have to deal with it. They don't care about if the door got locked and that they forgot to lock it, and they all have *"I'll just do it tomorrow attitude."* There are a lot more like these mindsets that we may compare.

Where someone that owns a business that has that 1099 attitude they have the *"If it's meant to be, it's up to me attitude."* As an entrepreneur or business owner, you think very differently. Essentially, the buck stops (and begins) with you. You're responsible for the success and failure of your endeavor. And you are the one who makes all the huge decisions (including who to designate littler decisions to!).You care about how many pens, post it notes or paper that needs to be purchased, or are the lights off and the doors are locked. There's a completely different mentality. A lot of W2 employees are there from eight to five, they punch in, punch out and they can't wait to get out of there

If it's close to the time to go home and they need to get something done, the entrepreneur finds a way to get it done. In a lot of cases they will try to avoid pushing it on to the next day.

There are several employees out there with theW2 mindset. Not all of them but a majority of them have that attitude. It's just a give and take and push and pull relationship. Being an entrepreneur and having what I call the "The Traits of a Champion's Mind," is having tenacity, being persistent, being fearless, having passion, tolerance of ambiguity, having a vision, creating an unshakable self-belief, being flexible, stepping outside the box, have a rule-breaking attitude, have a positive attitude always, showing strong integrity and leadership, being very helpful, having ambition, taking responsibility, being compassionate and giving back. These are all critical traits.

The other aspects of successful entrepreneurs that are leaders they are also readers. They are constantly into personal development. They are always educating themselves and learning. A lot of employees won't take time to feed their minds outside their job. It seems that the minute they are done with collage they stop learning unless the job requires it. A lot of them are more interested in what the next reality TV series is versus developing their mind with non-garbage.

Like my friend Les Brown says, "It's like me going into the middle of your living room and pouring garbage all over your carpet and stomping on it again and again, how would you feel if I did that? You'd be mad, right?"

Everybody would be mad. I know I would be!

But yet, this is what we let people and reality TV shows do to our minds. If you're not consistently reaching out to be the best entrepreneur that you can be, it's going to be a slow run and a slow path. I'm big supporter of constantly learning to be better than what you are.

All the very successful entrepreneurs that I have met are constantly doing things to improve their mind. Matter fact every successful person I know has some type of personal development program.

You can tell which ones have personal development program and the ones that are not. The ones that are put themselves into a position for success. You can't be in a position to have success unless you prepared for it yourself. It takes personal development.

A good example of instant success where they were not ready for it is the folks that won the lottery, 90% of the people in the lottery are bankrupt within the first couple of years. Why? Because they didn't know what it took to make that type of money. True success is not the end destination. The true success is the journey to it. It is who you become on the way to the destination. Everybody's definition of success is different. Mine is different than everyone else's.

What I can tell you, though, is that success is always an ongoing process. Everyone I know that's ever achieved some type of success, they've created another goal and their now off and running to achieve the new one. There goals are always ongoing and they are flexible and adjusting the whole time. I related to NASA sending a rocket to and around the moon, it is said that as rocket is going towards & around the moon and back that 90% of the time the rocket's off course. They're constantly adjusting to stay back on course. If they are even one percent off course it could be millions and millions of miles off the track to what they want to achieve.

Success is no different. Once you hit your definition of what success is, you're going to find the next level, and so you're going to adjust and keep going and keep building from that point on. Your goals are going to change they are just the road map to that destination. You're going to adjust and keep yourself on track to achieve what it is that you want to achieve.

At the end of the day and what I learned at an early age is that the entrepreneurial life is a blessing and a perfect personal growth opportunity that allows me the flexibility of working my professional life around my personal life instead of having to work my personal life around my professional life, as it often is when you're working for someone else.

Levi:

I completely agree with you on the concept of mindset. I'm thinking back why I read my first business book I think in middle school or early junior high and I was hooked from there and became a business nerd. But a question that I have is, for me I was always interested in business. Even from the age of a young child, I'd take things at school with me to trade. I come back with something better. I just use this as a process to continue to get better stuff. But the question is do you believe that entrepreneurship is that something we're born with? Can anybody become an entrepreneur?

Mike:

Anybody can be an entrepreneur it is a skill learned not something we were born with. Some learn it earlier than others, even though the potential is in us all. My other son, he finds and sells things on *Craigslist* and by doing so he makes money. He is always finding things to sell. He sells old games, remote cars, cell phones, tablets, clothes; things like that. He goes to garage sales picks stuff up or trades something with friends then he sales them. The old saying one man's junk is another man's treasure. That's entrepreneurship at its lowest level. What is it that we do, we have our product or service and that fills a need for something someone wants, and we sell that product or service. We all have it in us to design a business and become an entrepreneur. As I mentioned before, most of them start out as an employee for a particular product or service then they create a company providing the same product or service. However it's the skills that you develop to be able to develop your business. It's the fundamentals to running a business that you go out and learn.

One of the greatest books that I have read about business was from Michael Gerber called the *E-Myth*, he says, "Contrary to popular belief, my experience has shown me that the people who are exceptionally good in business aren't so because of what they know but because of their insatiable need to know more."

I kid around with everyone about my vehicle; I literally call it the, "University on Wheels." I learned that the phrase from someone in my career not sure who but I like it because the amount of driving time someone does to and from work in a short period of time can equal one semester at collage. I thought just how powerful that was because it's so true. You cannot get in my car without listening to something in personal development. Here's the amazing thing. It doesn't even have to be in what you're doing as a profession. You could be learning about cooking or gardening. When you're constantly feeding your mind, it's like watering a plant. It grows and it comes up with ideas and it's creative.

Ideas will flow to you. I always say that when the student is ready the teacher will appear. When you're feeding it, it reacts and it flourishes.

Levi:
It takes a certain level of sacrifice and discipline to become an entrepreneur to actually be good at it?

Mike:
Yeah, absolutely. But that goes with anything in life. The biggest thing is overcoming the 4 letter word called FEAR. The fear factor is the biggest obstacle that people have to overcome which a big part of that is dealing with the 6 inches between one ears. This is where people have the hardest time, they want to but they're afraid. Even my fiancé who I've been coaching and training right now to be on her own, her fear factor is what's been the barrier. We're busting through that. I tell people, "Approach the fear." I love the definition that I've

heard that the word FEAR stands for False Evidence Appearing Real. The reality is that it's exactly what it is.

If you face fear head on, what is amazing is that things will start falling into place for you to go around, over, and underneath. Things will start coming to you. Resources, thoughts, things will break through that fear barrier. Things just start happening!

Let me give you an example let's say that I have a wooden beam stretching from one center block to the other center block about 12 yards a part with the beam a foot off the ground. Now, I put $10,000 into a bag on the other side and told you can have the money if you walk across the beam to get to it, would you? Absolutely! Now I remove the ground and what you see is this same beam is stretched between two sky scrapers 100 floors up with no net would you cross? Majority of the people will not but if I add a million to the other side would you? Maybe a few more would. Now let's say your child is on the other side and that building is on fire couple floors down and there is no way down and the only way you can save them is to cross the beam to get to them and bring them back. Now I know if you are like me you will cross the beam with no hesitation to try to save your child. If the "why" is big enough you will find a way.

Now, the moment you commit to be an entrepreneur, life steps in. It's going to throw every obstacle that it can at you and that's okay. There's nothing wrong. Just know right now, you're going to fail sometimes. Every successful person that has ever been successful has failed once in a while. They failed their way to their top. What's most important is how you handle it and how you move forward that will determined your success. You have to fail once in a while. You have to learn somehow. You have to go through the journey to be able to succeed. Who you become on the journey and on your quest to reach your goals or success is going to be a whole different person than you are today. Don't be afraid to attack it head on, because the faster you learn how to do that, the more successful you will be, because then you're not going to be afraid to take on a challenge.

That's where I think a lot of people get stuck is when that fear factor steps in. It's not even a real fear factor. It's what you have had programmed into your mind.

It's what you've been programmed from others that say, "Oh, you'll never be good in business or you'll never make anything out of your life or you'll never make money." Or maybe, "You need to get a real job."

It's these subliminal messages that get programmed into people's minds. That fear factor. When you're younger, you did not have these types of fears, think about it in most cases you were fearless when you were younger.

Levi:
I have to ask, how someone can get over that "fear factor?" A lot of people are afraid of failure. They're afraid to fall down. They're afraid of the financial pain, as I tried it and it didn't work. How do people get pass that?

Mike:
That's a very good question and I get that all the time. The first thing that you need to identify the type of fears and know what is classified as fear. The definition of the word 'fear' is: an unpleasant emotion caused by the threat of danger, pain, or harm. It also means: To be afraid of something or someone. Fears come in all sizes and with varying depths of intensity. No two people are going to demonstrate the same type of fear for the same thing. This is one reason why facing your fears can be difficult. First step is to acknowledge and admit that you have the fear in the first place. Sometimes Fear can be a good thing. Fear is a survival instinct and without it, humans would not survive life-threatening situations. Fear keeps us alive by alerting us to imminent dangers. When humans fear the right things, they survive and pass these traits on to the next generation. Some fears are cooked into our genes. Have you ever been bitten by a snake, probably not, and yet you are fearful of snakes. Why don't you walk down a dark alley at night? Your internal warning system anticipates danger. There may be something hiding in the shadows.

While living with fear is very common place, serious problems begin to develop when these fears turn into chronic fears. A chronic fear is something that you just can't get out of your head, no matter what. You find yourself constantly thinking about this thing all the time and fear it intensely. If you develop this type of fear you should visit your doctor and seek treatment and possibly counseling to overcome your fears. This type of fear is not healthy at all and could lead to developing severe anxiety and/or depression.

It is very common for you to not want to face your fears. Most people prefer not to even speak about their fears. There is a process to facing your fears and this is known as exposing your fears. Exposing your fears involves gradually going into those situations that make you fearful. This is a slow process where you place yourself in a certain instance for a very small amount of time. Over time you will start to feel less anxious about facing this particular situation and this helps to reduce your fear of it. This process works best when you begin by facing a situation that makes you fearful, but not one that you are terrified of. By facing your smaller fears first, you can build up to facing and exposing larger ones.

I'll tell you, the biggest thing that's going to help you get over fear and is going to drive you strait through it is your "Why." Why are you doing it? If your why doesn't make you cry, then it's not strong enough for you to succeed or break down the barriers of the fear factor. Every master was a disaster before they learned how to master their trait. You have to have a strong why to drive you through any type of obstacles or fear you may have. To support that why starts with having your goals in place. I take the goals and build them around my why and then create a cause. I look at my yearlong goal for example and break it down into smaller goals. I look at what are the top five mini goals that I need to do to achieve that main goal. Once I have the top five mini goals identified I then break those down into smaller top five goals. Having these in place gives me a solid foundation for my why. This will help me face all obstacles and fears that I may come across.

I then track my goals and achievements in 90-day increments. Similarly to the rocket that goes to the moon, I need to make sure that I'm on course and it's easier to track in 90-day segments versus a yearlong segment. If I break it down from there to weekly goals, and ask what do I need to stay on track? I try to re-engineer backwards to where I am looking at every day. This way I know what I am doing and what I need to do to accomplish my targeted goals. By doing this it keeps me focused on my why.

Matter of fact, before I go to bed, I ask myself the question, "Have I done everything I could possibly do today to help me achieve my goals or my success?"

Whatever it is that I have as my destination my goals keep me on track and I have them written down. See, a lot of people, they think about their goals but they don't put it in writing. Here's what I tell people, "If you think it, ink it," because there's so many things in life that will take over in your life that your goals get lost in your mind. You may think of a goal but then three weeks later, you don't think of it again until then.

I look at my goals every single day, every morning and every night. I look at what it is I need to do. Goals are the driving forces to my why and it is my GPS to my ultimate destination. Without them I would be lost or more importantly not sure if I am on course.

It would be like me asking you to get in your car and then saying, "Hey, you need to drive to New York from California without a map to pick up a million dollars for doing so. However, you need to be there in 5 days. If you don't get there in that time then you can't have the million dollars"

You're going to have a hard time because you're not going to know the best or even, the right route. You're going to do whatever it takes to get there and guess but you're not going to be sure if that is the right way or what's the better way? Where am I going to get gas? Where am I going to sleep? What restaurants can I stop at? You will do everything in your power to get there because you have a big WHY the million dollars but without that map it is going to be hard. You've got to have a road map and that's what goals do for you. They give you that map and the goals keep your why alive.

If you do not have a strong enough why while you're trying to achieve your dream as an entrepreneur, then you're not going to succeed. You are going to come across all types of obstacles. You may be tough in the beginning, but over time you're going to get hit and then hit again and then again you're not going to be prepared to go through them, because your why is not strong enough. You really have to drive that home. Like I said, if it doesn't make you cry, then it's not going to be strong enough for you to succeed.

Levi:

I love that you brought the why and it's especially funny, because it's a reoccurring theme with all entrepreneurs that I talk to. It's that central raising or central motivation. The next step in the process that really I think trips up a lot of people is the how. Another concept that gets brought up—especially recently—is whether entrepreneurs have an ability to recognize profitable relationships. Relationships that will help them move from where they're at to the level that they want to get. Talk to us a little bit about relationships and the importance in achieving goals?

Mike:

You know, it is funny because I actually dropped out of high school. I was an entrepreneur and making money I wanted to get out in the real world and make more money.

I got to the point where in my senior year, I felt that "Hey, I'm making more money than I would from spending my time going to school."

Plus, I remember telling my dad that I did not like collage because they didn't teach you how to succeed for yourself. They don't teach you how to be an entrepreneur. Please understand, I am not knocking college. College does a great job of creating the discipline of what it takes to go out in the real world. I didn't really understand the true value of that education until later. The education is important for all the fundamental principles behind it but the relationships out of collage are as important as the education. The connections and the people you meet through collage lead to opportunity's later down the road. I eventually went back to school and receive my diploma. Then, I went to college and received a degree.

The point is that in the whole concept of going out there and building friendships and developing relationships leads to opportunities. I've always told my son, "The more people you know, the more relationships you establish, the more opportunities you have in "life."Get connected face-to-face with people in all aspects of your life, whether they be family, friends, business associates or casual acquaintances. Try to make brief encounters and lengthy visits a chance to really connect with someone and not just a passing of time. You never know what may come of a conversation where you are truly in the moment and making the most of your time with someone. Today, I have more opportunities than I ever had before. For example, the opportunity to write a chapter in this book came to me through a friend of mine. I'm always meeting new people. I love building relationships because one, I love hearing other peoples stories and two; you never know who somebody knows. It's not about them. It's about who they know.

When you're out there in the world, you may come across something that is the next big idea, or someone that can help you and may have a great idea that leads you to something big that creates an opportunity. Look at Steve Wozniak, who helped found Apple with Steve Jobs. You just never know. That goes not only for the networking, but also for mentorship. I have different mentors for different parts of my life that I report to on a daily, weekly and monthly basis.

A mentor is an experienced and trusted adviser, an individual with more experience in business or merely in life than you. They are there to help an entrepreneur hone her or his powers and advises him or her on piloting fresh challenges. A mentor may be a boon to an entrepreneur in a broad array of scenarios, whether they supply pointers on business technique, bolster your networking crusades or act as confidantes when your work-life balance becomes out of whack.

Mentors are there to help guide you, making sure that you break through the barriers of fear and keeping you accountable. Having accountability partners and mentors help you bounce ideas off of them and/or have access to resources that you may need to call upon. They also help keep you on track.

You should always ask for help when you're stuck or have an idea, they are there to help you and don't be afraid to ask. It's in our nature to help others. It really is. I have mentors for different things I am doing in my life. For example, one of my mentors is Dr. Patrick Porter, who's probably the leading expert in hypnosis.

I have subliminal music with his voice where he talks about breaking through procrastination or preparing for success. I listen over and over, and I consult with him on a regular basis and I read all his books. Then I have a different type of accountability partner on goals. I have an accountability partner on somebody that I know that's very successful in the area business that I want to be successful in. I tell him, "Here's what I want to do. This is what I'm trying to achieve. Here are my limited beliefs and obstacles that I may have or face." All my mentors and partners keep me accountable. It's a lot easier to give up on yourself when you only know about it. It's a lot harder to give up on somebody that also knows your goals and are keeping you accountable.

I turn to them for guidance and leadership and also, for motivation. Sometimes, I may be down. You need that person to be there for you to pick you back up.

Thus, you often find yourself saying, "Okay look, that didn't work. Let's go a different direction kind of like a river."

When you throw a bolder in the middle of the river the river changes the way it flows and adjusts to the situation. The flow of the river is always changing. You have to adjust to the situation. You adjust and then, go different way. But that did not work so you go a different direction. Having that mentorship is critical and that's part of the relationships. You always want to strive to associate with people that you feel are smarter and more successful than you.

I heard this when I was younger and I am not sure if it was true but it made great sense to me and that Harvard did a study. They said that the five people you hang out with the most, you become the average of. If you're not hanging out with people that are better or smarter than you, people that are going to stretch your mind, stretch your vision and take you out of your comfort zone, then you'll never going to grow as a person. You want to look for those types of mentors or partners to aligning yourself with.

Levi:

I've heard the concept of mentorship basically from everyone that I've ever met that's successful. One of the questions that I get asked a lot is, on that concept of hanging out with the five people that have an impact on who you are, what if those other people, how do I attract those other people to hang out with me? The concept that I often go back to is, either you have to be on their level or you have to pay for their services. Would you agree with that concept?

Mike:

Absolutely. Mentors come in all sizes and shapes and everyone who I know that is successful has a mentor; even Bill Gates has a mentor—he has Warren Buffet. A lot of times you can pay for some of these mentors that can guide and help you become successful in the direction you want to go. However, before you seek out a mentor you need to start with ascertaining what type of mentor you require. It is an imperative to the first step in the mentor hunt. Beginning with a list is a good opening. You might want somebody who's a great listener, somebody socially connected, somebody with expertise in marketing or a person with great resources.

Ideally, you may find a mentor with all of these characters, but the reality is you might have to make a few compromises to get a good mentor. After you count the characters you're looking for in a mentor, split up that list into wants and needs.

The first step is to "do an informational interview" with many different candidates and then, go back to your standards that way you don't get blown away by chemistry and you remain centered on your business or personal reasons for needing a mentor. By judging a combination of the qualitative and quantitative properties of each of your likely mentors, a prime candidate will come forth.

Bear in mind that it might be advantageous to have more than one mentor. If you think that you might monopolize too much of your mentor's time then several mentors might be the answer. The benefits of having multiple mentors is that you are able to get a lot of assorted viewpoints and when you have many mentors at a time, if they're seated around a table, the synergy between the mentors truly helps move your thinking along.

So how do you go about discovering a mentor? Depending on the level of mentor will determine how you start discovering the type of mentor you need. My suggestion is begin with loved ones and friends—When seeking a mentor, begin close to home. Really close to home. Occasionally, you are able to talk to your own relatives or friends, individuals who you trust, who you know, who you are able to sit and say what they feel about it.

Think about those in your broadened network—if your friends and loved ones provide you enough unsought advice already and you don't believe that's the route for you, then your leftover options are individuals who don't know you as well or don't know you in the least as of yet.

Okay, so how do you ask for such a huge commitment from a virtual stranger? The opening move is to get hold of your network of contacts. A positive word from a common acquaintance may go a long way toward getting a mentoring relationship off to a great start.

Additionally, you shouldn't pick out a mentor overnight, which implies you ought to keep your antenna poised to pick up on likely mentors at conferences, trade shows, and so forth. Meeting with a future mentor in person helps construct a rapport and you may wish to wait till that connection develops before tossing out the question.

Think about total strangers—perhaps none of the individuals in your network seem like a great fit for you. Begin doing a little research. Profiles of business owners in magazines and papers may key you in to somebody who equals your style. But when you have a few prospects go forward delicately.

Discover as much as you are able to about the likely mentor. One of the first things to do is search online to see if they have any websites or if they have any social media sites set up so you can start following them. Follow them online and subscribe to any and all of their stuff. Read their blogs or articles about what they do and what is it they're doing, start getting into their environment. Maybe they have an advanced program to buy or coaching program. A lot of coaches and experts out there have some type of mentoring or coaching program. Read their books if they have any on the market. Example you may or may not like Donald Trump but he has several books out in the market. I read his books because you can't deny his success. If they do not have anything available for purchase or any resources online then attempt to schedule a brief interview by telephone saying you have a few particular questions or generally wish to pick their brain.

You ought to travel to them and particularly at first, make it as simple for them to help you as you are able to. At the end of your interview, if it appears to have gone well, you may broach the idea of speaking once again, whether by telephone or in person, sometime in the time to come.

Over time, if they feel receptive, you may bring up the idea of a more conventional mentoring relationship with more particular parameters and goals.

Think about the rivalry—Well, not your direct rivalry. For instance, if you're in retail selling barbeque pits, somebody selling Patio furniture isn't in direct rivalry with you but may still have a few insights into the outdoor product industry.

If you have a brick and mortar store, you may even call somebody who does precisely what you do in a faraway location, suppose you're in New York City and they're in Arizona. However the web is increasingly placing retailers even on different continents in rivalry, so step lightly. A different hint would be to seek out counsel from somebody at a business larger than yours who may be less likely to view you as rivalry.

Another way is to tap into your field for mentors. For example look to some of your suppliers, or your local chamber of commerce, and or relevant trade publishing's as great sources for likely mentors. These are all great places to come by knowledgeable individuals, but how do you find somebody who matches your personal flair? You should look for a mentor the same way that individuals seek medical professionals; also, seek out recommendations about whom is best in your field.

As I mention earlier, paying for mentoring is another great source. Let's say you have an awesome idea that you wish to get off the ground rapidly and you need a fast jolt of expertise? Great informal mentorships are cultivated bit by bit and may frequently last for years. However if what you require is a crash program, it may be time to bring in the paid consultants who can help you get started.

The key to winning over any mentor is the more you get into learning about them the quicker you can establish rapport and they will respect you more.

There's a great book that I would recommend that everyone read over and over which is called *How to Win Friends and Influence People*, it is one of the most powerful books you can ever read for business. This book teaches you how to develop those relationships. It teaches you how to build a network. It's one of the most powerful books in the market that I can talk to as far as entrepreneurship.

That is one of many books that will help you especially in developing relationships. Some others that are good and are classics are

Think and Grow Rich, The Four Hour Work Week. The new one I am reading now is called *Peaks and Valleys*, by Spencer Johnson, who also wrote the book *Who Moved the Cheese?*

It talks about when you're having hard times and good times and how to manage them, it's a very powerful book. I couldn't stop reading it. Of course, my new book that's coming out soon after this book hits the market called, *"The 1099 vs. The W2 Attitude—Learn How To Break The Barrier From Being an Employee to Being Self Employed."*

This is where I go into more detail on what it takes and the mindset of being an entrepreneur. My current book that is out, *Mastering the Mindset, the Power of Affirmations*, is where I teach people how to reprogram the bad habits which are active in their minds. In this book, I give you a 33-day exercise to reinforce it and then follow up quote. All of these—plus more—are books that are important to have on your bookshelf.

Levi:

It's one of my favorite books, as well, I think that it's not the first business book I read, but it was one of the first. It definitely had an impact on me and my relationships. Another concept that was actually developed by Woody Woodward is the currency. We all have currencies that we can exchange. There's mental currency, emotional currency, financial currency, spiritual currency and physical currency.

A lot of times I think we get stuck in this notion that makes us think, "Hey, why would that person want to do anything with me? What do I have to offer them?"

There really are additional things that we can offer. We just have to take a step back and understand how currencies work and how the law of exchange works.

Mike, you've given a lot of great advice. One question I absolutely love to ask for people that are inspiring as you are is, "What kind of legacy do you want to leave behind?"

Mike:

That's a good question. In truly being an entrepreneur in business obviously, people want to leave financial legacy for their families, and I defiantly want to leave financial freedom for my family and my grandchildren and on. But I think the true legacy is the library of knowledge, the resources, the books that I have that I can pass on my experiences, a journal of thoughts that I've had throughout my career. I truly believe that is the most valuable legacy I can leave behind is the knowledge and resources to do what I have done but better. It's like this story I heard that I can give you a fish and you will eat for the day but if I teach you how to fish you will eat for a life time. These are the tools that are going to help you go out and be successful and eat for a lifetime.

Levi:

In conclusion, speaking to entrepreneurs or the people who are already in business or people that just want to make a change in their life, if you were to give one piece of an advice, one call to action that's the most important thing that someone could do it right now to start changing, what would that one thing be?

Mike:

Start by changing the way you think and act. Act as if you are already there. There are a lot of employees who are longing to be their own boss, yet, they are fearsome of what the future may hold if they were business owners. I would like to advise those people about the following—if you're among those individuals, you'd do well to become a great 1099 employee first! Act and start thinking as if you're already an entrepreneur.

There's a great movie out called *"The Longshots"* that I saw starring Ice Cube, in the movie he was coaching a pop warner football team with the first girl quarterback in history. In one of the scenes, one of the kids during practice gets the ball and runs it in for a touchdown.

The boy that scored the touchdown then jumped up and down and did a touchdown dance. Then Ice Cube asked, "What is that?"

The boy says, "That's my touchdown dance."

Ice Cube then ask the whole team, "Do all of you have a touchdown dance?"

Everyone responded by saying, "Yeah."

Ice Cube then asked "Let me see it." So the entire team all started showing and doing their touchdown dance.

Then at the end, Ice Cube said, "Okay, are you guys done?"

Then, the team respond by saying, "Oh yeah."

Ice Cube then said, "Here's how I want you to do it. When you score a touchdown, I want you to walk over and hand the ball to the referee and act as if you had already been there once before."

If you train your mind to think, you're already an entrepreneur and you start taking the path towards that, there's a ton of ways to be an entrepreneur. There's so many opportunities these days to be able to get started running a home—based business with very little investment. You can start out by just doing it part-time or full-time. You don't have to go full depth and full-time right away.

The key is to just begin; start acting like you're in business for yourself. Start training your mind and acting as if you're an entrepreneur. Start aligning yourself with other entrepreneurs, organizations, or groups of business owners. Develop a personal development program and start reading about entrepreneurship. Do all this and you'll start becoming an entrepreneur. Then, over time, you will develop the blueprint of entrepreneurship for you to the point where you're ready for success. It has to start with somewhere and the first place is with you and in your mind.

As the saying goes, "How do you eat an elephant? One bite at a time."

Entrepreneurship is no different. Just one bite at a time and work your way until it get easier and easier and better and better for you.

Sharon Wahlig

Sharon began her career in the corporate world through cultivating expertise in sales and management. However, she later found true joy in being an entrepreneur. Her desire for independence and her passion to make a difference led Sharon down the road of entrepreneurialism.

Sharon has trained and mentored hundreds of individuals across the country on a one on one basis. She has helped people to improve on both a personal and professional level through her live events, such as *"Live Life by Your Design, Because You Can"*. In addition, she has assembled, trained, and developed successful leadership teams as well as women's organizations and sales teams.

Sharon is a self-titled DreamKeeper. Today, with a team of experts, Sharon assists others in the process of changing their lives by creating cash flow through business ownership and investment in real estate. She advocates a simplified approach, so that they feel more secure and therefore more able to spend quality time doing more of what they enjoy.

Websites: *www.Sharonwahlig.com*
  www.lifessupposedtobefun.com

Levi:

So Sharon, you have been able to do something that a lot of people before the technology revolution just dreamed about, which is to create a business around your lifestyle. You've gone through a journey here. Perhaps it was Tim Ferriss that kicked it off in the minds of most of us, but this whole idea that you can start living your dream life now, and you don't have to wait until you build up a public company to retire now, you can start experiencing life the way you really want. And to jump in your introduction, I'd like to just explore your journey a little bit. Talk to us about how you started this living your life by design, perhaps when you fired your boss, and just give us a little bit of insight into your journey.

Sharon:

Yes, Thank you for asking. I officially started my entrepreneurial journey when I was in Corporate America. I thought I was doing really well. It happened to be at a time during the dot-com industry in the Bay Area. Everyone was hoping to land a pre-IPO Company that went public. I had great jobs, plenty of stock options, and thought I had "arrived," until the jobs I landed disappeared and the Companies didn't end up going public. One company I worked for reduced our salaries every month until we were at zero, instead of letting us go over night. Gracious, but I was still downsized out. Thousands of jobs were lost during that time, and I realized that the "secure" model was really "insecure." I couldn't get ahead and realized the system I had been taught to follow was not working for me. I always knew that I would do something independent, something outside the box, even before the downsizing started happening. I knew I wanted to experience more, I wanted more freedom, I wanted more control, and I knew I wasn't going to find my "it" job that I would invest 20-30 years in. Then what was happening in our history made nearly unavailable for most. In the end, I really did end up getting what I wanted. I wanted independence and it happened.

During my time in Corporate, I began attending Anthony Robbins trainings to assist me in my career to reach higher levels. Not being satisfied in my jobs, I was also hoping to figure out what I really wanted to do and gain the courage to do it. Through my work with Tony, I was so inspired by what he was doing; assisting people in identifying their dreams and then bring them into reality to accomplish them. That's when I realized that was what I wanted to do. I wanted to be able to create with those who knew what they wanted to do, but just didn't know how to go about it or had fear in doing so. The work was truly transformational.

At a time of uncertainty and insecurity in the job market, an opportunity came up to potentially secure a position as a Results Coach with Robbins Research International, I decided to go out on faith, and I walked away from my job; fired my boss. I spent 30 days training with Tony and his team which was well outside my comfort zone, but I stayed focused on what I wanted and earned a position as a Results Coach. (Ironically, not long after, the Company I left closed its doors anyway). I worked for Robbins for a couple of years until it was no longer an option.

At that point, I made the decision. I felt confident that I found a true passion; I was making a difference and had gained courage to go and figure out life on my own. I knew I had to figure out how to Live Life by my Design while also making a Difference. It hasn't always been easy, but I have never looked back.

Levi:
That's awesome. So, you fired your boss, and then you jumped out into trying to help other people to live their dreams. Can you talk to us about what that entailed and what that dream was like.

Sharon:
Actually, I went with my gut. So, for people who are thinking; is this the right decision? For me, it worked out. I fired my boss before they ended up firing me when they shut down the company anyway. So for me, in following my heart and my intuition, in looking back, it was a really great decision, I would have ended up without my job anyway. It was risky, but it felt right. For those who have jobs and can begin their entrepreneurial journey on the side, it is a good way to go. I am truly grateful for every Corporate and employee experience I have had, as each position gave me knowledge, mentors, experience, training and belief in myself. It's all part of the journey.

Levi:
No, that really highlights though the current marketplace for people that are out there, and who are working for someone, that are working for a boss, and they really don't know the security of their job. There's a lot of moving parts, and so the option of entrepreneurship seems to be more secure in today's market space.

Sharon:
Yes, I would agree. I have that conversation with people almost on a daily basis. Being an entrepreneur is the way, it is the solution to creating leveraged income & exponential growth. I believe we come by it honestly; it's how our ancestors got their start. Entrepreneurialism is what this country was built on. Not that it's always easy, but it is worth it. I talk to people every day and hear their stories of feeling insecure, and they are looking for solutions. There is a way. I wasn't getting ahead with linear, insecure income. I had to create another way. Being an entrepreneur allows me to have control of not only my time, but also my income, and then ultimately my future. I'm not telling everybody to go out and quit their jobs, but if you have a strong enough passion, commitment, and determination, and if you have an idea, or a thought; at least, try. America loves and embraces success and comeback stories of those who give it their best. To at least attempt something, win or lose, inspires others, and gives them hope because you had the guts, and the courage to go for it. What's the worst that can happen? I knew I could always go back if I had to.

I recommend being smart about it; surround yourself with the right people. Find people that have talent and expertise that you can model. Create or model an intelligent, effective & proven system. Be disciplined. Commit, believe, and at least go for it; give it a shot. You don't have to completely cut the cord like I did, there are ways of stepping into being an entrepreneur that you can do while also keeping a job.

For me, I found that creating my plan and Living by my design allowed me to have control over my income and time. I am able to generate more income, if I want to; I don't have to ask permission to be sick, to take a vacation, to pick up kids in the middle of the afternoon or come in late because I had another commitment in the morning. I have choices, control, freedom and a chance to live on purpose. If I want to work from an office, I do; if I want to work from the beach, I do. Freedom of choice is liberating.

Levi:

You have a motto that I actually love, which is "Live Life by Your Design, Because you can." Tell us what that means, and why it's meaningful to you?

Sharon:

It means living on purpose. Meaning that when I had a job, I was living what showed up, and what I needed to do to survive. I took jobs because they came with a good paycheck. Now, I get to work "on purpose," a double meaning; 1. I decide my work, and 2. My work is fulfilling my purpose in life; I'm on purpose with my path. I know I am here to make a difference. There are people who have their career because it is by design. They love their work. I happened to have fallen into mine, and I was working a job to fulfill a need. Then, through downsizing, I realized it wasn't even doing that. It wasn't something that I was doing on "purpose" or found joy in. I was living/working for necessity. Today, I choose to "Live Life by my Design, Because I Can."

What I realized through my journey; as cliché as it may sound, I really just wanted to make a difference. If in my work, I can, in some way, assist others to create something more for themselves or breathe a little easier in knowing it's possible, then, I feel fulfilled. For me, to venture out of the box of Corporate America, allowed me to live by my design and do what I felt was important to me, which was being a part of others keeping their dreams which is why my brand, or company name is DreamKeeper; because I'm keeping my dream it means I am assisting others in keeping their dreams.

Levi:

Now, you've talked about your journey. You launched out. You started living your own dream. You became a DreamKeeper. You started helping other people do the same thing, living their own life by design. But you mentioned in a prior conversation that you came to a point where entre-

preneurs come to where we realize, "Hey, I can't do everything by myself, or I'm going to snap." Talk to us a little bit about that.

Sharon:
Yes. As part of our life journey we learn through personal development, mindset training and studying success. Most of us have some limiting beliefs that can paralyze us. I saw some of my less skilled areas and equated that to mean, that I had to overcome those limitations and be great at all things. One of the things that held me back from really going full speed ahead was I felt like I had to be all things to all people. I was attempting to do it all. This is pretty absurd when I finally stopped to really consider that idea.

If I walk into any company, there are several departments, a team; each person bringing their best talents to the table. There's an executive team, accounting team, the fulfillment team, a sales team, a marketing team, customer service team and so on. As a solo entrepreneur, I was attempting to be every department, until I realized something very important; I needed a team. I began to notice, not many businesses or ideas were truly accomplished without a team. Even as good as Michael Jordan was, he was never going to win Championships without his team. Another limiting factor I discovered in my journey; is that I believed I needed unlimited capital to have a team. Not true. Collaboration with others doesn't always require capital in the form of dollars.

I would hear the term "self-made millionaire" and falsely believed I had to do it myself. Personally I don't subscribe to self-made any longer. One might have the drive, the determination, the desire, and a creative plan, but chances are that unless living on an island by themselves, at one point or another, we align ourselves with others' talents, or resources to get to where we want to go, and to really complete the process; Collaborative creation.

With that profound breakthrough that I had early on, I started aligning with talented individuals who were better in a particular area than I was. I used to work for a well-known international company, and I remember a conversation with the divisional director overseeing the US market saying "I'm not the smartest one here; I surround myself with people who are smarter or more talented than me." It's very important to understand this because it's very liberating.

In my business today, I have coaches, partners, and mentors. I create with people who have very specific talent and expertise in their areas. When I surround myself with a talented team, it allows me to focus on my strengths. I used to believe it was a weakness to involve others, now I realize it's really a strength. I believe when you can identify your strengths and align yourself with those of opposite strengths, and outsource what you don't enjoy or excel at, it is optimal for success. When you create partnerships and a team environment with like minded individuals with opposing strengths, all moving forward toward a Common Cause; magic happens. You win Championships—Together. I know today, that I could not have the success I have without the talented team around me, and in return, I get to be a part of their success as well.

We are all in this together. When I look at our economy, for instance, in this country, even if you have the largest bank account on the block, you need everybody in your community, city, state, and country to also be financially secure because if they're not, you're not really secure and vice versa. It's very important that we all work together and support each other's mission of financial security because we are only as successful as the rest of our team or the rest of our economy is. I knew I could either be part of the problem or part of the solution, so I chose to be part of the solution.

Levi:
I love that you brought up the economy because while you've been talking, I was thinking about Adam Smith who is considered the father of economy. One of the components that he proposed that was necessary to grow economies is specialization. So, what you've been talking about adding team members that are better than you, it sounds like what you've been doing is aligning people to have those specializations. The next component that he recommends for growth is actually trust in order for exchange. You capitalized on that with this concept: We're all working towards the same cause.

Now, a question that other entrepreneurs may want to know is, how

*do you go about selecting those individuals that have those specializa-
tions, and then how do you build trust so that that they continue to offer
their specializations to your unified cause?*

Sharon:
That's a great question. My natural approach in building trust is service. Be of service. I let people know I care, I do what I can, I show up,
and I give back. I don't expect trust; I earn it by showing up.

Specialization is also a key word in your question. Back to my comment about attempting to be all things to all people. Aligning yourself
with people who have specialized skill is vital. What I also subscribe
to is six degrees of separation. In surrounding yourself with people who are moving forward toward a common cause, or people who
have specialized skill and levels of success, an interesting thing happens, the right people show up. I believe it's in part to what I mentioned earlier about service. I know through experience that when I
serve it always comes back. It may not come from the direct area of
which I served, but it does always come back. So if I'm contributing,
if I'm surrounded by an immediate group of individuals, a nucleus
of people starts to build, and, they serve back in various ways. We
create business; we share ideas, resources, and connections and so
on. When you are like minded and surround yourself with those of
integrity, solution thinking, and strength, you find yourself in their
environment which also happens to be full of talented, individuals
with integrity. I guess what I am saying, from my experience is that
when you do things for the right reason, surround yourself with other talented people, and add value and service, what you need ends up
showing up.

I'm not shooting in the dark so to speak. I don't open the Yellow
Pages and say, "Oh I need a person with these talents. Who's it going
to be?" I surround myself. I put myself in likeminded circles. Tony
taught, if you want what others have, you have to do what others do,
which of course means, you have to be in the vicinity of them; watch,
learn & apply. You mentioned Tim Ferriss earlier, I recently read his
book. He has some great content and 'cut to the chase' resources. Tim
has proven himself that he can live life by his design. He invested

time investigating some of the best of the best, which has expedited his successes.

So, in my day to day life, I put myself in solution oriented environments, and in those environments I find truly great people. And if I come from a place of genuine service first, somehow what I want or need comes back. Zig Ziglar said: "If you help more people get what they want in life, you end up getting what you want." I have experienced that to be true.

I believe, to reduce it all down; for me it comes down to knowing what it is that I want to create, believing that I can create it, and then putting myself in environments of likeminded individuals who all believe in the ability of moving things forward, serving others and taking action, then whatever it is that I need ends up showing up. Whatever is left, I set the intention to either seek it out, or create it. Does that make sense?

Levi:
Absolutely, that makes sense. I have some other business associates that proposed the client set that value follows value. So, what you're explaining, makes perfect sense to me, that when you serve, you put value out there into the marketplace. We have something that we call the laws of exchange and that basically one of the principles is that we're only willing to trade for something of greater value; otherwise, no transactions would happen between us. We all have our own individual currency so to speak. We have things that we can trade, whether or not that's knowledge, or whether or not it's money itself, whether or not that's physical assets. But, if you offer those things up first, and if you've already given somebody something of greater value, because they didn't give you anything before they wanted to exchange something, so now they're going to be inclined to make that exchange with you. Does that align with the concept that you've been describing?

Sharon:
Yes, exactly. We absolutely all have something to offer each other. Also, not wasting the gift is a good idea. Show up by utilizing the talents, knowledge, skill or resources others share with you. Be an

example. So, if you're not living an example of someone who takes it seriously, they might feel like you are a time waster and will lose interest in aligning with you. How you show up, I believe, is what comes back to you. Sometimes, it is in the form of attracting the right mentor. If someone invests time in me, and I don't gift back by utilizing the knowledge, then I have taught them that I am not serious, or a good investment of their time and I probably won't be on their list as someone to consider working with again.

It's how you show up, "going first" as Rosa Parks said; "Each person must live their life as a model for others." I think that goes back to most of this conversation, being willing to go first, stepping outside the box and deciding to become an entrepreneur, being brave enough to look your boss in the eye and choose a different direction.

Rosa Parks is someone who inspired us all because she went first. Because she had the guts and the courage to go first; she lived by example, and changed our history. So it's her quote that each of us can gain inspiration from to live our life as a model for others.

When I remember that, I have enough courage to go first and live life by my design. I get to contribute and show other people that they can, too, and then they in turn show others, creating the ripple effect. The Pebbles in a pond concept. An end result as I mentioned earlier, it ends up coming back to you. It doesn't matter from where, doesn't matter the source, but somehow, whatever it is that I need always ends up showing up.

Levi:
You've brought up a couple of times the concept of a mentor, and right now you've been describing mentoring on the other side. So, once you've been mentored, you need to mentor others. Could you define what does it mean to be a mentor?

Sharon:
It is what it is all about. For me, it's fulfillment. To be able to be a part of someone's journey in a positive way and be a mentor, is what fills me up more than anything, more than money. To set a desired outcome, and work together with them toward its achievement is an amazing reward.

I'll give you an example and maybe it can help understand what it is I'm attempting to express. When I was in Corporate America and decided to cut the cord and fire my boss, it was a scary proposition. When I ventured out, honestly, there were times when I really questioned it, asking myself "what am I doing"?

Not wanting to give up, I knew I needed to create a name for myself, I had to get a reference, and a success story so I donated my time to a high school and worked with their football team. I worked with them on the mindset side of the game. How: 1st we got clear; what did they want, why did they want it, what would it give them in having it, what were they willing to do make it happen etc. Then, identified their limiting beliefs and language patterns that held them back. From there we got to work. We removed language such as try, can't, "we're the worst in the league" etc. Each week we focused on what they wanted (to go to the Championships), we rehearsed each game over and over in their mind of how they wanted it before they played; they used new language congruently with passion and emotional intensity that they were 'the best', that they were 'Champions.'

This was a team that had only won one game the season before, so they believed they were the worst in the league. The preseason stats said they would finish the season last. I went out, and worked with them every week. I taught them everything I had learned from my mentors on; How to re-write the predetermined destiny someone else had for them. Week after week, by what they were doing with their coaches on the skill side of the game, and what they were doing with me on mindset side of the game they became stronger and stronger, and they started winning more and more games. They showed up as the "Champions" they decided they were.

We stayed focused on what they wanted, reinforced and celebrated all the wins, big and small: games, belief changes, eliminating defeating language etc. That was a scenario where all of us were moving forward towards a common cause. What they wanted to accomplish was to make it to the Championships. That was their goal. So each week that's what the conversation was about. I worked with these kids every single week. It was an investment, time energy, and at times, tears. All I wanted from the coach was an arena to see what we could accomplish with them, and earn a referral or a testimony.

There were times during this process when I was building my company where money was extremely tight, but I kept going. I saw people who took over my previous sales position, who took over all of my accounts. They started talking about the money that was coming in. There were times I felt doubt, like, "What am I doing? I'm not getting paid, why did I leave my job?" My own limiting language showed up, "I can't afford to keep doing this" but each week, I was reminded Why I was doing it, and what I received in return. I kept believing I was on 'purpose.' What I was getting back was seeing these kids, watching their life change. Not just on the field, but in their life. The principal pulled me aside and thanked me, he said, "It's not just who they are on the field, it's who they are becoming, it's when I look down the hall and see who they have become off the field that I see. As far as I'm concerned you are part of our school improvement project."

I remember being at the game, the last game of the season. This game was the deciding factor for who would be going to the championships. There was a lot on the line for these kids, for both teams. This was the one and only team they beat the year before. This was a hometown rivalry; it was the "Battle of the Bell," and whoever won would also be going to the championships, which in their minds also meant being hometown heroes. So, it was the battle of the season for them. It was an intense game. They fought hard, they were in it to win it; you could see it. With 3 seconds left in the game, they kicked a field goal and won! It was amazing! A total rush of tears and exhilaration. It was a made for TV moment. Cheering fans rushed the field. The young men were so proud. When I went down to the field, they charged me, giving me big sweaty hugs and thank you's! For some it was probably just because I showed up for them, and for some it was for believing in them.

The emotion I felt week after week, mentoring these kids and hearing them tell me what an impact it made was irreplaceable. Seeing how they became better and better each week. Not just on the field, but in life, in school and at home. They wrote me thank you letters, some of them said, "You know, because of you I'm going to college." "Because of you now, I'm happier at home," or "I got a job," or "Now I believe in myself." At times, it was incredibly difficult, but I kept going week after week, driving an hour each way, as well as attending almost every game, not knowing if it was really 'getting in' or making a difference. I just believed, "If any of this assists even just one of these young men, if this impacts even one life now or somehow makes a difference in their future; it is worth it."

There were many times during that process, during the season that I had goose bumps, chills, or prideful tears, every week. After the games I'd go on to the field, win or lose and they'd charge me... "Shaaaron." They'd say, and give me big sweaty hugs. I was so full emotionally and thought. "There has never been a single pay check I ever received from a job that filled me up so completely as that did."

A pay check never moved me personally, never moved me emotionally. It was, as I mentioned earlier, just living for necessity. Being a mentor to me is being on 'purpose.' I get to make a contribution to another life and be a part of their journey; that fills me up with more joy, love, inspiration, and emotion than a job ever could have. Today, I get to mentor others in business, and I receive mentoring from amazing and talented people as well. We are all creating a ripple effect. Incredibly rewarding!

Hopefully that expresses what being a mentor is for me. And why I do what I do in assisting others in keeping their dreams.

Levi:
Wow! Oh, absolutely. What a wonderful story. I mean what you're really talking about is redefining what wealth means because to most of us, it's the number of zeros after the dollar sign. What you've just shared is that there are some things that only come by following your passion.

Sharon:
Yes. For me it's more than money. I know how to monetize this now and be fulfilled. What I want, I can't get simply through dollars... Money is not my sole motivator.

Today, I get to provide specific solutions for others in getting what they want; I get to help increase their financial circumstances or overcome an obstacle, or take it to the next level so that they can Live

Life by their Design. I love it! It is what brings me the most joy and the most fulfillment.

Levi:
I've talked to several other entrepreneurs that have hit on similar concepts, and for them, a lot of them have mentioned that as they started living their life and applying those principles, that not only did their level of happiness increase, but they found that actually the dollars did follow their happiness, the dollars did follow them living life the way that they really felt fulfilled. Would you say it's the same for you?

Sharon:
Absolutely. I don't serve for the purpose of getting back. I don't say "hey, if I go serve this person, I'm going to get something in return from them." I do it authentically, because it's where I'm in joy, and when I can assist others in getting what they want, let go of the result, the byproduct somehow results in me getting what I want/need. And it doesn't mean that it always comes from that exact source, and it doesn't always mean dollars. I may not have received a check from that school, but the emotional reward was far greater, and there are other areas of my life that abundance just started showing up where the "easy" wins came. I believe it is because I paid it forward somewhere. So I agree wholeheartedly that when you're living in your joy, when you're living your passion & purpose, and you let go and decide to Live Life by Your Design, that the dollars start showing up.

Levi:
So, for someone else out there, maybe a budding entrepreneur or basically anyone on any walk of life that's considering living their own life by design, where do you recommend they start?

Sharon:
I would recommend that they first start with deciding. Take a look at what it is they truly want to do. Then, once they've decided that they really would like to become an entrepreneur, even if it's on part time basis; Start.

So, first decide what it is that you want, and then start surrounding yourself with the right team. Start chatting with individuals about how you can contribute to them, find your team and learn from each other. From that knowledge and the knowledge you already have, create the plan. Then implement, and take action. Consistently.

When I started creating real success, it's because I aligned myself with the right team. I have a team that if anyone would like to talk to me about how to create or how I may assist them in assembling a team, I am very open to that.

Levi:

Wonderful. Yeah, sure. So you've given just some absolutely wonderful advice and taught some incredible principles that I think all entrepreneurs can learn from. In conclusion, if there were just one single call to action or piece of advice that you would want every entrepreneur or individual out there to know, what would that piece of information or that call to action be?

Sharon:

I would say the number one is getting clear.

Levi:

Explain what you mean by that.

Sharon:

Sit in a quiet space and get clear. Remove fear and doubt, brain congestion from the day and get clear; write the story of your life.

The reason I say that is because what I've learned in working with hundreds of people, and myself, we don't often know what we actually do want. Most know they want something different, they know where they are, they know what they "don't want, they know that they're not satisfied where they're at, but they don't know clearly what they DO want. The main quality question in the science of Neuro Linguistic Programming is, "What is it that you want?"

We don't often ask ourselves. So, getting clarity would be the call to action. Sit down, get yourself in a quiet spot and really see it, get a mental picture of what it does look like, feel the experience of having it light your fire. If it moves you emotionally, chances are you have found it.

As simple as it sounds, it's no different than setting a GPS. When you pick up your GPS, what's the very first thing you need to do? You've got to tell it where you want it to go, right? On mine I can virtually watch it calculate 1000's of routes to get there and ultimately, it chooses the fastest path. How you get there doesn't matter. There are many options.

Surround yourself with great mentors who can act like the GPS and help calculate the straightest route, I assure you, there are many ways to get there, some are long, some are fast, some are more scenic, some are more fun. But there are many routes. So find the fastest most enjoyable route for you and enjoy the journey. Be in service, notice what is showing up, be grateful, keep the faith, believe you will get there and keep going. Create your plan, take consistent daily action toward it, learn the lessons, adjust, and improve where you need to and of course, celebrate all along the way.

Final thought, to get yourself in a great place, start by doing something for someone else. Contribute in one way or another. It could be a compliment, a gesture, pay a toll for the car behind you, or any kind act; it doesn't matter. Making a contribution helps us to feel great. The giver and the receiver benefit, when you feel great answers and clarity are easier to come by.

Susan Bond Ross

Susan is a successful real estate investor, national speaker and trainer, coaching on how to think bigger and effectively utilize real estate and other diverse tools to quickly grow a sound financial portfolio and prepare for retirement. She is a proud mother and entrepreneur, running her own business and enjoying the benefits and freedom to be both an active parent, as well as a successful professional.

Working with some of the top trainers and mentors in the industry has provided a wealth of knowledge and created incredible opportunities that she now shares with her colleagues and clients. Her passion is opening minds and empowering people to think and act outside of the box. With teams of hundreds throughout the country, Susan's business continues to grow daily and is poised for record-breaking earnings in 2014.

Contact: *SusanBondRoss@gmail.com*
              PlanYourResults@gmail.com
Websites: *www.SusanBondRoss.com*
              www.PlanYourResults.com

Levi:
Susan Bond Ross. So, I've got to ask, are you the 007 of entrepreneurs?

Susan:
You could say that. My father was James Bond, and growing up a "Bond Girl" has been a lot of fun. I also happen to be number 7 of 8 children, so yeah, I am the "007" of entrepreneurialism.

Levi:
So, I think even more so than our favorite character in the movies, who gets himself into tight situations and has to overcome odds, your story is rather intriguing. You started out of what most would consider very modest means and I'd like to have you share with us a little of that journey. Also, you became an entrepreneur, but you came through the psychology and social services avenue, which to most people that seems like a completely unlikely route. Talk to us about your beginnings and a little bit about your journey.

Susan:
I'd love to. Well, I grew up in a big family in Southern California. There were 5 boys, 3 girls, 2 parents, 2 bedrooms, and 1 bathroom, all in less than 1,000 square feet, in a house that was 10 minutes from downtown Los Angeles. We had our challenges financially, and it wasn't easy. But, my parents had unwavering faith and conviction. They were devout Catholics and they trusted that God would not give them anything that they couldn't handle. So, when the Lord blessed them with 8 children, they embraced it lovingly, and we basically just learned how to make do with what we had. I did not have my own bed until I was 12 years old. I did not have my own room until I was a Junior in college at the dorms. But, I believe that love grows best in small houses. When there are so many people existing in a tight space, everyone just tends to keep an eye on each other. The combination of a strong moral foundation and close general proximity proved to serve us well. The guidance was always there, as was the support, positive reassurance, and reminder that we were strong as a family, but also as individuals. It was the constant faith and encour-

agement of our parents that gave us the confidence to branch out and to find ourselves.

We were fortunate to have help from our aunts and grandmother, as well as to receive aid from government programs. Yet through it all, our parents raised us to know that assistance was a blessing, not something that we should ever expect. It was our responsibility to become prosperous and independent so that we could not only sustain ourselves, but also, more importantly, to have the ability to give back and show similar kindness to others." Keep making good things happen," is what Dad always used to say. Because of the selflessness and devotion of our parents, all eight of us worked hard to attend college and have gone on to be professionals in our own right. And, though I believe that our government aid system is flawed, I feel like we are an example of what the system was meant to do. The goal is to give a helping hand up, not a permanent handout. We never once entertained the sense of entitlement that seems to run through society today. My parents were very clear about our future being up to us. They constantly assured us that we could accomplish whatever we put our minds to, so we did.

Growing up in the Bond Family was an incredible experience! Regardless of the circumstances, we got through it together. But, even as a child, I knew that I was a bit different from my siblings—more inquisitive and audacious. I was very outgoing and social; I was not afraid to ask questions and go after things that I wanted. In school, I was a floater, easily interacting with almost every social circle. I soon became aware of the extreme variances in personality types and realized that there were distinct ways to work more effectively with different people.

Because of where I had come from and what I had been through growing up, I inherited my parents' attitude of servitude. I knew at a young age that it was my passion to help people. I wanted to give back. Plus, I had a knack for identifying with individuals and getting to know them quickly. That skill allowed me to assess needs and solutions faster. In fact, in college, I was able to be a tutor for subjects that I'd never previously studied simply because I took the time to get to know the student. I had a better understanding of how he learned and could identify the key factors that made the subject click for him. This is where my fascination with psychology and desire to better understand people really took off. I attended Menlo College, a private business school in northern California. It was not the typical venue for such a degree. However, because of the smaller class sizes and focus on more personal teacher-student interaction, the school attracted an extremely high caliber of Ivy-League professors who savored the education process. Dr. Harvey and Dr. Bales both had profound impacts on me, encouraging me to stretch my comfort zone and to better consider the world around me. My mind opened to possibilities; I threw myself into the social mix and became involved in most of the major clubs on campus, including being elected to Student Government. The experience of such diverse interactions, all while studying the science of people in a business environment, definitely helped cultivate my entrepreneurial spirit.

After graduation, I moved to Utah and used my degree in psychology to get into social work. I became the case manager and guardian ad litem to 13 teenagers in state's custody. Wow! Talk about a job that rips your heart out every day.

There I was, barely 24 years old and now the legal guardian to 13 teenagers. I'd get a call in the middle of the night telling me, "Your kid's on the run." Or, a call letting me know that one of my kids had been attacked by their parent who had come to visit them. It was surreal. Strange and bizarre things occurred that one could scarcely imagine, yet it was my job to try to somehow reconcile these issues and get these kids back together with their families.

As much as I completely believe in the sacredness of family, there are times when reunion and cohabitation are simply not the best options. I witnessed firsthand that the social service system is broken. It became clear that working through the system was not going to get me where I wanted to go. There had to be more. I realized that I didn't want to just help people, I want to help people to help themselves. It comes back to the idea of giving a man a fish, versus teaching a man to fish. That's the difference. I can't do it all for them. They have to want to do it for themselves. And, when you encounter a person who is open to change, who genuinely wants to improve his or her life, then it is truly a gift to be the catalyst, and to be able to impart knowledge and share the tools needed to manifest that change.

Recognizing that formal social work was no longer in the cards for me, I found myself wondering, "OK, now what?" After months of unemployment, I took a temporary job as a receptionist at an insurance firm. This was not exactly a thrill a minute. Then again, my father sold insurance for 30 years, but who wouldn't want to buy insurance from James Bond? The company put together self-funded insurance plans for businesses, and my job soon progressed into a position of negotiating with carriers to bid for and bring in new business. This was my first real exposure to aggregate protection and leverage, and it made a big impression on me. Still, the reality was that insurance was not my passion, and I was stuck in a job. And, we all know that one of the biggest dream killers in the world is the J-O-B.

I was caught up in the grind, exchanging hours for dollars doing the 9-to-5 thing, and I wanted more. I knew that to build wealth I needed to either leverage my time, or leverage my money, and ideally both; though neither felt possible at that point. Then, one night, around 2 a.m., I was watching a late night infomercial. They were talking about how they made a fortune in real estate without using any of their money or credit. I was watching the program and thinking to myself, "I know I'm smarter than that guy." And, I caught myself laughing and saying out loud, "Why NOT me?" That was it." Why not me?" became a mantra and I made it to that seminar the next day.

What I heard there intrigued me enough to buy the course and move on in the program. I stayed open-minded and coachable; following through, finding mentors and taking guidance from those who had been successful. Still working full time, I spent another 20-40 hours per week gathering clients and building my power team. Within a few months, it all became too much and the job had to go. Armed with knowledge and without a safety net, I jumped in with both feet. I soon turned that late-night infomercial into multiple properties and I was able to save several families from foreclosure. It was SO liberating! However, as I touched base with some of the other people who were in those real estate classes with me, I found that no one else had even closed a deal, not one. I thought, "Are you kidding me?" That's when I knew that my results were far from typical—that I was doing something different. Yet, I don't think that it was rocket science. I think that the key to it all was just the idea of laying the plan and following it through. A phrase that has come to govern my life is, "Don't just set goals—plan your results! The only difference is *commitment.*" Back when I was struggling, I would remind myself, "I have to do this. I'm going to set myself free."

Another massive motivator was my desire to help people. I don't know if you know this, but people going through foreclosure are usually facing some of the most challenging of life's obstacles, including divorce, death, medical bills, and job loss... I mean huge, overwhelming things. I heard several horrific stories of people who had been victims of unscrupulous vulture-like "investors." Predators who had swooped in while these people were at their most vulnerable, taking advantage of their fear and ignorance just to make a deal. I couldn't stand it. That just couldn't happen anymore, not on my watch, at least not to anyone that I knew.

So, I chose to specialize in negotiating pre-foreclosure situations. My clients knew that I genuinely cared about them and their situation, and I firmly believe that is why I was successful. With the benefits of my social work training and my degree in psychology, I had the compassion and the understanding of where they were coming from to connect with them and to give them the confidence to work past those scary moments. I was creating my financial freedom while making a real difference and improving people's lives. I just don't have the words to tell you how amazing that felt.

Levi:
So, you mention that it's not enough to just set goals. And, you also talked about the importance of planning results, but you actually cut it down to one component that I think is missed by most individuals that don't achieve goals, and that's commitment. The question that I think many people would have is how do you stay committed? I mean, you obviously had to have been committed earlier in life to make it through, to graduate from high school, to overcome your circumstances, to get a degree, to work at a normal job, and then to launch out and

start a business and start producing results. That commitment is what
got you through, but how do others apply that same commitment, how
do they latch onto that?

Susan:
You know, honestly, there's definitely a component of faith. And, I don't
necessarily mean religious faith; I mean faith and belief in yourself.
You must understand and accept that in the end, you are the only one
that you can count on, and you are powerful. We all encounter
obstacles. Life can often take turns that we didn't expect. Everyone has
their down days, but the key is to embrace your humanity and to forgive yourself. Patterns and habits are comfortable. But, you can't have
change without changing. Sometimes, the discomfort of your current
circumstance has to become greater than your laziness or lack of desire to move. It's unfortunate that people are not better motivated by
reward, but that is human nature. I know that fear of loss and discomfort are big motivators in my world. When I face a challenge, all I have
to do is to think about my family and to redirect my fear into a greater
drive to succeed. Leaving my job at the insurance firm solidified my
commitment by making it sink-or-swim time. That level of conviction
is what has to happen. Something as real as, "I've got to succeed or my
family's not going to have food on the table." That's what they mean
when they say, "You've got to be hungry."

There was also a wholehearted belief in myself as a strong and
capable human being, a deep knowing that I have the tenacity and
the strength to see it through. I trusted that if I didn't have the answer, then I knew where to find it. I left myself no other option,
and success became inevitable. So many people leave themselves
a back door, or they give themselves an excuse. They choose to live
in their story, often blaming the challenges that they've faced or
where they came from. Those things are all inhibitors. They don't
help you. Excuses are nothing but that. Sure, we all have our down
days. Heaven knows that I've had more than my share. But, you've
got to forgive yourself for the moment of weakness, shake it off, and
find your strength. You can achieve anything if you just commit and
say, "Look, I'm in this to win this, and I'm going to get it done. Come

heck or high water, I'm going to make it happen."

I actually started in real estate before I was a mom. But, the whole world changed when my son was born. They are not kidding when they say, "Don't mess with Mama Bear!" Being a parent is a whole different level of motivation. Talk about emotional leverage! Circumstances that may have overwhelmed you or scared you before become just are another thing for you to tackle It's funny to think about the silly little things that once seemed so big. It reminds me of my mom, and how she was our "Master Spider Killer." As kids, whenever we saw a spider, we'd call Mom and she'd just come in and take care of it. One time, as she came in to save the day again, I found myself in awe of her immense courage. I said to her, "Dang, Mom, aren't you scared? Aren't you afraid of that spider?" And, my mom looked at me intently and said, "Yes, I'm afraid of spiders. But, the possibility of that spider hurting one of my babies is not an option. So, that spider's got to go." It was that simple, and all I could think was, "Wow! She really does love us more."

I've killed plenty of spiders since then, because I can think of my son as my why. The love of a mother for her child is a big deal, but any love can stir this courage—familial love, friend love, and especially love of self and the belief that you are worthy and that you deserve better. With love, we can do more than just overcome fear; we can also choose to redirect that energy and to become an even more powerful force toward the good that we hope to attain.

Levi:

So, I see a reccurring theme, that basically what you're talking about is leverage. Getting emotional or psychological leverage on yourself to where that component of commitment, driven either by fear or by gain, can work for you. And, as you mentioned is the case, fear is a primal motivator. It sounds like that's something that you use to your advantage.

Susan:

I do. I do very much so. It's an understanding of human nature. Rather than hold resentment toward the experience, I choose to look at every challenge and say, "How can I turn this around? What can I do to optimize this situation?" It is a conscious decision. Often, people tense up and do not take action. But, choosing to not act is still a choice. Why not make the choice that benefits you? This is something that I am passionate about guiding people toward and helping them to understand. It doesn't matter what your circumstances are, nor does it matter where you're coming from. Where you're going is what matters, and what you're doing to progress, and how you're moving forward. Fear is one of the biggest dream stealers and business killers in the world. But, fear can also be your friend. Choose to take responsibility for your situation and to accept your challenges. The power that comes from your accountability can help you to harness your fear and to channel that energy into the strength to persevere. Courage is acting in spite of fear. It's when you say, "Yeah I'm scared, but I'm going after that spider anyway." You do it because it needs to be done.

Levi:

So, I want to go back just a little bit to your transition from having a job, and then firing your boss. You saw an infomercial that inspired you, and then you actually went to a seminar. You took action; you went to the meeting, and there you got some knowledge. You then paid for additional training and built your power team. How important, in your mind, is it to gain knowledge to follow the plan and to stay committed so that you can achieve results?

Susan:

Oh goodness, it is absolutely vital to have a thirst for knowledge—a constant desire to know more and improve your situation. Seek the truth and find mentors to guide you. A good friend and mentor of mine once said, "The idea that keeps me awake at night is how my life is being affected by what I don't know." That thought resonates within me to my core. It's such an impactful concept. What knowledge is out there that can better the world around me? Ignorance is not something that we can control, but should be something that we constantly strive to overcome. Talk to the experts. Do the research. Attend the seminars. READ! Your thirst for knowledge should be unquenchable!

A perfect example of a little information going a long way is with money management. I do not want to get on a financial guidance soapbox, but one of the major concepts that we've discussed, and something that our school system fails to teach us, is that leverage is imperative. Most people do not realize that as long as you are dependent upon exchanging hours for dollars you can never be financially free. Financial freedom comes from passive residual income. You're human, your body will eventually break down, and then what? In a job scenario, if you don't work, then you don't get paid. Thus, to attain financial freedom, you need to either leverage your time or leverage your money. You can leverage your money through interest, diversification, and investment growth. But, what if you don't have money? Then, you need to increase your income through leveraging your time, like using a system or building a team. We all get the same 24 hours in a day and it's up to us what we do with it. Leverage is how wealth is created, and the average person isn't even familiar with this concept. Yet, how would they know if they've never been taught and have never inquired?

Likewise, most people don't know that they can leverage the same dollar in multiple locations. Imagine using the equity accrued in your whole life insurance policy to purchase a rental property, and then have the monthly cash flow from that rental property make your car payment. That's how the wealthy get it done. So many people living paycheck-to-paycheck have thousands of dollars locked up in job-related investments and retirement plans thinking that they can't access them. They don't know that often 401Ks and IRAs can be used to buy real estate. With the discounts that are available in today's markets, they're missing out. The truth is that even most financial advisors don't know these tips. They'll tell you that it's not possible and discourage you from looking further. Don't listen to them! It's your money, you should take back control and make the most of it! Keep asking questions until you get the answers that you need. These are just more examples of how what you don't know could be affecting your life. But, I'll get off my soapbox now.

Levi:

So, you've been talking a lot about the components of wealth building. This is something that you've applied in your own life, something that you've done for others. You've helped individuals and businessmen to grow their wealth, to gain on this principle of leverage. I know that we talked a bit about your background, but why do you do what you do?

Susan:

I knew a long time ago that I was destined to help people. I inherited my attitude of servitude from my parents, who led by example. My father was the most generous man that I've ever known. I cannot tell you how many times he gave me the last two dollars in his wallet for lunch money, and he was always willing to help anyone any way that he could. My mother, Allyne, had a grace that seemed to touch everyone who knew her. Her love, kindness, and generosity were so pure that they often became contagious. While I was in junior high, Mom volunteered to be the head of the gift-giving committee for the PTA. She gathered donations and lovingly put together beautifully decorated boxes of food and presents to give to the underprivileged families of our school during the holidays. She said that if she was not the head of the committee, then they'd probably want to give some to our family and "we don't need it." I didn't quite understand what she meant until she asked me to go with her one night to do the deliveries. I had no idea that other kids were struggling with such difficult circumstances. I remember delivering a box of food and presents on Christmas Eve to a family of five who were homeless and who had the money for a motel donated so that they could have a roof over their head that night. Looking back, I'm sure that there were times when my parents faced losing the house, or had no idea where that night's dinner was going to come from, but we never knew it. Their love protected us, and we always got by with little realization that there was even a struggle. And, through it all, they raised us with encouragement, confidence, and a belief that we could be anything that we wanted to be. Like them, I know that what I want to be is someone who gives back and makes a difference.

Delivering those gifts that night was an eye-opening experience for me. I learned compassion and a deeper understanding of the human condition. Mother taught me to only take what I needed, and that the rest is surplus meant to be shared with others. It is up to us to recognize that and see how we can utilize what we have to improve the world around us. And, though we may not have had a lot of money when I was growing up, we were never taught to revere money, nor did we think that money was evil. Money is a tool with which we can help others. You hear, "money can't buy happiness," but I can say with conviction that the lack of stress regarding money can definitely better enable it. That's the reality. The only times that my parents ever really fought were over money. The challenge of trying to provide for the many different needs of their children sometimes became overwhelming for them. Experiencing their strain, and feeling that pressure, I decided early on that that was not something I wanted in my life. Rather than a mentality of doubt and scarcity, I chose to embrace abundance and freedom. My parents worked so hard because they loved us. And, I learned that the best way for me to show them my love and appreciation was to love myself enough to try harder. My parent's sacrifice is one of my biggest inspirations. My heart smiles to know that my son learns from them every day through me. He is being raised to love and honor himself with an attitude of gratitude and spirit of servitude. I could not ask for more.

I have experienced many blessings along my life's journey. More than a passion, I feel that it is my responsibility to impart the knowledge that I have gained and to do my best to bless others. I live in gratitude for the loving family in which I was raised, and I work to pay-it-forward for my parents who taught us that we really could make a difference. That's why I do what I do. And, I am rewarded every time that I see that spark in someone's eyes as they have that moment of clarity. When I meet a person who has been beaten down and who is struggling, feeling like they're in a hole that they can't get out of, I can show them that they have options. And, when they realize that they have the power to take back control of their life and find that place of strength, that means everything to me.

Levi:

So, in conclusion, you're obviously giving back and that's very central to your value system. You've gained knowledge and you've been able to share it in part as mentioned earlier. But, you've talked multiple times about it, the importance of commitment, that that's the differentiating factor. If you were to speak to another, maybe a budding entrepreneur or maybe somebody that's just kind of struggling, and you could tell them just one thing, one commitment that they need to make today, what would that commitment be?

Susan:

I would say to identify your soul purpose—to find out for yourself that which you feel you were placed on this earth to do, and then go for it. Make that impact and improve the circumstances around you. Once you know what you're meant to do, it's your responsibility to do it. When I say commitment, there is no person to whom you should be more committed than to yourself. As my dad always said, "Talk is cheap, but action is contagious." When you act, and you do what is in alignment with your purpose, you will have people gravitate toward you. Before you know it, you will be working with the kind of people that you were meant to be around, who will boost you, and guide you, and lift you, and impart the information and the knowledge that you need to continue to grow in your purpose. I would just say, find out who you are and commit yourself to sharing it with the world.

Teresa R. Martin

Teresa R. Martin is a sought-after speaker, lecturer, business keynote speaker, consultant, facilitator, and educator for executive conferences, ministries, and educational events. She demonstrates a deep understanding of the importance of financial education in business and in life. Born in Long Island, NY, Teresa began her career in the legal industry in the late 90's. Despite a lack of mentors, Teresa was inspired to move up the corporate ladder to self-employment; creating her own successful law firm in the areas of real estate, bankruptcy, and foreclosure defense. Teresa speaks passionately about self—realization, real estate investing, the importance of financial stewardship in business, and the responsibility of personal development and influence in the pursuit of financial freedom.

After 15 years of legal practice, Teresa made the conscious decision to focus exclusively on real estate and financial literacy as an aspect of business and social economics. Her core interest and passion is financial literacy for women, young adults and other emerging markets, which represent the most disenfranchised segments of the population concerning money issues.

Teresa, has two adult daughters, is the very proud grandmother of two grandchildren and currently lives in Brooklyn, New York.

Websites: *www.teresaRmartin.com*
www.womeninvestorsexchange.com
www.mywealthzone.com
www.reianyc.org

Levi:

One of the questions that entrepreneurs ask is, "what does it take to get started?" One of the most intriguing things to me about your message, Teresa, is that you truly believe that you can overcome anything. I'd love to jump in and have you talk about why you believe that, and maybe give us a little bit more about your personal entrepreneurial journey.

Teresa:

I would love to do that, but first I would have to share my journey from a teenage mother to a legal, real estate, and wealth building maven. My journey actually started early, as a single mother. I learned early on that the obstacles in life can be overcome no matter how difficult or overwhelming that they may seem, including having a child at a young age. Being a single mother is a journey that never ends. You'll grow from nurse to teacher to inspirer to become your child's confidante and friend for life.

I was immediately placed into the role of a role model. I refused to be a statistic and that's what most people have to do. Teen mothers are at a greater risk to drop out of school than their non-parenting classmates. By this, I mean that I refused to let anyone tell me that I wasn't going to make it just because some people in my situation weren't able to do it. I set out to prove that the statistics were wrong. While I knew that some high risk, teen moms faced the challenges and obstacles of finishing school, I knew that I was going to graduate. I knew that I wanted to be an attorney. I don't know how I knew that, but I actually knew.

My success as a teen mother, graduating from high school, definitely hinged to some degree on my personal transformation within myself, which spurred from my family background. I came from a two-parent household, but I was actually an only child. My parents really were unique in and of themselves because they encouraged me that "I can do all things through Christ who strengthens me." You understand what I mean from Philippians 4:13. That was bred in me. "I can do all things." Most people do not make an intentional choice to be a single parent. Life is not always what we want it to be and it's not like what we would carve out for ourselves, but how you handle the challenges will make the difference in your life. Situations are unique to everyone and it will differ depending on the unique circumstances and personalities of the individuals that are involved.

My circumstances were not going to define me, and I knew from an early age that I was going to be an attorney, from the time that I was in junior high school.

I don't know how or why this thought entered my mind. I never had any personal point of reference of attorneys in my life. I graduated high school at 16 years old and I went on to achieve my Associates degree, my Bachelor's degree, and my Jurist Doctorate. And, the journey began from that point. As a highly paid corporate attorney, the world was my oyster. You couldn't tell me anything. My career eventually took me to the New York City Law Department where I worked on litigation cases for NYPD and things of that sort. My world was turned upside down on that fateful day of 9/11/2001 when the World Trade Center was attacked. My office was one block from that attack. So, my only thought was to get home to my children in the Poconos.

The devastation of this one incident changed my life because the attacks left me jobless for months, and my home went into foreclosure despite my numerous pleas to the bank lender, "Help me, help me, please don't foreclose." My lender was very unsympathetic and eventually they took my home to the foreclosure sale, which I stopped on the courthouse steps through a chapter 13 bankruptcy filing through a pro se action. They actually took me to the foreclosure sale. My only thought was how could this happen to me?

Here I was, a one-time corporate attorney with a very impressive financial portfolio, who was now being forced into financial desperation to save my home from foreclosure. I truly didn't understand how this could happen to me. I did everything that I could just to embrace my outer strength through my spiritual beliefs and I just heard the voice, "Just trust in me, trust in me with all your heart. Do not depend on your own understanding." I really embraced that and I did exactly that. The bankruptcy was dismissed. The lender allowed me to sell my home, and I even learned of a large profit from that situation.

After this humbling experience, I finally understood why God allowed me to endure such an experience and I just smiled. If you understand everything that

I just said, my journey was never to become a corporate attorney and it definitely wasn't to allow me to build up my storehouses on this earth. My journey was to withstand the test and to empower others to do the same. The mortgage meltdown didn't start until late 2007 to 2008. I emerged from my situation and I became a real estate, bankruptcy, and foreclosure defense attorney with a special focus on helping others to build wealth through real estate.

My story is for single parents, students of color, and disadvantaged youths to encourage them to dream and to give them hope beyond their most difficult circumstances. You cannot have a testimony without a test. I went from losing one home to now having a large real estate portfolio, and the ability to help others to achieve their dreams of home ownership, financial security, and business ownership. I help people to build generational wealth instead of generational poverty. Real estate and financial empowerment is now my ministry and I love it.

For those people who actually desire, despite their financial resources, to become an entrepreneur, what I tell them is to know what you do and do what you know. Don't start a business simply because it seems sexy or it boosts large hypothetical profit margins and returns. Do what you love. Businesses are built around your strengths and talents. It will give you a greater chance of success if you do what you love. It's not only important to create a profitable business. It's also important that you're happy. Managing and growing it day in and day out. If your heart isn't in it, then you won't be successful.

The other thing that I will tell them is that they have to learn under fire. No business book or no business plan can predict the future or fully prepare you to become a successful entrepreneur. There is no such thing as a perfect plan. There is no perfect road. So, you should never jump right into a new business without any thought or planning, but don't spend months or years waiting to execute. You'll only become a well-rounded entrepreneur when you're tested under fire. And, I was tested under fire. The most important thing that you can do is to learn from your mistakes and never make the same mistake twice.

That is the best advice that I can give to anyone who wants to become an entrepreneur because lack of finances or lack of resources has never stopped anyone from doing anything. If somebody has the will and they have the determination, then they can do anything that they set their minds to do. It's called the power of a network. If you don't have the finances, then networking can put you in places where you can meet someone with finances. If you don't have the credit, then you can be put into a situation where somebody can help you to improve your credit or help rent their credit to you while you getting your credit under way.

There are so many different things that you can do to be successful and it's not necessarily about profits. I never put profits before people because you can't be successful that way. That's my best advice to entrepreneurs just from my journey and my own personal test.

Levi:

You would say that you believe in favorable disadvantages. Malcolm Gladwell recently wrote a book where he talked about people who have got learning disorders, or who have come from financially challenged backgrounds, or things of that nature. This works as a catalyst that forces them in one way or another to become successful.

Teresa:

I would agree with that. If I didn't become a mom at such a young age, then I don't know if I would have been as determined. I do know that it definitely was a catalyst because I had an entire generation to think about and I also didn't want to be a letdown. It doesn't matter whether or not you come from middle-class or whatever, circumstances are what push us into situations that we never would have thought that we would be placed into. I think that sometimes the disadvantage is your vantage point because you know what struggle is. You know what you need to do and I think that you just fight a little bit harder to do it.

Levi:

I think that perhaps that's why we admire entrepreneurs so much because they're constantly in situations of overcoming obstacles, and recognizing opportunity amidst the ashes. Would you say that for yourself that since you've become a successful entrepreneur that you define success differently than you did before?

Teresa:

I think that I do. If I wanted to say what success means to me, then I would have to tell you what failure means to me. Failure, to me, is not achieving the desired end or the ends that I set out to accomplish. That means that I wasn't successful in that task. Before, if asked that question, my answer would have been defined as by getting a nice job, making sure that I have made enough to pay the rent, or that I've made enough to meet my expenses. Success to me, now, is saying that I want to do something and actually doing it. The achievement of something that I desired, I planned, or I attempted. There is no better sense of success to me! Somehow, success just feels better as an entrepreneur. It is being able to change the way that I do things in the marketplace. As an entrepreneur, I can be anything that I want to be. However, as an employee, I'm a little bit restricted because I am now working in a master plan of someone else.

For me, as an entrepreneur, my design can be anything that I want it to be and I always can have an eraser. I can always say, "That's not working out" and start over. However, as entrepreneurs, we work hard. Entrepreneurs know that they have to keep pushing because our paycheck is not in a piece of paper at the end of the week. Our paychecks, if you will, comes from the clients that we serve, and the students that we coach. That's what success is to me. If I deliver a positive product and my client is satisfied, then at the end of the day that makes me successful, and that's how I define success right now. I didn't define it like that before because it was defined in my bank account.

Levi:

The entrepreneurial journey is laden with learning experiences. What would you say was your greatest aha moment?

Teresa:

My greatest aha moment? I think that my greatest aha moment had to be when I actually was able to learn that I did not have to be perfect. I think that would have been my aha moment because remember I told you where I came from, my journey. I always had to prove something. So, I couldn't start anything unless it was actually perfect. However, I learned that my time management skills and the way that I actually delegate to others were more important than being perfect.

I can be the catalyst to so many things that are going on, but I actually did not have to be the person that was doing it because a true entrepreneur understands proper delegation. He or she understands proper systems and making sure that you align yourself with people and leverage yourself with people that actually can help you to move the ball forward. That you don't always have to have the answers, but you have to be able to be a resource to be able to find the answers should you need to.

That was my biggest aha moment or my biggest aha moments as an entrepreneur.

Levi:

You've been talking about people that helped you to move the ball forward. Did you use mentors in your journey?

Teresa:

I didn't have formalized mentors, but everything that I learned came from someone who has done it before. I find myself in any venture that I jump into, and I try to latch onto the person who actually has had success in that thing or venture. I do this so that I can actually pick their brain and be able to have a "give and take" partnership with them, an accountability partner, if you will. Then, I can reach out to them and I can avoid the land mines that they have avoided or went through and survived. I can also render some of my expertise for some of the things that they may need. I say that now; I did not have a formal mentor, but I have always had informal mentors in every venture that I have undertaken.

The one thing that I look at when I'm looking for that person that I want to work with as a mentor, if you will, is their experience. I want to look at whether they actually have been there, done that, whether their character is that of someone I actually admire and respect. Whether they have similar goals and whether they're going to be available to talk to me. I won't waste their time or overburden them, but I do want them to be available to share with me. Those are the things that I look for and I am so happy to say that I have never been short of informal mentors but it's definitely important.

Levi:

There's definitely more than one way to approach procuring a mentorship.

I think that it's a formula that I have come across with every successful entrepreneur that I've ever met; it is important that they are able to align themselves to attract individuals that know more than they do in that chosen field to get them to that next level.

It's good to hear that formula is consistent in your story as well.

Teresa:

Absolutely.

Levi:

Speaking more about your journey, you started very poor, and then you went to school. You wanted to be an attorney. You were working. You went through all these challenges and you talk about the advantages of being an entrepreneur. That you're not limited by someone else's dream. Has your dream changed and evolved and what is your current dream? What is it that you are trying to achieve?

Teresa:

I was born and raised in a place called Long Beach, NY on the South Shore of Nassau County in a middle class family as an only child. My mom is a retired nurse and my dad is still a working electrician. According to the pictures of me, I don't think that I was the cutest baby on the block, but I do remember that I was a happy child. I was spoiled rotten and raised to believe that I can become anything that I wanted to become and I was just young enough to believe it!

My goal is to help 5,000 families achieve financial security, affecting five generations in five years within my network. I want to be a catalyst through that and that's why I created *Generational Wealth Zone* because *Generational Wealth Zone* is just that, creating generational wealth by breaking the chains of generational poverty, affecting one family at a time, and then affecting at least 5,000 families. The challenge begins on Jan 1, 2015.

Of course, I can't do that alone. That's why I talk to people and I encourage people to form networks because together we can do so much more than we can do individually. That is my dream (my goal) and I've been working towards that for the last ten years. I'm not giving up until I have that goal accomplished in five years, so I'm pushing towards that. I can't wait to tell you the stories and lives that will have been changed in 2020.

Levi:

That's a fantastic dream. That's a fantastic cause that I could see people just latching onto. What kind of people do you see coming into your circle of influence and what kind of people would you like to come into your circle of influence that you want to help?

Teresa:

I see a group of women and the reason why I see women is because if you look at consumers, women are the biggest consumers in the economy today. If we can affect the women, then we can actually change the world because we are raising up the next leaders. The people who I am targeting, my audience is women. People who are financially in debt will now have a resource that they can go to and actually get empowerment tools to find out how they can restore their credit, and how they can eliminate debt.

The influencers that I want to be a part of this movement, this crusade, are insurance people. People who can tell people how they can use their whole life or universal life insurance as an empowerment tool. People who are custodians or work for companies that deal with self-directed IRAs to show people that they can use self-directed IRAs to help build towards their financial future. People who are involved in real estate. Not necessarily people who are looking to sell people real estate, but people who know that real estate is one of the vehicles towards wealth and teaching people how if they put themselves in position, they can be their own bank through the different real estate investment models. People who are in the stock market, financial planners, and people who can actually help people to align themselves and to get themselves straight, to get their financial house in order. These are just a few but we are looking for all influencers with large networks to help move this movement forward.

The one trait that separates the *Generational Wealth Zone* leader is their stewardship and their heart to serve people. They have something to give, but it's not about the profit. It's about the people. When you service enough people and become a good steward of financial resources, I believe that the profits will come. It's just destined to be that way. That's who I'm trying to attract. That's who I am attracting and I'm looking to get more influencers into the circle that will help us on our tours because we're taking this citywide, and then statewide, and then countrywide. We're looking for people that will help us to sponsor these events. We're not charging people for the event, but we will need to charge a fee to cover the out-of-pocket expenses. Also, we need sponsors and places to host the events. We need people to help us to get where we need to go so that we can give the information to the people who need it.

That's what the movement is about and I just believe that I was given these skills and talents for a reason. And, I'm going to use them to help the most people that

I can. That's what I'm hoping to get, and that's what I'm hoping *Generational Wealth Zone* will do.

Levi:
What are you teaching at those events?

Teresa:
Excellent question. It all starts with the foundational principles of financial education and personal development. We cover one or all of the five main areas of money management, depending on the type of session. We cover Assets, which are things of value that you own, like cash, stocks, real estate, mutual funds, bonds, gold, and silver. We

cover Income, which is money that we earn from work; it's money coming in from investments or from businesses, and any other money that we have coming in from any source. We cover Credit, which basically refers to your ability to borrow and access money. We cover Insurance, which protects our things—like our assets, our income, and our credit. Insurance is really important, and we'll talk more about it later. Our last area is Debt, which is money that we owe—in loans and other obligations. Being in debt isn't always bad; debt can be used to buy assets that will benefit us in other ways.

Breaking it into its simplest form, we help individuals to understand how money works. We dissect the credit scoring system, letting people understand how credit is the center of all business. Also, if you have not paid your bills on time, that 35% of your credit score is based on your payment history, and that look back periods for banks are 12 to 24 months.

When you're trying to go for a mortgage or a loan or anything, we show them how they can look at the credit report, analyze their credit report, and see when they will be in the best position to actually get approved for a mortgage. Your insurance premium is based on your credit score. If you're trying to apply for a rental unit, not just apply for a house or a mortgage, your landlord is going to check your credit score. We show that credit has to do with everything. We provide coaching services for credit and financial health. We provide credit restoration services and do it yourself tools so that people don't have pay an exorbitant amount of money to get those things done. That's a big piece and we are just helping them to feel better about themselves, giving them affirmations as well as sustainability tools, so that they can actually hold themselves accountable. And, we assign them accountability partners. That's what we do at our events, as well as at our home study courses and coaching sessions.

We have a real estate investing component. We teach them the basics of real estate investing from turnkey to lease options, and all the other types of strategies in between so that they can choose and make the best decision for themselves if they want to get into real estate investing. Also, under real estate comes home ownership because there are so many people who are renting and they want to be home owners. That's the tag that we focus on, real estate.

We also have a stock market component to our wealth building tools, and we talk about DRIPS (dividend reinvestment plans) by teaching people how they can take $25 a month and start their stock portfolio and to build their wealth portfolio $25 a month at a time, a minimum of $300 a year. And, people are doing that successfully right now through our program. Lastly, we also have business ownership. In the business ownership module, we discuss everything from start-ups to home-based businesses, but not the mid-size or large businesses. We discuss areas such as compensation plans, bookkeeping, taxes, and formations.

People come out and they say, "I thought I only wanted to own a home, but I want to own my home, and then I want to pull some money out, and then I want to invest." It's always a circle of motion and that's why we deal with the holistic woman, the whole self, and not just one aspect. We also have a health aspect because some people that are financially in debt are stressed. It's helping them to realize that we can help you and you don't have to struggle on your own. It is about telling people that here are some free resources, in some instances, which can actually help you to get back on track. So, then you don't have to be stressed anymore. We do those things in our webinars, our blogs, and our video chats.

Levi:

By the way, fantastic. I love what you're doing. It sounds like that really is what people need to do; that they need to make their way down to one of your events. They need to find their way into one of your seminars. They need to get themselves educated. They need to get exposed to the material so that they even know what direction that they can take. What would you say to someone who right now is just questioning whether or not they can do it?

Teresa:

I think for the people, who are just pondering the question of whether they could do it, I really think that they need to acknowledge that fear and whether it's imagined or real. The first step to overcoming that fear is to admit that it exists because for most people, who are used to a paycheck, entrepreneurship is a scary, scary thing. We all have fears. It's human nature, but saying that that fear doesn't exist doesn't make those fears go away. If you want to take that step, then you should know that I offer free consultations. I would just talk to anyone who is interested in actually making that step towards entrepreneurship, or just thinking that they have too much debt that they can't even possibly think about it.

There are such things that we could help to reveal, such as building business lines of credit, even if you are personally credit-challenged. There are so many different ways and angles that we could actually assist you in your situation, but reaching out for help is the first step. You just need to come to us and say, "I don't know what to do next?" Reach out to someone who can actually help you to make informed decisions so that you are not operating in fear, but you are acting on information. Then, if it is determined that after all the information that you have received and all the research that you have conducted that you are not ready for entrepreneurship, then at least you have made an informed decision and you haven't acted in fear. I would just say take that first step. Do your research. There's a lot of information out there.

I do free, 30-minute consultations with women so that we can discuss their options. They just need to request an appointment directly on my website for a 30-minute consultation, and we talk about it in a clarity session. We operate nationwide, not just in New York, which is why we're doing the national tours beginning in 2014.

Levi:
For anyone that wants to get involved with your movement that wants to help with the effort, what do you recommend for them?

Teresa:
I recommend that they get in contact with us. They can go to *www.womeninvestorsexchange.com* or they can go to *www.teresaRmartin.com* and they just fill out the contact request form. We have so many different resources that they can look through just to see where they think that they could fit and what they are in need of. We can definite-

ly point them in the right direction. The one thing that I love about *Generational Wealth Zone's* women empowerment network, which is called Women Investors Social and Strategic Exchange, is the solid network of super-fantastic women. We have many free resources, including our newsletter, accountability program, and action guides. It's just resources where people can connect. It's a free membership that people join just to stay connected.

We wanted to have a resource that was fully accessible and not cost prohibitive for everyone, and we wanted people to be able to have a forum. For example, if I have a question, I may not want you to know what I'm going through. We wanted to be able to have a place where people can feel secure and to not feel as though they're being judged, and just be around women who actually have been there and/or done that. I just think that this is a great way for people to just check us out and see what we're about. If they want to get involved, then they can send us an email, or fill out our interest form, and we'll get right back to them. We are always looking for influencers in the area because we need help with this movement. We have a long way to go to reach our target 5,000 families, and we only have five years to do it. We are hoping that we have people that come on board. A thousand millionaires a year, that's a great goal.

Levi:

That is a wonderful cause, and a wonderful movement. I admire your efforts and believe in what you're doing. In conclusion, do you have any final advice that you want to give to entrepreneurs out there with regard to your cause?

Teresa:

One of the things that I want to leave you with is to say that whether you are already wealthy or whether you're in debt, you're still phenomenal. Whether or not you are divorced or single, you are still phenomenal. Whether or not you are with child, have children, or are unable to bear children, you are still phenomenal. We are a group of individuals that want to encourage the best you in the areas of financial education and personal development, investment portfolios, business ownership, and eventually being your own bank where you don't have to depend on anyone to tell you yeah or nay. That you can make your own choices because it is the unique individual that we care about. If you believe in you, as well as we believe in you, then we say come on board and let's work together to make our dreams come true. That's what I would leave with anybody who believes that "anything is possible."

Levi:
I love everything that you said and recommend for anyone that's interested to absolutely follow your advice and to reach out to you. And, I just thank you for your words of wisdom and encouragement.

Teresa:
Thank you so much Levi.

Wylene Benson

Wylene Benson's first entrepreneurial experience was at the age of 13, which was when she encouraged neighbors to pay her $3.00 per hour for weekly house-cleaning services. Working for multiple employers with very different standards, she quickly discovered that she had a gift for organization, problem-solving, and flexibility. Since that time, Wylene has been involved in several business ventures. She created a thriving direct sales business, which she maintained for 18 years—it was in these 18 years that she learning invaluable people and branding skills that still serve her today. She has worked with multiple organizations, building synergetic connection wherever she lands. Wylene is currently developing a Foundation and Mentoring Platform designed to reveal the Super-Hero behind the Mask of Addiction. She lives in Mapleton, Utah with her husband of 27 years, Clint, and their three daughters. She has a passion for art and creativity; she sees the beauty in all things.

Levi:
Wylene, you've had a lot of entrepreneurial experience in your life. You've helped to grow businesses. And, from what I understand, you have basically climbed the mountain that you had thought that you had wanted to climb, and then when you got there, you found that it wasn't the destination that you had thought that it was going to be. You had a heart attack and that experience transformed the way that you viewed your life, and the way that you've viewed business.

You feel that you can actually achieve more success if you enjoy business. I'd like you to just talk a little bit about that. What does it mean to achieve your success story?

Wylene:
I appreciate your mentioning that I had achieved something and maybe gotten there and hadn't really found what I was looking for. Because I actually did have an experience in a previous business that I owned where I had certain goals that I worked for, and actually achieved them. Once I got there, I kind of looked back and I was like "This isn't really what I want. I'm not really happy here."

I think that the reason for this was that I was so focused on my goal. I was so focused on business and what people told me that I should want and so that's what I was going for. After I had a heart attack, I had to have no stress, and no physical activity for eight weeks. I basically had to sit in my front room and my kids and my husband waited on me.

I had a lot of time to think about that, and I've always been such a go-getter all of my life that it was a huge blessing in my life to be forced to take that role of having to delegate and having to allow people to serve me. During that time, I had to think about how I wanted to run the rest of my life. This heart attack was caused by stress and I was able to really see, during those eight weeks, that there is another way... that I can listen to my heart.

I can listen to inspiration of what is really important and I was able to focus and narrow down to certain areas that really fit my purpose, my passion, my mission in life, and my vision. Really, all of my decisions now are based on helping me to move closer to becoming more in alignment with that passion and that vision. I listen to my heart on a daily basis in order to learn what I need to do to achieve that.

Levi:
You have told me, in the past, that you actually have experienced more success, and a higher income because you're listening to your heart. Is that correct?

Wylene:
Yes, that is very accurate. I feel like in past businesses, and even right before my heart attack, I was actually working for someone else, and all of those experiences I felt like work was, work. I tried really hard, and I was always just working my hardest to achieve that goal, or whatever, to get to that next level, or to move up to a supervisor position, or whatever I could do to raise myself up within the companies that I had worked with or with my own businesses.

Now, I go at it in a lot more relaxed and peaceful manner. Every morning I just sit down and ask, listen to my heart, and I wait for inspiration of who I need to talk to, what I need to be doing. There are many times when I will just receive these wonderful ideas, creative ideas of events, or things that I can do to further my business, and honestly it's not something that I could have thought of on my own.

I really do believe that I've tapped into this higher Power that is leading me, and teaching me, and mentoring me from a higher level. Because of that, because I trust that inspiration and take action on it immediately... I think that's a huge key... when you have a feeling that you need to do something, not to go to everybody that you know, and ask them, "do you think that this will work?", or whatever. That, I think, kills the inspiration. I think that when we trust it, and when we believe that this is from a higher source, and somebody that knows more than we do is bringing it, then we can use that to our advantage. However, it does need action immediately. Otherwise, it loses the magic if we doubt it.

Levi:
I like how you said that it loses the magic if we doubt it. And, it sounds to me like that is the process. I mean if you're truly being guided into

this sense, then that's a wonderful secret weapon to help you to not only achieve results, but also, as you had mentioned earlier, to enjoy those results. We live in a very mechanistic world. The question that I would ask is how does someone set aside all the noise, and how do they recognize the source that you're talking about?

Wylene:

It's a really good question. And, that is difficult for most people, I think, in the world that we live in today. That is probably the biggest challenge that we have, to consciously set aside that noise. I get up every morning; I get up before my kids and my husband, and I have a room right across the hall from my bedroom that I call my Creating Room. I go in there, and I sit in a comfy chair, and I ground myself. It's sort of a meditative process.

Many times, I don't even turn the light on. My palms are up, my body is in an open position, and I just breathe. Just really concentrate on my breathing, concentrate on listening, and I try to always have my head forward a tiny bit, so that it's more focused on my heart and not my head. And, I just kind of shut my brain off and listen to my heart.

It does take some practice. There are times when I'm really focused on an intention, or maybe I have a deadline that I'm working towards. I have to really, really concentrate to shut that off, and to allow the inspiration to come. Sometimes, it comes in the form of a person's name. Sometimes, I get an idea of an event that I can hold. I don't ever know what it's going to be. Many times, it seems to have no connection whatsoever with the question that I had originally asked. The whole key is to not question it, to not judge it, and to allow it to come. I have a pad of paper sitting by me and I'll just draw it out, whatever image that comes to me. And, usually it becomes my list of things to do for the day.

As long as I follow that, I find that I don't think anything really falls through the cracks. I sometimes think that might happen because I don't have a very structured schedule. I have come to believe that I'm given everything that's important.

Levi:

That's fascinating. Steve Jobs had his own ideas about higher powers and things of that nature. It's interesting that there's something that you tap into, and for him it was a similar, traumatic experience in his life that triggered it, which allowed him to take a step back and say, "Wait, I need to recognize that something different has to happen in my life."

One of the things that I frequently teach is that if you want a different outcome, then you have to change the process. The way that you beautifully describe the process that you've gone through is absolutely fascinating.

What about when you're out and about, and you're actually in the middle of business, is there an impact there?

Wylene:

Yes, definitely, I feel like I have learned to kind of keep myself open throughout the day for changing plans, inspiration, or whatever. I'm not so rigid that I can't make a change. I'm out a lot of times during the day, and if I have a feeling that I need to go somewhere else, then I go there. One particular example of this is when my husband and I stopped in Costco. We don't have a Costco card, but we stopped in just to walk around to see if we might want to get a Costco card. This was a decision that was made in the moment.

As we were walking around, I noticed how busy and crazy it was in there on a Saturday morning. Then, all of a sudden, I just got a feeling, and it hit my stomach that we needed to leave. I said, "We've got to go." Clint, my husband, has learned that I live this way. He's fine whenever I say that we've got to change directions. He's like "Okay." We started heading towards the exit, and I ended up running into somebody that was on my team, someone that I had considered 'at risk'. I felt that they were probably on their way out of the business. We stopped and talked to him. There were so many people rushing by that we had to move into an aisle to not get run over by the crowd. By the time that we had finished our conversation, the man had tears in his eyes and I had committed to work with him on a personal basis. And, actually the very next day, I just showed up at his house, because it's what I felt that I needed to do. And, we all shed tears and he has become recommitted, and I know that I was divinely guided.

I know that there was no reason for me to be in Costco that day. There was no reason for me to automatically just say, "We need to go, we need to leave." To run into him, and have that happen so beautifully, it could not have been planned. Those types of things, again, you do have to get to the point where you can let the phone ring or that you can allow the craziness of Costco to be going on, but that you still are listening to what is really important.

Levi:
One of my heroes as a child, because I grew up in a martial arts home, was Bruce Lee. He basically said that we have to become as water. What you're describing is that you just have to go with it. We've been talking about some of what many people would consider the soft skills in business, i.e. how you could apply soft skills to achieve things. I have to ask the next question on a personal level, how do you define success?

Wylene:
How do I define success? Wow, gosh, I'm not really sure how to answer that. I think that I define success by living at my fullest… at my fullest capacity. In times past, that would have meant working my hardest by giving it my all. Now, it means reaching inside of myself, finding out who I really am, knowing that I'm living on a daily basis to the best of my ability, and doing it in a way that fulfills my highest ability.

When I say that I am fulfilling my highest ability, I'm talking on a spiritual level. I'm not really sure how to explain it or how to describe it, but I think that all of us have gifts that we've been given and talents that we have that can be improved upon. I also believe that these gifts and talents are given to us to make a difference in this world. Everything is about relationships. Everything is about serving people, and about building those relationships with people.

Success to me really doesn't have anything to do with money or status or anything like that. I think those things come when you're fulfilling your higher purpose and if you can figure out who you are, where your power lies, and what you can give on a daily basis, then you'll be paid really well.

Levi:

I completely agree with you there. You had mentioned relationships, i.e. how important relationships are to business success. What relationships have been the most impactful for you in making the transition from high stress?

Have there been individuals that have made a big impact in that transition?

Wylene:

Yes, two individuals come to mind. After I had this heart attack, I went in for my follow-up checkup six weeks after, they did another echo-cardiogram, and there really had not been any improvement in my heart. The doctor had told me that I would probably not improve any more from where I was at that time. She said, "you know, a lot of people live with this, and have a normal life." And, I remember driving home from that doctor's appointment.

There's a mountain behind my house, Maple Mountain, that I attempted to climb two or three years earlier, and I hadn't quite made it to the top. I had always wanted to get back on that mountain and make it to the top. As I was driving home, I looked up at that mountain and I thought "why me?" and "why is this happening?" and "I don't want to just live with this and have a normal life!" I was really having a lot of negative emotions. I finally settled on anger, and I was just mad! I was mad for two to three days, and then I finally realized that wasn't really where I wanted to stay. That wasn't good energy and it wasn't going to do me any good to feel that way. I decided to change.

I contacted my daughter's boyfriend, Dylan Mooney, who wanted to be a personal trainer. I knew that he had done a lot of research and had a lot of knowledge about good health. I called him and I said, "Okay, I want you to work with me; I want you to give me a heart healthy diet, and I want you to give me exercises to do to strengthen my heart." I was so dedicated to everything that he told me to do. He was even amazed at how dedicated I was.

He was a very good coach for me because he would push me but he did it with love. That was one person who really helped me. The other person was a mentor, Kris Krohn. He helped me to see what caused my heart attack and that it really wasn't anything to do with my heart. It was the choices and the way that I was living my life.

He helped me to work through that and to figure out a healthier way to live. It's interesting because through this mentoring process, and being able to change my belief about my heart, my beliefs about the way that things had to be, that life had to be hard, I had to work hard to be successful. Through this process I've discovered my gift is connecting heart to heart with people. So, within our struggles, and perceived weaknesses, lie our strengths and our power.

Turning those beliefs around, I feel like I have a stronger heart than I ever have had before, even in my 20s, and I have not had any problems since then. I actually recently committed myself to hike Mt. Timpanogos, which is even higher than Maple Mountain. I am doing it this summer, and I'm also walking a half-marathon in March. That's kind of my halfway mark to help me to get ready for this hike in the summer.

I don't have any fear about that at all. I don't have any doubt that I can do that. It's all come about because of this change in my belief and doing the work to have a healthy body and a healthy heart, taking care of those physical aspects of it. I think even more than that, it is this change in my mindset, this ability to trust myself and to trust my body. I'm not going to have another echo-cardiogram. I don't need one. I know that I have a healthy heart. My heart is strong.

Any success that I enjoy has all come about because of the journey that I've been on to feel a lot more confident in listening to my heart and knowing that I do have strengths there.

Levi:

That's wonderful. One of the reoccurring themes for every successful person that I've ever talked to is the concept of mentorship; the concept of someone coaching them. You mentioned a couple of people. A question for others out there, be they entrepreneur or not, how do they choose, or what should they look for in a mentor? I am asking you this because you mentioned different qualities. One person that pushed you (but it was with love) and one person that had helped you to open your mind and to change your process. What should someone look for when they're trying to find a mentor or a coach?

Wylene:
I think that there are a few things that one should look for in a mentor or a coach. Number one, I would look for somebody that has love and whether that's love for what they're doing, being a mentor, or love for people. There has to be an element of love. Another thing that I would look for is someone who's happy. If they're not happy with their own life, then I don't think that they could help me to be happy. To me, that is one of the most important things in life, just to be happy.

Another thing is someone who's committed... committed to you. Someone who is committed to being there for you when you need them. That's one of the things that I appreciate about a mentor, just knowing that if I have a dark day or a dark time, then it is important that there's somebody that I can turn to, to guide me up.

The last thing that I think is really important is that you trust them. Because when you are working with a mentor, you have to be willing to be completely vulnerable. When I look over my experiences with the mentors that I have had, I could never have achieved the heights that I have achieved, if I had not been completely open to baring my soul and sharing anything and everything that comes to me that I need to share.

There's a lot of unpleasantness that we have, that we maybe don't necessarily want everybody to know. If we're going to share those things, then it needs to be with somebody that we can trust.

Levi:
Another question that people often want to know about successful entrepreneurs is the type of legacy that they would want to leave. And, so my question for you, Wylene, is when someone writes up the history of your life, what are those highlights? What is the legacy that you want to have written about you?

Wylene:
Well, I will share just one experience that comes to mind. I met a lady at an event and she was inspired by something that I had said. So, she

came over and talked to me. She was struggling with her business and she said, "I just don't even know… what's the next step, where to go from here?" I… instead of just spouting out some superficial thing… I looked into her eyes and I asked her a few questions about herself.

I spent a little bit of time finding out about her, what her interests and gifts are, and why people would want to work with her. I didn't realize that it had made that big of an impact. I found out later that from that conversation, she went on to have a highly successful event that really kick started her whole business. She gave me the credit for that. She came back later and she told me that that conversation was what had sparked that for her and what had just really started her on the road to success.

That is probably the legacy that I would like to leave. That maybe I was a small part of someone being inspired to discover who they are inside. That they see their powers because of a conversation that they had with me, or because of something that I might have helped them to create. That would be the legacy that I would like to leave.

Levi:
Well, Wylene, you have a wonderful spirit about you. You've definitely shared some things that are helpful both to me and I'm sure to those that are going to read this book. If you could give just one, last piece of advice, either to a budding entrepreneur or to someone that perhaps is further along in their career, then what would that one piece of advice be?

Wylene:
I would tell that person to trust yourself. Trust your inspiration. Be you. Don't try to duplicate somebody else's business or someone else's success. Find out who you are on the inside.

We have what we call weaknesses. I used to think that I could never inspire anybody and that I was not a good leader. I found that this was really the clue that I was looking for. That was really the key to my success. Once I started stepping away from that weakness and actually acting as if it didn't exist, I discovered that I had a gift in that area. If you have a weakness, then look at it as a clue. Embrace it, your power lies within it.

If you're inspired to do something, then do it. Have courage to stand out, to be different, because I don't think that anybody can be successful if they copy somebody else. I think that every person on this earth is an individual and has something to give and some power that is their own. If you trust it and if you allow it to happen, then your own unique qualities will emerge and YOU will be the catalyst that you have been searching for in your own life.

Kevin Wallace & Carolyn Johnson

Kevin Wallace and Carolyn Johnson are motivational speakers, business consultants, and financial literacy educators with more than ten years of financial experience, they have helped countless people get their finances in order by investing in real estate franchises, rental properties, and home ownership.

Contact: *kcholdingsllc@strongbrook.com*
Website: *www.kcholdings718.strongbrook.com*
Ph: 718-930-9031

Levi:
Kevin and Carolyn, you're really pursuing what most would consider to be the American Dream. Certainly, it's not exclusive to America, but that dream is the dream that you can achieve financial freedom if you get the right knowledge, have the right tools, work hard enough, then, you can really break out of being employed by someone. You can build your own future. To start out, I want to find out where this dream for

financial freedom began for each of you. To start out, Kevin, where did the dream for financial freedom begin for you?

Kevin:
The dream of financial freedom began for me when I was temporarily laid off for approximately three months due to contract negotiations between the union and management. I knew that, at that particular moment, I needed to do something different and I needed to do something now.

Carolyn:
For me, the dream of financial freedom came because I've always wanted to be free from my job. However, I didn't know how to do it or which way to go. Once I started going to events and reading educational books, it helped open my eyes. Real estate is the way to go.

Levi:
It's interesting that both of you hit on points that normally do motivate us to get into entrepreneurship. It's usually something that happens in our workplace. We learn that we're really not as secure as we think, or it's because we've been exposed to new knowledge and new skills. For each of you knowledge and skills is always an important part of succeeding in business. Are there books that you encountered that really made a difference or are there individuals in your life that really opened your eyes to what could be done?

Kevin:
For me, there was a guy by the name of Robert Kiyosaki. I read his number one bestselling book which was named *Rich Dad, Poor Dad*. I knew that once I finished reading that book, I needed to do something different alongside me being laid off for a couple of months due to contract negotiations.

Carolyn:
To add on to that, Kevin has probably read more books than I have, but I'm just coming basically into it within the last year or two. I began to educate myself reading books also. I've read Robert Kiyosaki. I've read

Kim Kiyosaki's books, she's his wife. I've also read quotes from Warren Buffet, things of that sort. They're doing it. Why can't we?

Levi:

Great question to ask any of us at any time in our entrepreneurial journey. If someone else is succeeding, then why shouldn't I be able to? Typically, that just means following a pattern. I'm just curious. You obviously went into business together, and you chose real estate as your vehicle. Can you tell us why you chose real estate?

Kevin:

The reason why we chose real estate is because that's one of the largest parts of asset in our portfolio. Everyone needs somewhere to live. Everyone needs a space, a shelter. That's a part of each and everybody's lives. Real estate makes the most sense to us.

Carolyn:

To add on to that, in addition, everything we do on counter is real estate. We walk into a store, that's real estate. We go in a building to go to work, that's real estate. Everything is real estate. Real estate is a money-making investment tool.

Levi:

Real estate definitely has a longstanding history of creating wealth, both in America and throughout the world. In your opinion, what does it really take to be a leader in your space?

Kevin:

What it takes to be a leader in this space is being ethical, being honest, and being passionate about what you do and helping others to obtain what we have as of today.

Carolyn:

In addition to that, I definitely agree with Kevin, but to add on that real estate also is being passionate and taking charge. You have to take charge of your life by doing something different. Make a difference not only for you but for other people, as well as, for family members and friends. It trickles down the line to help others out.

Levi:

When you look at real estate, people think that when one gets involved in entrepreneurship, there's always that fear that there's a risk factor. What do you say to people when they're thinking about taking a leap from being employed, getting a paycheck, to creating their own future. How do you help them through that fear factor?

Kevin:

What helps the fear is taking action and also, taking a calculated risk and financially educating yourself. We always have to inform individuals that we partner with or do business with that this is not going to be easy road. You're not going to receive a paycheck every week or every two weeks or even once a month. There may be some times where you're not going to receive a paycheck from your business for a month or two. With that being said, you have to remain diligent and have a strong belief in you, that you can accomplish anything. It's not going to be easy, but you can accomplish anything.

Carolyn:

I definitely agree with Kevin. Fear is taking a risk. Stepping into faith. You have to overcome your fear. You have to just step out. Take that risk. See what's going to happen. It isn't going to kill you. It can be positive or it can be negative or it can be great. Just don't be afraid. Just do it.

Levi:

I love what you said, Carolyn, that it's not going to kill you. I remember reading something in one of Tim Ferriss' books when he came to a crisis point.

He had to just go back through the process and just say, "Alright. What's the absolute worst thing that could happen in my business right now?" That was never really part of it, so he realized that there's always an option to move forward. As soon as he realized that, then everything opened up for him. He could see the solutions going forward. For each of you, when you get in those situations where it could be discouraging and you might be back against the wall, what techniques do you use to pull yourself out of it?

Kevin:
The technique I like to use is to take a look at your vision board. Look at each and every single thing that represents something that's the closest—and has significant meaning—to you. Just remind yourself why you're building this business. For example, time, money, family, friends, associates, etc.

Carolyn:
I agree with Kevin. You do have to take a step back and look to see why you're doing this. The question is why? Everything is done for a reason. You've got to dream big. It's true. Go back. Look at that vision board that you have. That vision board is there for a reason. You make what to do and what's to happen on a vision board. You go hard at it. You press.

Levi:
You both have big goals, but at the same time you both came ... you made the crossover. You came from working at a job. I'm sure that, at the time, that you were working, you had one definition of success. Now that you are in entrepreneurship, how has your definition of success changed?

Kevin:
Our definition of success has changed drastically. To be able to wake up when we want to, not because we have to wake up, in order to get to work. To be able to serve others as a part of our business as far as our client base. We should learn it is valuable to sit down and receive more inviting information from our mentors. It is fun and exciting to be able to travel the world. To play with our children. It just brings joy to us. That's our definition of success. Time plus money.

Carolyn:
I agree with Kevin. Time means a lot. I can also add that it's putting a plan into action and making it work for you. You got to go for it. You got to give it a try. It's like I said, again, it's not going to hurt you to try.

Levi:

I find that one of the things for entrepreneurs is the time, but it's also that ability to take your own risk. There's a fulfillment in doing so, in paving your own path, even though you could mess up and you could make mistakes and often time mistakes do happen, but at least they're your mistakes. Would you say that's true in your business?

Kevin:

That's very true in our business. When we make mistakes, we sit down; we speak about it and strategize. We also contact our mentorship for extra guidance. Then, we go at it again.

Carolyn:

I agree with Kevin. You make a mistake, you get the mentor involved. See where you went wrong. Don't give up. Go at it again. Stay focused.

Levi:

We've been talking about mistakes. We've also been talking about success and how the definition has changed. I'm just curious. How do you define failure?

Kevin:

Define failure means—at least, to us—not giving a shot, just giving up when you're so close to your goals. Listening to naysayers, people who don't believe in you and tell you why you're building a business. You shouldn't be doing that. You should go back to your nine to five. To us that is failure. Those are the naysayers that want to... It's like a crab in the barrel syndrome that goes on everywhere. When the people see you rising up to success, people will pull you back in the barrel. That's what I define success as.

Carolyn:

I agree with Kevin. Success... I find it as... no, I think it was failure, your question. Correct?

Levi:
Correct.

Carolyn:
How do define failure? Not even giving it a try. Not taking that risk. How do you know if you're going to fail if you don't try? How do you know if you're going to succeed if you don't try? Also, I look at it as how you respond when it happens. What do you do next? Do you pick up and go on, or do you stop? Most people pick up and go on. Some people stop.

Levi:
You've both talked about the importance of having a mentor. Tell me a little bit about the process of choosing a mentor.

Kevin:
First and foremost, before we even choose a mentor, we have to find out if he or she is in our industry. Once we locate he or she in our industry, then we've got to find out their successes, their failures, their years of experience. Just to build a strong relationship with your mentor. I think that's really key to any business, any industry, in any area.

Carolyn:
I agree with Kevin. A mentor should be a person that's definitely in your industry that has the same understanding, knowledge, and experience. I want someone with experience that can guide me in the right direction.

Levi:
I like that you mention direction. One of the quotes I heard—and I have no idea who it's from—but basically, it states that you can't return from somewhere you've never been. How that applies here is that if you're trying to choose a mentor, someone that hasn't done what you're hoping to do, it's really hard for them to come backwards and tell you the steps on how they got there, because they've never been there. One component of mentorship that maybe doesn't get mentioned as much, but the con-

cept of being a mentor... in your mind, how important is it, not only to find the right mentors, but to be a mentor?

Kevin:

I think it's very important to be a mentor to others who are coming up the ranks—the ranks and files of becoming new entrepreneurs, because knowledge is key. It only makes sense to pass off as far as what you know, what does she know, to other individuals so they can become successful too. That's a great way to leverage. Leverage it out.

Carolyn:

Definitely agree. Finding a mentor. I need to find someone that has already walked that path, who has done it and has proof that it works.

"Look, hey, I did it. I have proof. Look at me. Look where I'm at now." Having a mentor and a strong mentor at that; that is key.

Levi:

What do you do to fight time management issues now that you're out building your own business or is it an issue, at all?

Kevin:

Since we became financially free, time management is no longer an issue. The way we have managed our time more appropriately is the old fashioned way for us, by utilizing the calendar and just putting dates, times, and locations on our calendar.

Carolyn:

Yup. It's true. We utilize the calendar as best as we can, making appointments, attending events, whatever we need to do we have that time to make these appointments.

Levi:

It definitely demonstrates that some things don't change. Some things are real stable in business and life. However, we are in the middle of a technology revolution. How much has technology impacted your business? How important is it?

Kevin:

Technology has done awesome things, not only to our business but just to make things much easier. For example, if we're doing a business meeting, we have partners in China, one in Australia, and one in Africa. We all can attend a meeting from different locations. To be able to communicate through emails, go to *meetings.com*. It's done wonderful, absolutely phenomenal things for our business. I give it two thumbs up.

Carolyn:

I agree with Kevin. It has come a long way. Technology changes often, such as every three months. It helps where you need to put out events on things that are going on, make it known. You still have to pick up the phone, but technology is just more advanced. If you can click a little bottom, it's so much easier.

Levi:

Is there anything that each of you do specifically to keep up with technology?

Kevin:

Specifically what we do for our business is that we hire a technician. We hire someone who stays abreast as far as the technology curves. That makes it much easier. That's our personal advisor, technical support.

Carolyn:

Yes, our technical support person also keeps us abreast of what's going on and what the new technology coming out is. How does it work? How does it function?

Levi:

For each of you, what do you like best about what you do?

Kevin:

What we like best, as far as what we do in our business, is to be able to make a difference in somebody's life, to empower individuals to step into the world of entrepreneurship, because at nine to five there's little security there. Social Security is a joke. We can no longer rely on companies and governments to take care of us in our senior years.

Carolyn:
Definitely true. What Kevin says is definitely true. We like to share the word to people about other ways to make money, such as, cash flow, possible early retirement, and help them become financially free, just as we did.

Levi:
That's wonderful. For someone who was say, considering leaving their job and leaving their boss, what advice would you give to them as far as to where they start?

Kevin:
The advice that I would give any individual is to go to franchise, network marketing. The reason why I say that is because it has a low-cost startup and a phenomenal education system, depending on the company that you choose. You have to do your due diligence.

Carolyn:
Don't be afraid to fire your boss. You don't know what's out there until you reach out and try it. I love real estate. I think that's a great tool. Try it. Try investing in real estate. See how far it goes. You might be financially free before you even thought you were going to be. For instance; 401Ks, Social Security, you know, all that stuff is a joke. Fire your boss.

Levi:
What legacy do you want to leave? At the end of your life, what do you want to have said about what you're doing right now?

Kevin:
The legacy we would like to leave behind is that we impact; we change people's lives, throughout this phenomenal country we live in, which is called the US of A, and abroad in other international countries. We

want to make a difference by empowering people financially, mentally, emotionally, spiritually, and even, physically, if possible.

Carolyn:

That's true. We also want to leave a legacy of, hopefully, wealth. Besides, wealth, we would like to explain how one can have financial freedom where people can free up their time to do more with their time. Then, they can spend time with their friends and families. That stuff is very important.

Tracy & LaVieve Roberts

Tracy and LaVieve have been married for 19 years and they are the parents of five children: Andrew, Carolyn, Katherine, Thomas, and Joseph. In their retirement, they enjoy having more time to teach others the values of financial freedom, prosperity, and abundance.

Tracy has served his country, church, and community in many capacities. He served in the United States Air Force. He is a member of the American Legion as well as a member of Veterans of Foreign Wars. In addition, he served terms as Deputy Sheriff-Colonel of the Sheriff's Honor Guard and City Councilman. He has also served as a scout leader, missionary, mentor, motivational speaker, and teacher.

LaVieve raised her family and those around her to change the world in a positive way. She established an endowment, Louis E. Parks, Jun. Endowment House, LLC, to help fund missionaries to spread the Gospel of Jesus Christ throughout the world as well as to fund youth projects of hope and possibility.

Contact: *tracy@abundantlifeministriesintl.com*
             avieve@abundantlifeministriesintl.com
Websites: *www.Abunantlife.strongbrook.com* &
             www.abundantlife.strongbrookdirect.com

Levi:

So Tracy and LaVieve... you've built a business together. Tracy, you've been called the Pastor of Prosperity. You're very passionate about helping people to achieve financial freedom so that they can start living the life that they want to live. Talk to us a little bit about... each of you... a little bit about how you go about helping people to achieve financial freedom.

Tracy

We have chosen real estate as the vehicle that gets us where we want to go. We have also brought mentors in our lives that have helped us move in a positive direction. Now we are becoming mentors and helping others improve their lives. I come from a rich heritage of pioneers in my family history. My ancestors crossed the plains pulling handcarts to their promised land. I personally don't want to come to my promised land pulling a handcart. I prefer to drive in a Mercedes with heated seats. Each of us are moving toward our promised land, the only question is how and how long will it take to get there?

There are many vehicles out there to create financial freedom. I have found that real estate is one of the best vehicles that you can ever get into. Not real estate by itself, but, real estate done right is what makes the difference in a person's ability to become successful and obtain financial freedom. We've been able to work with mentors that have shown us the "Strait Path to Real Estate Wealth." They have helped us create cash flow and financial freedom and now it is our goal and mission to help others do the same.

LaVieve:

I love what Tracy said about working with a mentor. In the beginning of our financial journey we had a mentor who helped us identify our beliefs about money. A lot of mine were negative. If you have negative beliefs in your mind, you're just going to be blocked... you're not going to be able to achieve the prosperity that you want. Our mentors helped us identify where we were stuck and helped us move to a more positive place.

Levi:

Since you brought up the topic of mentors and the importance of them in your journey for financial freedom, I would actually like to know how... basically you're perspective on how to best learn from a mentor.

Tracy:

I am open minded, willing to change and willing to learn, not thinking that my broken ways are the way. If you think you've got it going on, then you may find it hard to get where you want to be. For me, it's being willing to listen to what your mentors say. They have been able to teach me and show me some of my blind spots. They were able to take me to the mountaintop because they were standing on higher ground.

One of the mentors who helped change our financial future and increased our real estate portfolio took me aside one day and said, "Tracy, do you think I've been teaching you these principles just so your bank account can get bigger?" My answer to him was in the affirmative. I said, "Yes, I believe that's what you're doing for me." He gave me a look that only the most important people in your life can give and have you willingly receive it, then he said, "No. The reason I'm teaching you is so that you can be a blessing in the lives of others and help them on their journey toward financial freedom."

That started moving me in a different direction, where it became clear that I was going to be able to bless the lives of hundreds and even thousands of people. As an afterthought, this mentor, who happens to be a multi-millionaire, said to me, "Oh, and by the way, your bank account IS going to keep getting bigger and bigger."

LaVieve:

Tracy and I have been fortunate in the last few years to have many mentors in our lives. We appreciate them so much! We just seem to attract them, almost. If we need to learn about something, then someone will come into our lives and we recognize in them that they have that knowledge and understanding that we need to help us grow our business.

Our teachers have helped us so much financially, but I have experienced so much personal growth as well. I feel happier and more fulfilled than I ever have before. Every area of my life has improved. I communicate much better with Tracy and my relationship with our five children is better than ever. I just can't say enough good things about working with a mentor!

Levi:
In your opinions, finding people that have already done what you want to do is essential. Beyond that, are there certain characteristics that an individual should look for in finding a mentor or mentors?

Tracy:
If I'm trying to find a mentor that is going to be a spiritual mentor for me, then that individual should be very spiritual. If I'm looking for a financial mentor, he should already have obtained millions and millions of dollars. I look for people who have great skills in the area that they're trying to teach me. If I'm trying to learn Hebrew and I'm trying to understand the Old Testament, then I go to my rabbi, Rabbi Daniel Lapin and he helps teach me things I may not be able to learn by myself. For me, seeking mentors that are way above, and way past where I want to be, makes all the difference in my life and has changed me mentally, spiritually and emotionally.

LaVieve:
Tracy and I have a different way of approaching things sometimes. In my opinion, mentoring is accepting someone into my life and be-coming their student. I need to have a strong, emotional connection. It's more of an intuitive thing… like I just know I'm going to connect with someone and be able to learn a lot from them. If I don't feel that connection, then I'm just shut off, and it doesn't work for me.

Tracy:
And when LaVieve uses her natural intuitive nature, those mentors that come into our lives are beneficial to both of us. The thing that I have found with mentors, over and over, is after they're teaching me then they want me to be passing on the knowledge. Because their mission is to endow the world with their gift… whatever their area of

expertise happens to be… and they want other people to be blessed with the information they have found and put a laser focus on.

Levi:
I would totally agree with you on the concept of finding mentors that not only have been where you want to go but those that, as LaVieve pointed out, that you can relate with, that you can form a bond or relationship with, because it just enhances the experience. Just switching gears a little bit, in your own business, what's been the greatest 'Aha' moment for you?

Tracy:
I'm going to have to defer to LaVieve on "Aha's," she is the great identifier of lessons learned.

LaVieve:
I have learned so much! It is hard to narrow it down. Recently, I had a major breakthrough when one of my mentors suggested that instead of blaming others for my failures, I should take accountability for myself. Everything I do is because I do it, not because someone made me do it or influenced me to do it. So all of my successes and all of my failures come from me. Instead of wasting time being angry and blaming others I dig into myself and take accountability for my actions. I progress much faster now!

Tracy:
One of the 'Aha' moments for me is in finding that some of the sayings in the world that have oftentimes become trite phrases, do have truths embedded in them. Here's an example, "If it is to be, it is up to me." What I learned is that I am the captain of my ship and responsible for its direction. If I'm going to be successful, it's not going to be just because there is a great mentor in my life. It's going to be because I AM willing to change. I bring those people into my life as helps and guides, they can spoon-feed me knowledge and wisdom all day long, but I have to take it in and make it a part of me. My willingness to change and apply the new knowledge is what brings positive change into my life. Individuals who are willing to do what they need

to do to get the success they are looking for will use the knowledge they receive from others and apply that knowledge to life. I AM the captain of my own ship, and I AM the master of my own destiny.

Levi:

I find that as a common trait among successful entrepreneurs, is that they really take ownership for the things that they're trying to change, whether or not in their own life, whether or not in their business, whether or not in the marketplace in the world at large. We've talked a little bit about success and failures and that's a common theme in business conversations. In your business and for you as individuals, how do you define success?

Tracy:

I truly define success as a person's ability to have and to be free to do what it is they want to do with their time, and with their life. Oftentimes in this world there are individuals who spend the best years of their lives working for somebody, having a job, doing something to help build someone else's dream. They put their own dreams on hold because they don't have the finances and the freedom and the liberty to go out and do what they want to do. So for me, success is driven by the ability to do and be and act as I choose to and to relate with and to associate with whomever I want.

LaVieve has a great passion when it comes to her idea of success. And her passion is now becoming my passion, but she views it from a different angle. Her angle is one that has made a difference because she looks at it as the queen of our castle, she looks at it through the lens of the family and it has changed our world greatly.

LaVieve:

There is so much negativity in the world. Success for me is just being happy living and doing what you're doing. I lost my brother and we have lost other friends to suicide. I have learned how to be happy by forgiving myself, letting go of the past and learning to trust myself. It is a passion of mine as we learn from our mentors to pass that knowledge on and to mentor other people. We are able to help other people discover those negative things in their minds that hold them back, whether it's emotional, physical, financial or spiritual. We just love to see people bloom and blossom when they're not anchored down and held back by those negative, limiting beliefs. So for me, success is dads and moms and children discovering how they can be happy in their own lives!

Tracy:

And that makes us harbingers of hope. Because we believe that we are trailblazers, we're pioneers. We are preparing the way for people that are to come after us. As we help bring hope in this world, there are going to be children and parents and other that aren't going to have to experience this hopelessness, and keep believing the LIE that there's nothing that they can to change their situation. One of our great passions is to help people see that there is hope. We are able to help individuals whether they've got money or not. We have been able to help them start creating some financial freedom. Oftentimes when the finances are removed from the equation, then individuals actually see help is on the way start feeling some hope. They're willing to carry on, and stay on this earth another day.

Levi:

I love that both of you brought up the more private and personal side we often like to separate in business and there have been studies that demonstrate that when you're doing something that makes you happy or when things are going well on your home front, they actually go better in the business world. You both decided to go into business together as a married couple, which perhaps that's something that was very common earlier in the country's history and then it became less common with the invention of the corporation. Now in the new technology revolution age where it's easier to connect with people, it seems to becoming more common that you see husbands and wives coming up with ventures that they run on their own. Talk to us a little bit about what it's like to do business in a family relationship.

Tracy:

It is wonderful. One of the things I want to perpetuate on my posterity is to teach them things of finance and financial freedom that I was never taught. LaVieve and I both have wonderful parents. But they didn't understand about finance and they didn't understand about wealth. We both came from fairly poor circumstances, and so for us to work together as a family, that is the greatest joy. Because I can take my children with me when I'm going and when I'm doing presentations to people or I'm talking with folks.

And now my children, who are young, they are better able to handle things of finance at a young age than probably 90% of all the people in America. My seventeen year old son... if something were to happen... I'd be willing to turn over my finances to a seventeen year old, right now, because he knows more about those things, and he's also been mentored by millionaires. My children may even now at a young age be able to do a better job at handling financial matters than those that many deem experts. So we get to work together, we get to spend time together and for me, time is the only thing... it's the commodity for me that is most precious.

I don't know how much time I have and so I want to maximize it and be with the people that I love and care about. Now we get to spend time together, we're essentially together all day long. I hope that this is as great of a blessing for LaVieve as it is for me. Spending time with my family and my loved ones and my friends is the most precious thing. I love doing business that helps create financial freedom and hope for the future.

LaVieve:

I love everything my husband has just said. In the job that he was doing, one week out of every month he had to work night shifts. He basically slept and ate and went to work. I felt like 25% of our marriage and our family life, he was gone. So many important days and holidays he missed. We love having him home and all the time we get to spend together and all the things we get to do together. We have so many more opportunities to make memories than we ever had before. We were even able to take the kids on a cruise last Christmas!

Levi:
On a personal note, for each of you, what really inspires you?

Tracy:

When I see lives changed when people come up to me, or send me a text, or send me an email and the first words of that email are "I quit my job today." That's when I'm inspired, because I know that I've been of positive part of their life. I've made a difference in their world, and I've helped them achieve dreams and/or move towards their dreams. When I can see people living their life IN PURPOSE, and ON PURPOSE, then I get excited about it. I get passionate about it. I want to ring the bell of freedom and shout it from the housetops!

Every time when one of the individuals I have the privilege of working with comes to me and tells me that they quit their job today, I just get excited and start posting it on Facebook and let people know. When I've got doctors telling me that they're quitting their job because they've got passion for other things, I'm excited. We've seen this over and over again as we serve others. For me, I AM inspired by the success of the people in my life as I uplift them they put wind under my wings and help me sore higher and higher, and oh what a view.

LaVieve:

For me, I feel inspired when someone comes to give me a hug and says, "My life was changed because of something you said." I think there is no greater honor in the world than to be able to inspire other people. And so for me it's just a cycle that continues on and on. I'm able to speak to people and I inspire them, and then their stories of how their life has improved just inspires me more and it just continues on.

Tracy:

And we get to see this more and more often where folks will come up to us, that we've never met before, and they'll thank us, and they'll say, "Thank you for the message that you gave." What we're experiencing is awesome, you just don't know that when you drop that pebble in the pond what will happen, it is difficult to calculate what the ripple effect is going to be. We have some indicators that let us know how we are doing. One of the indicators is the show of gratitude for what we are doing, it is feedback, we know we are inspiring and uplifting others.

We are giving people permission, as if they needed permission, to follow their dreams and living their purpose and find their truth. When we see people making great changes I've learned that the best response I can give when someone comes to thank you, is not degrade yourself or downgrade yourself. The best response ever is just to say, "You're Welcome" and "Thank You." And when you say "Thank You," you receive what they've given to you and that encourages them, the individual, to go forth and do their greatness and living in their greatness.

We all have greatness in our life and often times in my life I have chosen not to play great. I wasn't standing in my power and being true to myself. Now LaVieve and I are standing in our power and being a blessing to others daily.

Levi:

In conclusion, if someone wants to live a new lifestyle, they want to… as you say… they want to quit their job or fire their boss, or change their financial circumstances, where do they start? What's the first step? What do they need to do?

Tracy:

They need to find a vehicle. They need to find something that is going to create passive income for them. The very wealthy in this world do not become wealthy by working harder. They come wealthy by working smarter. The first step that I would tell anyone would be this: Find something that is going to create passive income and that passive income is going to take you where you need to go. We believe that real estate is one of the great means of creating passive income. It created the first billionaire in the United States of America in John D. Rockefeller. For us, that is one of the things that you need to do. My houses are paying me, whether I'm talking to other people, or I'm sitting on a beach in Mexico or the Bahamas. It's paying me all the time. I like that and that would be what I would suggest to individuals is that they would find something that would be able to make money for them independently of any of their actions.

LaVieve:

I absolutely agree is vital to have an idea or a vehicle to get you there, the business you want to start. I think the number one thing that pops up for people is fear. So identifying the root of your fears, what exactly you're afraid of, why you're afraid of it, how that came to be, and then replace that with something positive. Create a new truth for yourself. Believe in yourself. You need to have a burning passion why you are doing what you're doing inside of you. When your desire to succeed, when your 'why' is stronger than your fear, then you will always succeed!

Levi:

I love that we actually got two perspectives there because I've talked to a lot of entrepreneurs that they'll either hit one or the other perspective. They'll either talk about the why or finding your passion or the other will talk about finding the right vehicle or the right opportunity and the very best result happened when you have both. So, wonderful advice. A challenge, I think, for all entrepreneurs out there to make sure that they're doing what they're passionate about and to make sure that the vehicle that they're using is creating value in the marketplace, it is creating residual income for themselves so thank you so much for your words of advice and wisdom.

Tracy:

And now you know why we're in partnership together, because of our partnership we have the ability to do more as a team and it makes it possible for us to do all things. We've got the Yin and the Yang working in harmony.

Levi:
Absolutely.

Dean Demos

Dean Demos is a serial entrepreneur, a Certified Public Accountant (CPA), Speaker, and Author. Dean is passionate about teaching people about tax strategies, personal finance and entrepreneurship. He has helped people from all walks of life, from Artists to Small Business Owners to Multi-Millionaires and Billionaires. He loves helping people go from being a-want-to be-entrepreneur to becoming an entrepreneur. Using creative strategies to leave a financial legacy and financial freedom for as many people as possible is his number one passion. If you or your group would like to work with Dean or have him speak at your event, please contact Dean through one of the websites below.

For life-changing tax strategies, go to *www.demostax.com*

To make any child in your life a millionaire, go to *www.makemykidamillionaire.com*

Dean has also partnered with Startup Shepherds to help people become an entrepreneur; go to *www.startupshepherds.com* and use code ONFIRE for a free week of education.

Levi:

Dean, you've been an entrepreneur pretty much your entire life. You started out as a very young child, you had that mindset. You've kind of picked up the torch, or the flag, should I say, to really help others that are young to actually become successful. But you've done it in kind of a unique way. You started this "Make My Kid A Millionaire" brand. To start out, just talk to us a little bit about that brand, your story and why you're doing this.

Dean:

The main reason I'm doing it is I had two very entrepreneurial grandfathers that taught me a lot. The first one made significantly more money than the second, and back in 1940 if you were to compare them, one made $40,000, the other one made $10,000. If you fast forward 35 years to when I'm six years old in 1975 and I was starting my own first business, my first grandfather, who had made $40,000 a year, lived above his means and never planned for a rainy day. He was in a bad situation. We had to help pay his rent.

My other grandfather, who made significantly less but always planned on a rainy day, and always planned for his future, he was taking us to Greece, to Mexico, to France, to the UK. Living the life of his dreams. That had a huge impact on me, so I didn't want anyone to ever end up my first grandfather. I'd like to see everybody end up like my second grandfather, and the earlier we can teach people the life lessons that they need to actually become millionaires and create that nest egg of wealth that they both use in their retirement, or to have and use in their current life, and that's really what my passion is all about.

Levi:

Wonderful. How did you get started into this project? Where did it all begin?

Dean:

I guess it really began back when I was six when I learned that lesson, that if you don't plan for the future, you end up getting bit. I experienced just what everyone else does in the country. I got all these credit cards when I went to college. I got myself into debt, and I vowed that wouldn't happen again. I went back and I talked to my grandfathers and I learned the lessons from them, and it's something I've been teaching my clients for a very long time, on how to create wealth not just for their family, but for their children, and methods that they don't normally think of.

I had a lot of clients for several years push me to create a book or a system that I could share with more people, because they said, "It's not fair that all your clients get this knowledge, and you need to share this with the world," so that parents can help their children without really doing much damage to their own personal pocketbook.

It doesn't take that much effort or money to turn a small child into a millionaire in the long run. It just takes a little bit of planning. Teaching the right lessons at the right times, setting up certain things, like retirement accounts. When my wife and I end up having a child, our child will be three days old when I set up their retirement account.

Levi:
Wow.

Dean:
That's literally the plan. There's always a way that you can do that. Obviously, you can use the child as a model in some advertising that you do for your business, so it's just one example. The work has to be age appropriate. You can't have a six-year-old being the head chef at your restaurant, that's just not going to fly.

Levi:
Sure.

Dean:
If you can find age appropriate work for the child, then you can actually create income and a Roth IRA, and a wealth building tool that will create a legacy and financial freedom for your child.

Levi:
I think, Dean, it's a wonderful message, especially in this era where a lot of parents are concerned their kids are going to be video game depen-

dent. They're going to move back into their basement or never leave, and it's content that you can help them generate wealth and learn how money really works, and I think it's an incredible approach. Does it start with the parents? You mentioned that it was two grandparents that helped you with the lessons, but where does this process all start with helping the child to earn money and become, as you say, millionaires?

Dean:
The school system lacks teaching anyone about this topic, so unfortunately we're not going to get it there unless something dramatically shifts in our educational system. So, it really comes down to the parents or grandparents teaching the children these lessons. Quite often, we're all taught not to talk about money, so a lot of people are ashamed of it, or they don't want to share the lessons. Reality is, the kid still learns the lessons, it's just that they're learning the lessons from what the parents are doing and not necessarily learning it from actual experience. I think parents have to take more responsibility in educating children on how to create money and how to actually preserve it, grow it and use it wisely. Some of that is, by example, but some of that is sitting down and teaching them strategies.

Although we're starting with the *"Make My Kid A Millionaire"* book, we are working on developing some gamified apps, and possibly a board game to get these lessons out there, so that way we can teach young people from a very young age. As board games always say, "For kids of all ages."

Levi:
Absolutely. You know I'm a big advocate of gamification, making things engaging and fun. I want to switch gears and take us back just a little bit, because I believe that success, it leaves clues. There are patterns and things that lead to, reveal to us how we should learn. How we should apply truths. I want to find out about your own journey. When did you first become an entrepreneur, in your mind?

Dean:
It's going to sound a little bit silly, but about the age of three. I didn't start my first business until I was six, but if you were to ask my

Mother when all the other kids are being asked "What do you want to be when you grow up?" and people are saying fireman or astronaut, I was saying businessman.

Levi:
Wow. I think for me, it was Buck Rogers or some other superhero, so I think I fit into the other category. You said you started your first business when you were six?

Dean:
Yeah, when I was six.

Levi:
Talk to me about it.

Dean:
At the age of six, I was walking by, there were two gentlemen talking loudly. One of them had a carpet store that just went out of business, and he had a truck that was filled with carpet samples. It looked like the biggest truck I had ever seen, but reality was it was probably just a pickup truck. He was mentioning that if he left the carpet samples in the store, the landlord was going to keep his security deposit.

He'd already gone to the dump, and they would not accept the load, either because of the material or that they thought it was too much. He didn't know what to do with it, and I offered him eight quarters, the two dollars that I had on me, for everything if he'd deliver it to my house. I hopped in the truck with him—it was a different time then. We drove to my parents' house. I opened up the garage and we ended up stacking all of these carpet samples that were about the same size as a welcome mat floor to ceiling, in three gigantic stacks, much to my mother's annoyance. Over the next couple of months I sold every last one of those carpet samples as a door mat for a quarter each. And that would be my first official business.

Levi:
Wow. One of the root definitions of entrepreneurialism is recognizing opportunities and then taking advantage of them. It sounds like this is

something that is almost in your genes. Is this the type of thing that you are helping parents to teach their children? Walk us through a little insight into your program.

Dean:

Sure. In the book, which is just a first step, it's giving people strategies on how they can save for retirement, even when they say they don't have enough cash. A lot of people say they don't have a way, they have a hard time making their bills as they are, but I teach them creative strategies where they can actually fund their retirement with what I like to call "found money." In addition to that, we're setting up a series of books and games to actually teach the proper use of money, starting with the basic lessons and learning how to grow it, respect it, utilize it and recognize those opportunities.

If we go back to the pre-industrial USA, everyone was an entrepreneur. There were no big mega-corporations, really. Everyone had the Mom and Pop shop. There was a person who made the bread, there was a person who made the chairs, a person that was the butcher, and everyone was an entrepreneur and it was a normal state. But as we got industrialized and more and more people became worker-bees, that entrepreneurial spirit got repressed. I think we're at a turning point now, where we can shift people's awareness and bring them back towards that entrepreneurial spirit that's in everyone, and just give them the self-esteem or the courage to step up and actually go for it, and let that spirit that's being suppressed actually out.

Levi:

All right, I absolutely agree with you. We're in the middle of a technology revolution that really changes the rules of the game. It makes it possible for anyone, regardless of age, ethnicity or background to be an entrepreneur and to do it with very, very little expense. I have to applaud not only the message and the cause that you're moving toward, but the timing to me seems impeccable.

Dean:

Thank you.

Levi:

For someone, either a parent or a grandparent, or maybe even an ambitious child, like perhaps you or I were, what is the first step? Where does somebody start their journey?

Dean:

They start their journey really by observing their parents, and some will have a little bit more initiative, or some parents will take a child under their wing and teach them. One of the cool things, I didn't get much of an allowance, and that allowance did not afford me the ability to buy the things that I wanted. My mother was very clever. She said things like, "If you want more money, you have to earn it." So, it might be if I finished reading two books, I got paid a dime. Or, if I vacuumed the stairs, I got a nickel. I still had my set chores I had to do for my allowance, but if I wanted to do additional things to earn more money, I could do that. I think that was one of the greatest lessons, that if I wanted to actually buy something, I had to earn it. I was taught that at a very young age.

There's a friend of mine, he's a CPA, so obviously there's lots of confidential documents that need to be shredded. His youngest daughter, she is five or six year old daughter and she has a job. She is in charge of shredding everything. And she earns money for doing that. If you ask her, she'll tell you that it's hard work, and she's very careful with how she spends that money. So I think not just giving them an allowance, but giving them a way to earn money, teach them the lessons with reality, with opening up a bank account, or saving money to purchase something, or putting money toward charity. All these lessons can be taught at a very young age with very little actual cash, but forming these habits very young is critical.

Levi:

What about teaching them about leveraging money, which is something that anyone looking at the future, looking at retirement, and even not retirement but looking at growing a successful firm, have to understand?

Dean:

Of course. You have to get them to the basics before you get them to learning how to leverage it. That's where you can gamify it, and you can use something like Monopoly to actually teach them the lessons of "you bought this for this much, but this is how it's now generating much more income," or "if you are the bank, here's how you have some advantage, you can get the mortgage or you can take the property," and there's various lessons that can be taught with games like Monopoly. In about another year or so (2015), we'll have our games out for "Make My Kid A Millionaire," and hopefully we'll be able to gamify a lot of those lessons in teaching them about leverage.

Now, if the child's in their teens, you could probably start teaching them about stock options and things like that, or teaching them about real estate investments in a serious way, but for a seven- or eight-year-old, it might be beyond their capacity. But there are many lessons that you can start, and then keep growing over time.

Of course, with the power of the Internet, there are tons of people out there that they've learned how to develop programs and apps, even at a very, very young age, and they're putting that out there and making some good money. There are certainly ways that we can teach them leverage, and the more advanced ones maybe when they're a little bit older, but we can certainly teach some of those lessons while they're young.

Levi:

Absolutely. We've been talking a lot about financial prosperity, helping parents help their children to learn the lessons about money and gain wealth. One question that I love to ask entrepreneurs is how do you define success?

Dean:

Success is the freedom to do what you want—enjoy life on your terms and nobody else's. You can still work for someone else and have that feeling of fulfillment, and it really is best when it's something that you've created. You have the freedom to travel where you want.

Last year, my wife and I took a month off and drove the entire length of I-10, from L.A. to Florida and stopped off at all the National Parks. We had the freedom to do that. That's not easy for most people, to take a month off and enjoy life. One of the ways I view success is that we're able to do those things and not have to think about it or worry about it. Really, success is living life on your own terms. There are times when I wouldn't call giving up on something a failure, because sometimes there are things where as long as you learned the lesson from it, that can actually be a success, too. You can have a business that went under, but if you learned the lessons that bring you to either financial prosperity or achieving some other goal of yours, even having something that failed sometimes, if the business went under, you can still grab the granule of success out of that, and bring that to make you much better off than you were.

Levi:
Absolutely.

Dean:
Success is kind of broad and different for each person, but I just view it as having the freedom to do what you want on your own terms.

Levi:
So, this freedom that you're talking about, obviously taking a month off, that's wonderful and that's something that a lot of people don't have the means or the security to do—leverage tools properly in order to achieve. You mentioned that there's something that you can do, even in an employment situation, but I'm just curious. Do you remember the moment when you first fired your boss?

Dean:
Wow, there have been so many times. Sometimes, I will go work with someone or for someone to learn a new skill that I can utilize. The first time I fired my boss—well, I had a hospital job back in the day, one of the things I did to put myself through school. It got to a point where it was sucking up too much time, and I was an accounting major, and people started coming to me to do their tax work back then. I started making much more money doing the tax work than I was at the hospital, and it just didn't make sense to actually commute half an hour to go to the hospital and work for $5.18 an hour when I

could do a tax return for an hour or hour and a half and get paid fifty bucks. It made no sense to me, and that was freshman year at college. I guess that would be the first time I fired my boss.

Levi:

I think for most of us, it's when we have those valuable "A-has." When we recognize that either I can trade my time for money and my time is valued at this, or I could do something of a higher value. For me, I remember, kind of like your carpet story, I realized that there were things that I could sell, and I could sell very quickly, and earn more money in the day than I could a whole month working at a job. That was another real revelation for me as a young child, the kind of experience as an entrepreneur that I want for my own children.

Again, I applaud what you're doing. I think your cause is wonderful. One of the questions that I always like to ask also, when any people that are passionate about their cause, is what kind of legacy do you want to leave?

Dean:

My goal is to create at least one million millionaires. Create legacy and security and freedom for at least a million people.

Levi:

Wow. Wonderful.

Dean:

I'd like it to be a lot more, but let's start there and see where we can take it.

Levi:

In conclusion, if there's one call to action that you think everyone needs to hear—every parent, every grandparent—what is that call to action, and why is it important?

Dean:

The call to action is to start early. The earlier the better. I'm sure you've heard of Einstein saying "Compounding interest is the most powerful force in the universe"?

Levi:

Yes.

Dean:

I'm sure you've seen the penny example. If you accepted $100,000 today, or a penny that doubled every day for 30 days? That penny doubling will bring you to over $10 million dollars in the 30 days. Imagine if you were to set up a Roth IRA for a child and put in $5500 today, and $5500 on their first birthday? Just let it grow at a reasonable rate of return, not really a high rate of return, but not really low, but reasonable. You would end up with $1.1 million by the time they actually hit retirement at 59 and a half. Obviously, you want to encourage them to save more, to have these habits. They can do it outside of an IRA as well. The younger you start, the bigger the impact it has. If you look at that penny doubling example, of that $10 million dollars, $5 million of that is on day 29, right? The difference between day 29 and day 30 is $5 million dollars. If you just use that as the investment in yourself and in your child, then the value of the lessons that they learn, it keeps growing and growing, so the earlier they start, the better off they are. Take action TODAY! That would be my give away.

Samuel Prentice

Samuel Prentice is the President and Co-Founder of Dove Ventures Financial Services Firm. Dove Ventures was founded in 2012 and has experienced record—breaking growth in the past two years. Starting with just two entrepreneurs, Dove has since expanded to 12 states— with over 25 independent sub—agencies. Samuel's business acumen and constant desire to provide a higher level of excellence, both to his organization and its clients, has attracted some of the most success- ful planners in the industry. Although Dove Ventures is a relatively new agency and Samuel is a relatively young entrepreneur, one of the strengths of youth is a proclivity toward having a finger on the pulse of development. Dove Ventures offers the most cutting edge solutions to today's complicated financial portfolios.

Samuel Prentice is a third generation entrepreneur. He has person- ally developed over four different successful businesses in his relatively short career. At an early age, Samuel identified some of his passions and found a way to turn those activities into profitable ventures. Many of these ventures centered about the field of communication—he focused on everything from conducting overseeing to developing curriculum for private instruction camps for baseball skills to a mobile technology solutions business to facilitate the implementation of electronics into individuals' everyday lives. As life progressed and more of his natural skill sets developed, he became laser—focused in the field of finance. This allowed him to combine two of his strongest skills: numbers and communication. Since entering the field of finance in 2009, Samuel has won numerous awards, including #1 sales person in Oklahoma for American Farm Life Insurance company in 2010. The challenges of to-day's marketplace have been instrumental in fine-tuning Samuel's focus, as his constant pursuit of the best solutions affords him an ample opportunity to exercise both of his most prominent talents.

In both his personal and his business life, Samuel constantly strives for improvement and development. He credits his success in business to his work-ethic, discipline, faith, and education. He is blessed to have been surrounded, even from an early age, with an environment that fostered a responsibility mindset. This mindset is what has motivated and inspired him to continue to improve and develop each business venture he has undertaken.

Contact: *Sam@doveventures.com*
Website: *www.doveventures.com*

Levi:
So, one of the components of entrepreneurship that is kind of a mystery to a lot of up and coming entrepreneurs, or those that are just looking at entrepreneurship, is actually investing for themselves. Sam, you've spent a lot of time in the investment side of entrepreneurship and you've developed some very unique and powerful approaches and tools that truly can lead to much higher results. To start out with, I'd love to know how do you do that. Please just talk to us a little bit about what you're working on right now.

Sam:
What I'm currently working on is developing an Elite General Agency ("EGA") called Dove Ventures. Dove Ventures is a full service financial firm with both a production and distribution arm. We equip both finan-cial representatives and our clients with the most cutting edge, efficient, and effective solutions that are available today. As an "EGA," we have

access to some exclusive financial products. No one else, aside from those through our distribution channel has access to what we have!

These products are at the top of their market sector, a market sector that has experienced exponential growth this past decade. This market sector deals with two of the biggest fears that an individual should have about their portfolio: Market Volatility and Future Taxation. The majority of the plans that we propose at our firm address both areas with accounts that don't lose principle due to a negative market year and that can be accessed tax-free at retirement. The exclusive (patent pending) product that we have is just an improvement on a tried and true strategy that is provided by the most financially stable companies in the world. This strategy has been utilized by a variety of financial institutions, including major banking chains! The improvement, this exclusive feature, simply takes a good strategy and concept, and then enhances it by lowering internal cost. As any good businessperson knows, lowering internal costs is one of the best ways to increase your profits. This new exclusive product has the lowest cost of any product in its class.

Levi:
So, for the average person, the takeaways of what it's really providing is a reduced cost of growing money, and an accelerated rate of growing our income as well. Would that be an accurate statement?

Sam:
I would feel that that would be an accurate statement, but there is more to it than that. It's a strategy that provides great flexibility and security with great returns. In the current times, it's more vital than ever for an individual, especially the self-employed, to have flexibility. However, that flexibility can't be obtained at the expense of a good rate of return or dependability. This strategy, backed by a proven asset class is an ideal foundation to a business owner's financial portfolio. People are steering away from market backed investment vehicles because the fluctuation and volatility of the market is not conducive to their base financial asset. This asset provides protection and guarantees that, should the S & P lose 50% of its value tomorrow,

your account will not lose one penny due to that market downturn. Combine that protection with better than market returns and incredible flexibility, and you can see why many entrepreneurs have owned this asset. In fact, Walt Disney and J.C. Penney both utilized the flexibility of this asset to either fund or maintain their businesses when no other funds were available. It's tremendously versatile, but also tremendously powerful.

Levi:
How did you get involved in this line of business?

Sam:
I got started in the business as more of a by-product of my nature than a specific calling. I say that, because I don't know that anyone wakes up one day, with the world of opportunities before them, and says, "Hey, I think that I'd like to be a financial advisor!" When I was born, my father, an engineer by trade, owned his own oil and gas operating company. You could say that I was born into an entrepreneur's environment. As a family, looking back now, I know that we were exceedingly blessed financially. Somehow though, growing up, that never really resonated with me. My parents didn't come from significant wealth and they never had anything given to them. I know that it was their intent to pass some of the life lessons that this upbringing teaches onto my siblings and onto myself. So I don't know that we ever had much of anything given to us! Any spending money, activities, and most possessions were tied to various household chores. The experience of having to work to be able to do the things that I wanted to do definitely taught me, from an EARLY age, the importance of taking responsibility for my actions and reactions in life. This was definitely a key component that led me into the financial services industry.

As I had mentioned, I grew up in a family that was definitely in the upper echelon of society. With that financial blessing comes the challenge of increased responsibility to maintain and properly steward your finances. This is where all my natural talents, core ideology, and opportunity met. I had a natural gift for numbers and communication, at the heart of my being was passion for responsibility, and now I had been introduced to a field that afforded me the opportunity to exercise all three. The financial services field provided me with tools and resources that enabled me to show people the most efficient ways to manage their assets. It also provided me with tools that could be used to enhance an active portfolio through increased flexibility, more predictable returns, and infinitely better tax treatment. Once I realized that the financial industry was my passion, I then sought out the absolute best products, people, and tools that I could lay my hands on. And, that's what has led me to where I am today. I'm very thankful to be involved in a business that allows me to employ my communication skills, attention to numerical detail, entrepreneurial nature, and leadership skills.

Levi:
Have you seen a shift in the way that business is being done in your market space as technology has evolved?

Sam:
Honestly, the financial industry is one of the slowest responding industries. I still do a lot of my work on a legal pad, across the kitchen table or the conference table from my clients. We have introduced some elements of technology, anything from digital meetings to infinite online resources for education, but as a whole, much of what we do has yet to be automated.

Levi:
Okay, okay.

Sam:
As far as reaching financial communication, in that light, I have seen a significant spike. Just being able to communicate with someone, via like we're doing right now, e.g. conference calls, virtual meetings, and the ability to share screens even from a cell phone, it has facilitated a wider reach.

Levi:

Sure. So, what do people not know about your industry and your approach to business?

Sam:

There are many things that people don't know about the financial services industry. Furthermore, our approach to how we do business and what sector of that industry that we represent is even more obscured from the general public. Oftentimes, I feel like I'm in the belief changing business. Due to the plethora of information that is promoted even within our industry, information that may not be inherently false, but is not specifically tailored to each person's individual situation, we spend a lot of time re-educating our clients away from 'traditional wisdom.'

We work with many business owners who have very diverse portfolios. Most often one of their largest assets is their business. When helping someone to structure their portfolio, we've found that it is vital to evaluate each asset, and to make sure that it is properly positioned and utilized. This individualized approach goes against mainstream marketing, but one of the mantras at our firm is: "Different is not always better, but better is always different."

Levi:

So, would you say that there is an information gap in your industry?

Sam:

That's a good question. There's usually a pretty large information gap. My goal in what I do is to give people an education on a variety of different subjects, to the point that they are empowered, motivated, or capable, really, to make informed decisions. However, what I would say is that there's a lack of understanding of what's available. Most often you are only exposed to one line of thinking when it comes to your finances. This narrow minded focus, perpetuated by institutions that would like to control your money, has created some degree of information gap. The most common thing that people have put in front of them, are options and vehicles that don't offer much flexibility, don't offer much control, and have you, kind of, conform to more of a herd mentality. The reason that this is perpetuated and it's so commonplace is because that's how the largest financial institutions make money; it is by having people in that "herd" mentality. What I would say that my industry does, and especially my firm, is seek to put the individual in control of their finances. We do this by not pushing one cookie cutter approach, one specific product, or one line of thinking, but by educating people on how to quantitatively evaluate a variety of assets. Now, you're more educated so that you're able to take a higher level of control over your financial portfolio. The goal is to help people to protect, grow, and leverage their money, to put you in absolute, 100 percent, complete control of your dollars while you're living, and help you keep as much money in the family when you pass away. We just believe in stewardship, family, peace of mind, and success.

Levi:
You mentioned earlier that you've taken an innovative approach to investing. Can you explicate a little bit further on how you have discovered this innovative approach, and then explain what kind of additional benefits or impact that it's having for your clients and for people in your market space?

Sam:
First, what drives me and what I preach to my clients is that good stewardship is at the core of an efficient financial plan. When you're developing a financial plan that's strategic, it doesn't matter what echelon of society or finance that you're at. At the core of a good plan is either being a good steward, or having efficient finances. This relates to how you approach what you do with investing, what you do with business ventures, what you do with planning for retirement, all these different areas.

The innovative approach is more centered around an exclusive financial product that enhances almost any portfolio. In fact, it is what I consider a foundational asset. I've personally owned and been involved in a plethora of different assets, and I honestly believe that if I had to choose just one asset to start and put at the foundation of my portfolio, it would be the exclusive "flagship" asset we have at my firm. What makes this product so innovative, is that it took a concept which already afforded clients the following benefits if structured properly: Tax-Advantaged Growth, Tax-Free Access, Creditor Protection, Market Volatility Protection, Guaranteed Loan Features, Arbitrage Opportunities, and More... It took that product, which already was a tremendous offering, and made it less expensive internally. It now has all those benefits and most likely costs LESS to manage than your mutual funds, brokerage account, or 401k.

Levi:

When should an entrepreneur start looking at financial planning? Because you brought that up on a couple of occasions. When is the best time for them to start taking a look?

Sam:

Obviously, at the core of building a business is a financial focus, that's typically why an individual starts a business. So, I would definitely recommend, even in the early stages, having some financial plan in place. Sometimes you are planning your finances with your cash, sometimes you're planning it with your credibility, and sometimes you're planning it with your credit. But, at any time, you need to be aware of what assets that you have available to you, and make sure that you're utilizing them and stewarding them in the best fashion possible. I would say that you should coordinate that evaluation into your efforts early on. So to sum it up, my advice is encapsulated in an old proverb: "The best time to plan a tree was 20 years ago, the second best time is right now." Although, being the very literal mathematical mind that I am, there are about 7300 days between 20 years ago and today, that would technically be the "second best time," but you get my point.

Levi:

Ha Ha! That's great. So, one of the things that I love to ask, when I talk to people that have strong financial minds like yours, is to talk more on the power of leverage. Because I really think that understanding finances, understanding the tools that can be used, at the core, is this concept of leverage. Would you mind, kind of, peeling back the curtains for us a little bit?

Sam:

That is one of the most influential pieces of what we do. When I talk about the three pronged approach of what strengths are in the specific line of product that we specialize in here at my financial firm; one of those strengths is the ability to leverage it as an asset class. Leverage is defined as positional advantage. So, you're able to take a positional advantage with your finances. I love analogies, so I want you to picture kids on a see-saw. Visualize 3 small children sitting on the one end of a balanced see-saw, and one small child sitting on the other end. In your mind, you likely pictured the three children lifting the one child up. Now imagine that the see saw-saw is slid towards the single child, but the fulcrum remains in its original spot. Now ONE child is lifting three! Simply by optimal position-ing the same child that previously was lifted far off the ground and had no control of his situation, was able to lift three times his own weight. It's the same way with your finances. The days of just having your one dollar do the work of one dollar are over. It is vitally important to make sure your dollars are not parked on the freeway of forward progress. Leverage allows you to have the same dollar working multiple places at one time. There's a very fine balance in between over-leveraged and not being lev-eraged enough. People often go to one extreme or the other. One extrem-ity never leverage yourself in any way, shape, or form and quite likely miss out on opportunities that may arise. The other extremity is to be 100 percent leveraged. Both extremities have had their adherents. We saw oil companies that over-leveraged themselves with this whole natural gas price explosion, and then when you have a series of depressions, or mar-ket corrections, that leverage can be a cancer that eats you alive. You also see people who didn't take those risks, who didn't leverage at all, and they were left behind and were not able to keep up, because it was necessary to have more dollars working for you.

Levi:

So, from an investing standpoint, is there a secret formula, a secret mix to understanding good leverage and bad leverage?

Sam:

Yes, I think that there is to a large degree there. It depends on your activity level with your investments. If you're going to be a somewhat passive investor in it, then unless you know that the people that you're investing with have real solidity, then I would say that your leverage percentage needs to be lower than someone who's going to be an active investor. I would say that the percentage of leverage should be a coefficient of your level of control over the investment. I wouldn't say there is a magic formula, but I would recommend erring on the side less leverage if you are unsure or uncomfortable. As always though, have your trusted advisors, counselors, mentors, etc, involved when it comes to leveraging or business ventures. As an entrepreneur, the buck stops with you, but don't let that responsibility mindset turn you away from valid counsel. No one has a corner on all knowledge, and everyone should be a continual student of their finances.

Levi:
So, you've mentioned the importance of finding people that are knowledgeable and this is a common trend for anyone trying to succeed in any area of life. How would you recommend that an entrepreneur, who is trying to grow his business, trying to understand leverage and financial tools, how would you recommend that they go about finding someone that truly can help them in this area?

Sam:
Honestly, the best advice I can give is: a multitude of counselors provide wisdom. Again, my literal mind says that a multitude of counselors can also pool ignorance... So at the end of the day, it's up to you and your gut to exercise discernment over what is presented to you. Good indicators I would look for are things like a proven track record, personal financial success, stable morals, and transparency. Bad Indicators MAY be personal bankruptcies, law-suits, dissatisfied clients, and non-transparent answers like: "you don't need to know about that, it's just not a good fit." That kind of talk is baloney—educating yourself on all options should always be commended and never discouraged due to a preconceived judgment. Many opportunities are missed, because someone was ignorant and transferred that fear onto another.

Levi:
Sure.

Sam:
At the end of the day, it's up to the entrepreneur to make the best and wisest decisions. So, definitely getting your counsel is important, but you have to trust your gut and make the final call. Now, I may be a little bit biased, but I think that my firm offers pretty good counsel.

Levi:
Sam, you did bring up that when somebody's starting out, or when they are in the earlier stages of the process that maybe they can't afford a CFO or maybe they're not even to that point yet in their business. So, how do they go about attracting experts, advisors, or mentors that can guide them on their path?

Sam:
As far as finding a mentor, that's something that really speaks to me because I've done that again actually somewhat recently in the last year. I guess a little over a year, probably about a year and a half ago. I greatly encourage any entrepreneur to go down that path. Finding someone who's got a high level of honesty, who's had some degree of success, and can shine some light on your path is invaluable.

If you can get someone involved who is willing to observe your business, and then cares enough about you to be blatantly honest, you have found something special! Letting my mentors get down to the nitty-gritty, letting them get their hands dirty, and just seeing what I had going. Being totally open with them, and getting some external perspective has been invaluable to my business. So, no matter how good you are at your business, how successful you've been, having that external perspective, a lot of times, will open your eyes to some things that may have been hindering your proficiency and efficiency and really put a cap on your business. I've yet to see somebody bring on a mentor that has good intentions that has not had improvements to their business. Oftentimes, the best mentors are not the ones who charge the most. In fact, I've found, a lot of times, the inverse to be true.

Levi:

That's a fascinating concept. Why would you say that would be the case?

Sam:

Just my personal observation that their interests are not always aligned with yours. Their interests are in being retained as an advisor. Whereas, if you've partnered with someone who has an active stake in your company, or who doesn't have an interest in living off your money, then their interest is more likely to be aligned with your success. Unlike a typical consultant, they would have no reason to drag out your success. On the other hand, if you're paying for a service, then their sole goal is to continue to be retained. The best input I have ever gotten came from either people who needed nothing from me, but simply wanted to influence me in a positive way, or from a mentor who is now a business partner. Our arrangement started with a production based compensation model, as my production increased, so did his compensation. My success was directly linked to his success — it was a very powerful and dynamic relationship. Plenty of accountability to be had with that model.

Levi:

That makes sense. Certainly, seeing a little bit of both sides of the fence. It actually brings up a very pertinent topic for entrepreneurship. Talk to us now about how your relationships have impacted your line of business.

Sam:

Oh, relationships are really everything. You've heard the saying, it's not what you know, it's who you know, and that is more and more evident in today's world. There are people who are handicapped because they're not able to cultivate and retain relationships. I've seen business crumble because they did not have the proper relationship base. So, you should be making sure that you take the time to cultivate relationships. Be intentional about it. Realize that it's not a fruitless endeavor; it should be considered just like developing asset class.

Personally speaking though, my line of business is nothing but relationships. Each client is wholly unique, so it's vital to have an active relationship with them. When trying to help someone further their financial portfolio, it's vital to understand their frame of reference- This can't be done without developing a relationship. I have over 300 clients. If you gave me a list of a thousand random names, with my 300 mixed in, I guarantee you I could pick all 300 out of the list. The client relationship is very unique. In fact, many entrepreneurs will never have clients, they will only have customers. See, Webster defined client as: "One who is under the protection of another." I had a client call me 20 minutes after her husband died, because she didn't know what to do. I had clients attend my wedding, clients who call ME on Christmas, and clients I see at social events. Relationships are the backbone of my business. However, I've had people who I had to fire as clients. As an entrepreneur, I've had to learn to guard my relationships; I've had clients who acted like customers and business associates who treated me with contempt and disrespect in spite of the fact that they were financed and employed due to my business. Relationships are everything, and you must be careful to avoid a relationship in which you are protecting and giving and another is manipulating and taking.

Levi:
I would absolutely agree with you 100 percent on that relationships are everything in business, and that your business really actually grows as you gain quality relationships. If you were able to give someone just one, gold nugget of advice that, regardless of where they're at on the entrepreneurial journey, when it comes to investing as a whole, would that one nugget be that everyone should know about investing?

Sam:
It really comes down to responsibility. I use the word stewardship often because I think that that's a very intentional, powerful, and purposeful word. At the end of the day, it's your responsibility to educate yourself to the point that you are able to make good decisions. There's a lot of information, but if you're really willing to do the digging, then you can get to the point where you're educated, and where you can make an informed decision. The problem is that the majority of people, I'd say probably 75 percent of people, make their decisions based on hearsay, what they've heard, what they've gotten in passing, what was traditional, what was

given to them by a party that may not have had their best interests at heart. So, at the end of the day, if I could preach one thing, it is financial responsibility. Have a will and desire to educate yourself on various financial topics. Surround yourself with people who will help you create a culture of financial awareness and good stewardship. Know where you are, know where you're going, take responsibility for it, own it, own where you are, and own where you're going. Once you know your current status, always look for that chance to improve. Don't ever become complacent or idle. Part of being a good steward is using your talents and resources to create continual improvement!

Levi:

Great replies. I like to talk to people about knowing the score of the game. If you don't know the score of the game, or how the game is played, then it's pretty near impossible to win the game. You might score a point here or there, but you're not really going to win the game.

Sam:

Right, and my analogy is really similar to yours. What I tell people is that managing your finances is like playing tic-tac-toe. The first time that you played tic-tac-toe, you didn't know the rules, you barely knew the game, and so you lost repeatedly until you learned the strategies of the game. That's what I have a passion for doing—showing people the strategies behind the game. There are only so many variables in tic-tac-toe, so if you learn them, you can guarantee that you will never lose. Unfortunately, life and your financial plan is a little more complicated than a 9 option game, but the principle applies. If you have the ability to learn the strategies, you'll encounter infinitely more possibility, and you're going to win more times than you lose.

Levi:

Alright, that actually speaks to my core concept of implementing strategies. One of the things that I see frequently is that you can change any outcome that you want, as long as you change your process. And, if you apply a strategic approach to it, then you're going to see a tremendous outcome.

Sam:

Correct.

Levi:

We have talked a lot about business strategy, we've talked a lot about how you got into this industry as well as some of the things that people can do to take action. But, for yourself, talk to us about your legacy. What is it that you're trying to build here?

Sam:

When I think of my purpose, my life, and what I'm looking to leave behind a few key things come to mind. I'm greatly influenced by a spiritual background. I do have a strong relationship with my Lord and Savior Jesus Christ, and this has an influence in every aspect of my life, whether it be personal, business, emotional, etc. And, that's a strong influence. So, when it comes to the kind of legacy that I want to leave, that is an influencing factor there, for sure.

Also, I have a passion for training. I've always been educating people in some form or fashion. I have a passion for taking what, I feel, has been revealed to me, what I understand, and then conceptualizing it, putting it into terminologies, and using communication skills that I believe I've been gifted with to transfer that knowledge to another human being.

What I want to build as my legacy is one that is first a testimony of my faith, second an example and encouragement to other entrepreneurs, and finally as catalyst for meaningful positive change in the lives of those I influence. I absolutely want to make a positive impact, starting with my family, then my clients, and finally my firms clients through all of our advisors here at Dove Ventures.

Levi:

Well, I definitely sense your passion inspired by the things that you've been teaching. I hope that those that read this chapter will be able to take some of the nuggets, take some of those gems, and apply them to their lives. If you were to give one last piece of advice for anyone wanting to invest, or wanting to get involved in entrepreneurship, what would that be?

Sam:

You should be taking control and responsibility for your finances and your business. Learn that "results" is the name of the game. What is common is not always what's best. Different is not always better, but better is always different. So, if you do the same things that you've always done, then you get the same things that you've always gotten. You need to be taking responsibility for what you have, be a good steward over what comes to you as you or your wealth grows, and look for the most efficient ways to protect, grow, and leverage your assets and your business. Surrounding yourself with people who have a mindset like I just described will create a culture that is proven to produce success.

Kevin E. Clayson

Kevin E. Clayson is one of the Founders and Executives of Strongbrook, a multi-million dollar real estate investment company that he and his partners created in early 2007. Kevin is lovingly referred to as the "Chief Officer of Awesome" and the "Vice President of Prosperity." As one of its primary trainers and educators, he has developed and created much of the company's coaching and mentoring curriculum. He has instrumentally assisted with the development of the company's corporate vision, strategy and products, and he largely is responsible for its nationally renowned and admired company culture. He is a seasoned, skilled, nationally acclaimed speaker and Emcee. He travels and speaks on a regular basis, entertaining, thrilling and inspiring audiences all over the country.

Kevin has been powerfully assisting thousands of Americans in achieving personal, financial and business success for 10 years. He has had the opportunity to personally mentor many successful people, working with everyone from struggling college students, to budding entrepreneurs to multi-millionaire business owners. He helps people learn how to "show up" in their lives in a way that has a profound impact on long-term sustainable results. His passion is people, and he has a desire to connect and authentically communicate with the millions of Americans who feel the sense that they have a greater purpose in life.

Kevin is the author of *"Sit On The Front Row"* and *"Gratifuel"* ™ and the Owner of Quadrefi, LLC.

He lives in Orem with his beautiful wife, spending every second he can with her and their three gorgeous children.

Websites: *www.Kevinclayson.com* • *www.Quadrefi.com*
www.Gratifuel.com • *www.SittingOnTheFrontRow.com*

Levi:

So, one of the things that we get asked all the time from entrepreneurs and people that are aspiring to be entrepreneurs is, "What is the formula for success? What is the secret sauce?" One of the things that I often tell people is that success happens at the speed of decisions. Kevin, you've developed an approach that actually enhances that whole process of decisions, and I'm going to let you go ahead and talk about that real fast.

Kevin:

Yeah, thanks Levi. You're absolutely right. I love the term you just used, that, "Success happens at the speed of decisions." I have seven decisions that I try to make every day. It's these simple decisions in seven different categories and in my experience, if I'm conscious to what the seven areas of decision-making are, if I'm conscious to it and I absolutely consciously try to make a decision, a good decision in each one of those areas every day, I find that over time, my results compound and become really differentiating from many other entrepreneurs and other people around me.

That's not to say that I'm anything special, it's just a simple truth that I've learned over time. I want to back up and tell you about a story of how I came to arrive at this daily decision concept that I've been implementing now, both in my business, as well as with a number of entrepreneurs and people that I've coached and mentored over the years. I am not built to be a runner, yet when I met my wife, she was training for, at that time, her third full marathon. I was blown away that this incredible woman had run three full marathons. For those that don't know, a full marathon is 26.2 miles of running—in the sun, usually. It is tough. It is really tough.

I'd had this lifelong goal of wanting to complete a marathon. Now, I get to stand before you today and say with tremendous accomplishment that I, too, have completed three full 26.2 mile marathons. I never even dreamed that I would be able to do one. It was the example of my wife that helped me see that maybe it was possible. What I watched my wife do, at that time we were just dating, but what I watched her do is I saw her take time and I saw her make a decision every day that she was going to go and pound pavement. She was going to get up and she was going to go running. It didn't matter how tired she was. I didn't matter if she wanted to or not, she made the decision, the determination every day that she would go and pound pavement. I just thought that that was really incredible.

I remember asking her, "How did you start running marathons?" She told me that all you need to have is a three-mile base and four months. If you can run at least three miles and give yourself four months to train for a race, anybody can run a marathon. Well that seemed fairly simple to me, I thought, "I think I could probably go a knock out three miles and if I wanted to make the choice to give myself four months of training, I think I can do that, too."

I watched her complete these marathons and was just blown away and at some point made a decision that I was going to put that theory to the test. If I had a three-mile base and I gave myself four months, maybe I could run a marathon.

I think it was 2010, and I ran the St. George marathon. What I did was I took my wife's formula, training formula, the fact that I needed to have at least three miles that I could run and I gave myself four months and I went through and I did it. I woke up. I was running five times a week, and I was able to complete my first marathon. It's a tremendous accomplishment. Well, the following year, I decided that I wanted to run yet another marathon. It seemed like a good idea to me. The following year, I also was able to get into the St. George marathon and I began my training schedule.

What was interesting is the second marathon, because I already completed one—by the way there's a lesson in this for every business owner and every entrepreneur, so pay attention to it—because I'd already achieved a certain level of success, because I'd already achieved my goal one time, I thought that in order the replicate that process, there was no way I'd have to work that hard. I know that I can do it. It was in my mind that I could do it. Therefore, I didn't need to train as frequently. So, during my training schedule for the second time that I ran a marathon, instead of running five days a week I chose to run three days a week, sometimes four. Many weeks it was only two days a week. I was still half-heartedly making daily decisions that would end up allowing me to run this marathon, but it was a completely different, I wasn't making daily decisions. It was "every now and then" I would make a daily decision to go and run a marathon.

The time came for me to go and run. This marathon happens in the fall, so you wake up and it's cold. You load up on these buses and these buses take you up this mountain. The buses take you up the mountain, you get off the buses and you see tens of thousands, it feels like, maybe it's just thousands of people that are also so crazy as to run 26.2 miles on their feet. I'm there and I'm looking at everything, I'm really excited and I'm thinking, "Ah, here we go again! I'm going to do this." I felt that I was prepared. In my mind, I thought I was prepared. In fact, I was even feeling pretty good about myself thinking, "Wow, here I am ready to run the marathon again and I didn't even have to train as hard. I didn't even have to work as hard, yet I still achieved my goal," thinking I had discovered, unlocked some sort of magical formula to success in this universe that somehow you don't have to work as hard, but you can still achieve a result.

Well, the marathon starts and everything's just fine. I'm pumped up. I've got my earphones on and I'm jumping and getting ready to go. The gun goes and people start to run. They cross the start line and here I go, I start pumping my arms, I start pumping my legs and I am so excited. I jump out of that gate significantly faster than I normally would in any other training run, but I can get out there because I'm excited. For the first seven and a half miles, I felt fantastic. I was going faster than normal. I didn't require as much nourishment, I felt like, as I usually do.

Everything was going great, but you see, at the St. George marathon at mile seven and a half, something happens. There's this incredible grade, you have to run over a volcano. It's a place called Veyo. You get there at seven and a half miles, and you are going to have about a mile and a half of some steep terrain and some steep grade, even though it is on the street. So, I start pumping up this thing, and I'm realizing, "Wow, this is really hard. In fact, this is harder than I remember it being the year before."

The way Veyo works, you come to the face of this volcano and you make a left, and then the road curves around right to get around this volcano. As I came around right, the sun was just starting to breach the horizon and the sun hit me in my eyes and I remembered, "Oh, I forgot my hat the other day when I was going running. Darn it!" I'm closing my eyes and I'm running and I feel like I can't even open my eyes. I started to notice that there was something happening inside me that didn't really feel great, something that I was not familiar with, something that I didn't understand.

I just kept going. Mile 8 passed by and before I knew it I was at the half marathon marker, 13.1 miles and I'm noticing, "I just don't feel well." See, after you get off the volcano, you go through an area, I believe it's called Dammeron Valley, and there's a gradual hill for a number of miles. I'm noticing that I don't even want to open my eyes as I'm going up this hill. I just not feeling well and I don't, I just felt like, "What is going on with me?" I would drink water. I would take some nutrition in. I would still be cotton-mouthy and I was drinking more water and before I knew it, I was sloshing around in my gut. It was like that water was not being absorbed into my body.

You have to understand, if you've ever run a marathon, there's a really cruel trick that marathon planners will play on you. They will send a bus that goes up and down the route of the marathon and I always thought of it as the quitter bus, because what would happen is if you weren't feeling good, if you didn't think you could accomplish it, you got to get on the quitter bus and they'd take you to your nice air-conditioned finish line. You wouldn't get a medal, but hey, at least you lived to see another day. I always told myself, "I will never be on that quitter bus."

Here I was, my second year running this marathon and I am looking at that quitter bus in a different light. All of a sudden, it feels like it might be my salvation bus, because I knew that there was something that was not right in me. I got to about Mile 15, and at Mile 15, I knew that I had 11.2 miles left. I seriously considered quitting. I didn't think I could do it, didn't think I could make it, felt that my body was not taking well to this run. Something hadn't happened. I wasn't hydrated. My body wasn't taking in the water. My kidneys had started to hurt, but I looked at that quitter bus, thought about it and I said, "No way. Not today. I'm going to finish this race. Regardless of what's happened up to this point, regardless of how ill-prepared I was for today, I'm in it and I'm running it."

I kept going, one step at a time. As I was running, I remember using all my mental Jedi tricks. I'd learned what it means to have a positive attitude. I'd learned what it means to create your reality. I knew that mind could overcome the weakness of body and I was doing everything in my power to use all of these tools that I felt had been learned by me, that had been given to me over the years with a lot of study and contemplation. None of them were working.

Levi, I couldn't get me to feel better. I couldn't get me to want to finish the race, but I made a determination that I would. As I'm running, I've got teenage girls that are running by me, passing me. They're ten, fifteen years younger than I am, singing Miley Cyrus and having a great old time. I've got 85 year-old barefoot men that are passing me on the track. I have pregnant women that are 12 weeks pregnant. They are passing me and on the back of their shirt said, "You just got passed by a woman who's pregnant at 12 weeks." I'm looking at this and I'm going, "Oh, yeah. This is going real good for me."

I'm watching these people pass me. I'm feeling my body and I'm wondering if I'm going to make it. I'd made that decision I was going to finish. So I came to a conclusion that day, and it was a conclusion that I had to come to, I don't know how many thousands of times, from the moment that I made the determination to finish the race. I did finish that day, but it was after a significant amount of pain, a significant amount of tears, a significant amount of fear and a lot of exhaustion.

Turns out I had begun to become dehydrated and luckily was able to make it across the finish line, but I learned something that day, Levi. As I reflect on that day, and I reflect on what happened, I realized that all I could focus on was the very next step. If I thought too far ahead, it was overwhelming. If I looked in the past at the steps that I'd taken, I'd be discouraged by how slow the steps had been. So, the only thing I could focus on, that had to become present, that it was the next step.

I learned something that day. I learned that we've been given these moments in time and this goes for entrepreneurs, this goes for business owners, this goes for fathers, like I am, mothers, anybody; we are given these moments throughout the day that I have nicknamed, "Divine moments of minute decision-making." I believe in God, so divine for me means it's a gift from God. Somebody reading this book may not believe in God, but I'm sure that you understand the word divine and believe that it can also be used for excellent. However you want to define the word divine, I believe those moments we are given are divine moments of minute decision-making that we get a choice to make.

I realize that at the conclusion of each one of my little steps, and by the way, my steps, I looked like a character from The Walking Dead; I could barely lift a foot, but I had to take one step after the other. I realized that when I would complete one step, I only had to make one tiny decision. The decision I had to make at that moment in time, that divine moment I had to make a minute decision, a tiny decision to take another step. It didn't matter of the step was a few inches or a few feet; I had to decide to take the next step. In your words, Levi, success for me at that moment came "at the speed of decision," the decision to take the next step.

Step after step, decision after decision, divine moment of a minute decision after divine moment of a minute decision, these compounded over time and I crossed that finish line. Nay, I did not cross the finish line, I collapsed across the finish line, but that is neither here nor there, but I made it. I learned something that day. I learned that these divine moments that we are given happen thousands of times a day and we have complete and total control, if we are conscious to it, we have complete and total control on how that little decision is made.

To give you an example that I love from Zig Ziglar: Zig Ziglar refers to them as stupid, I believe, but the person who sits at the stop light looking at that red light, feeling like they're in a hurry, so angry that they're stuck at a stop light that they rev their engine as if it is going to turn that light green. Zig says, "How stupid is that?" Revving an engine is never going to turn that light, but what if you looked at that light, not as a stop light, but as a go light and you saw your name on that light, and you saw that the minute that that light turned green, it was your cue to move forward in life?"

How often are we met with these tiny decisions, be it at a stop light or as Zig puts it, a "go light," or whether that's a marathon or it's one step at a time, or it's in our business and we realize that there are tiny decisions that we have to make on a regular basis: Whether to hire a certain employee, whether to fire a certain employee, whether to give an employee a raise, how we choose to view our P & L statement. There's so many decisions that we have to make on a regular basis, and many of them are not even large decisions. It's a simple decision that you're getting in a moment to be kind to the customer that you're interacting with at that moment in time, and if that's the only decision that you make, it's a decision that can provide some success.

As I learned this concept and as I learned about divine moments of minute decision-making, I started to apply it in my life. I started to seek out those divine moments, these tiny moments in time where all I would have to do is make a small decision and then that small decision, even though it seems inconsequential at the time that I made the decision, I mean, think about my race, one step that was only two or three inches as I shuffled along sure doesn't seem like a huge step towards my goal, but thousands and thousands and thousands of tiny little couple inch-long steps culminate in me achieving my goal in crossing that finish line.

So, I started to think about becoming conscious every day to the tiny decisions that if I could just make a certain decision, the same type of decision, every single day of my life, even though those decisions may be small, they would compound and culminate into something absolutely incredible. Levi, today I get to come to you and tell you that I know this has been true for me for my business life, I know that it's been true for me in my speaking world and going a becoming a nationally recognized speaker. It's been important in my life as a father.

I have these beautiful moments every day where I get to decide the kind of husband I want to be, the kind of dad that I want to be, how I want to discipline. I get to decide, when my wife asks me to do the dishes, if this tiny moment in time, it may be inconsequential, maybe it's only doing one dish, but if I choose to do that dish, I'm then given another moment where I get to do the next dish. If I were to just do that, how much happier is my wife going to be with me after making a series of tiny little decisions, as opposed to me making the decision when she asked me to do the dishes to say, "Eh, maybe not," or, "Isn't that your job?," or, "Nah, I'll do it later." Tiny decisions can culminate in incredible results.

Levi, with your permission, I'd love to go through the seven daily decisions that I implemented in my life that I've found if I'm willing to make a decision every day to doing something in each of these seven categories, I will achieve success every time, without exception. So, with your permission, can I go through what those seven are?

Levi:
Absolutely.

Kevin:
All right. So, the first one is The Daily Decision about Your Physical Body. Here's what this means. You've got to do something for your physical body. Now listen, you're talking to a guy that has struggled over the last decade with some extra pounds. When I am in a physical state that I'm unhappy with and I think about, "I need to lose ten pounds, I need to lose twenty pounds." I get all caught up in disappointment that I'm so far from my goal, but if all can do is simply focus on today.

I don't care about tomorrow, I don't care about the next day, I don't care if I did or didn't do it yesterday, I wake up in the morning and I make a decision, "Today, I will spend twenty minutes on the treadmill. Thirty minutes on the cross trainer." "Today I choose to do a workout video at home." "Today I choose to simply do ten push-ups between each appointment that I have." Whatever the decision is, it is a decision that must be made the second you spring out of bed and take on that day, you say, "Today, I choose to do something for my physical body."

I don't know if people out there are familiar with the story of Jared from Subway. He's a Subway spokesperson who lost a tremendous amount of weight eating Subway sandwiches. Now look, I don't know if the Subway diet is the right way to lose weight or not, but here's what I can tell you. As Jared chose to eat Subway sandwiches, it was a daily decision. He had to choose that today, he would forgo the Big Mac for the sandwich. He didn't have to think about five years from now, "I need to forgo the Big Mac for the sandwich," I simply had to think, "I just had breakfast. I look forward to lunch." When lunch time rolls around, he has one decision to make. That decision was to eat the sandwich as opposed to the Big Mac. Now, that had a physical effect on him. I know that there was exercise involved there, too.

I have a friend of mine, a guy by the name of Nick Hoyer. We've become Facebook friends over time. Here's a guy who at one point weighed nearly 400 pounds. Nick is now a triathlon athlete. He is a marathon runner. He is incredibly fit. He had to have surgery, not gastric bypass surgery, but surgery to basically get rid of all the excess skin from how large he was. This is a man who is very fit. I was interviewing Nick one time, just trying to learn from him and I said, "Nick, how did you get skinny?" He said, "Every day, I started by deciding that every day that I would get on the cross trainer, on the elliptical machine." He said, "I made that decision every day for a year, but it was only one day at a time. It was only one decision at a time, and I did that every day for a year, and you know what, at the conclusion of the year, I lost a significant amount of weight and I felt that the results were really good so I ought to keep making a daily decision to just go and get on that elliptical trainer."

Now, we have a man who has completely transformed his life, has transformed his business life, has transformed his love life, has transformed his physical appearance, and the joy that he can experience on a daily basis because he simply makes a daily decision to something for his physical body. So, that's the first one, physical.

The second one, as this one is very, very important, by the way, these are in no particular order, I'm not going to say that one is any more or less important than the other, but the second one is spiritual. I've already mentioned, I'm a religious person. For me, making a daily decision to do something spiritual is reading in the Good Book, it's reading scriptures. It's saying a prayer. Those are the two things for me, prayer and scripture study, that are the daily decision that must be made. What's interesting about that is that can be very, very difficult, especially sometimes those of us that are religious begin to entertain feelings of guilt if we don't do something the way that we know that we are supposed to according to our belief system. We love to entertain the feeling of guilt. That feeling of guilt certainly does not proliferate our desire to do more good, it simply robs us of a desire to make a change.

So, what I've found is in order for me to be right in my Godlife, meaning to be in good standing with my God, I simply need to make a decision, not about tomorrow, not about yesterday, but just about today—that at some point today, I will read my scriptures. I will kneel and I will pray to my creator, just today.

The third is one that I do think is very important is the daily decision that you make about money. There's a variety of ways that this could be done. You could choose to save a little bit of money every day. You could choose to create additional money every day. You could choose to read something or become educated about money every day, but you should have money on your mind. One thing that is very important for anybody reading this book to understand is that money is nothing more than a representation of value. If you want more money in your life, provide more value for others. The more value you provide, the more money you receive in return and the more you can grow over time your money world.

Most people think of money like this: "I hope I have enough to spend on superfluous nonsense." Hoping that you're going to have enough is not a form of creation, it is simply a form of diminishing what you already have. What we need to do in our money life is wake up every day and make a decision that, "Today I choose increase my money life." Now, when we increase our money life, that can be in the typical form of dollars and there will be paydays and there will be times when checks will come in and it will seem like you did, maybe you met your daily decision for money that day, but I disagree. The money flowing into your life is a direct result of the money decision that you made yesterday. Okay? So, when money actually shows up and you cash a check, that's not your money decision for the day. Your money decision for today should be, "I choose to read this book on my financial life." "I choose." If you are in a direct sales or a network marketing company, as a good example, or you're in sales of some sort, your daily decision should look like this, "Today, just today, I won't worry about yesterday and I will not worry think tomorrow, but today, I will talk to just two new people."

If you woke up every day, and think about this, Levi, if somebody that was in direct sales or network marketing and they are looking for a pool of prospects that they've got a great product for that they believe that they can serve with this product, if all they did is, every day, simply made the decision to go and talk to new people and open their mouth two times to someone new. If they did that every day for three years, what kind of results would they compound? We could play with the math, but I want you to think about that. Look at how powerful that small daily decision is. In fact, let me do the math.

If you just talked to two people a day and you did that for a full year, actually if you did that for three years, that would be over 2,000 new people that you would have introduced your opportunity to, as opposed to sitting and waiting and hoping that friends and family were going to approach you. Or, as opposed to hoping that somebody that you enrolled in your program at some point is going to perform for you, if all you did was make a decision that, "Today, I'm going to talk to two people." When it also comes to, that would be the type of a way to create money, I actually have a philosophy about money that is separate. I'll mention it here and recommend everybody, if you want to learn more, you can go to QuadRefi.com, but I believe in a money philosophy that is very easy to use on a daily basis if you are doing something in one of four quadrants.

I believe that QuadRefi, there's four quadrants to your financial life and you ought to be considering each one on a regular basis and just to give you an idea of what those are. The first quadrant is to "redesign your financial life." By that, what I mean is simply, we've been taught a lot of financial nonsense in this world and it doesn't work. We know that it doesn't work, yet we continue to engage in it time and time again. So, when you redesign your financial life, you simply look at it a little differently, and that could be your daily money decision. You could choose to seek out some form of knowledge that is different from what you already know, or maybe it's another piece of knowledge about what you invest in so that you can learn a little bit more, because you've got to be in your money, or else someone else will be in your money for you.

So, you have to redesign your financial life and question some of these nonsense that we've been taught for years and years and years. I've got a whole program on this. I've got ways that I've been literally impacting American's lives now for seven years on how to QuadRefi, so four ways to refinance your life, you redesign your financial life.

The second quadrant is you "refine your financial life." That simply you are going to create money at some point, whether that's from a job or whether that's from a home-based business or whether that's being an entrepreneur or business owner. You will create money. The question is what do you do with it once it's created? The second quadrant is to refine the decisions that you make and take out the financial impurity. Many of us don't understand how many financial impurities exist in our financial life. So, when you refine, it's, "How do I store money and how do I remove the financial impurities, the wealth-eroding factors that keep me from becoming wealthy?" There's many of those. You can go to QuadRefi.com, or I've got a video that I posted on *YouTube* called "How to QuadRefi" on my *YouTube* channel at Kevin Clayson on *YouTube*. I go into tremendous depth there. This philosophy is all about, "Could you do something today to look at your financial life differently?"

The third quadrant, I'll just mention briefly, is to recharge. Recharging your financial life is, "How do you generate some income?" You will be generating income in your life. How do you charge your ability to generate more income? It could be a home-based business. It could be network marketing, direct sales. It could be starting a business on the side, a variety of way you can do that and I go into depth there.

The fourth is to recreate your financial life, so four ways to refinance your financial life. I call it the Q4 Blueprint. You redefine, you refine, you recharge, you recreate. Recreating your financial life happens in your mind and in your heart. That does not happen in the physical world. All of those play into, "What is your daily money decision?" "Do you choose to recreate your philosophy about money by engaging in books that are powerful, or by learning from mentors who have made more money than you?" "Do you call them? Do you take them to lunch?" Just today, decide to do something to change your money life, to change your financial life, whatever that is. It's important that if we consider money every day, we'd be conscious of how much is being created, how much is going out and what we could do.

That's the third. The first daily decision, "Do something in your physical world," the second daily decision, "Wake up tomorrow and decide to do something for your spiritual life," regardless of what you believe, do something that allows you to connect with a power that is outside of you. The third daily decision is your money decision, "Read a book, learn some information, save some money. Go and talk to someone that can produce more income for you. Sit down and write a business plan of a new business you can start." Decide today you will wake up and put pen to paper just to write the first sentence of that new business plan. Whatever it is, make a decision and you'll consider your money every day.

The next one is one that I really, really love. This is one I found to provide an unbelievable amount of joy and happiness for everybody that uses it. The daily decision next that I'll talk about is that of service. Wake up tomorrow and decide, that just on tomorrow, don't worry about the day after that, don't worry about the day before; simply decide that today, you will go and render service to someone. It may be small, it may be large. It may be donating to a charity. It may be simply helping an elderly woman out with her groceries who's at the same store that you're at. It could be so simple as opening a door for someone. It could be so simple as providing a smile and a "Hey, how do you do?" to someone that looks a little down. Do something to serve someone every day.

I've got to tell you a story really fast. There's a gentleman that I worked with many years ago when I was in the retail world. I spent a lot of years in retail before I left to get into the financial world and then eventually start this very successful company that my friends and I that own now. There's a gentleman that I worked with. He and I sold shoes together. I was a different person back when I sold shoes. I was in a marriage where I was unhappy. I didn't know I was unhappy, I only found that out after she left me and I became happy after she left me, but I was in a type of mindset that was not creating success. It was putting me in the same broken philosophies and broken courses of action that the majority of Americans travel, by the way that's why less than five percent of the people in this life, especially in America, ever really achieve the success that they hoped for, because we buy into broken paradigms and broken patterns. That was me.

I was somebody who showed up as being victimized by others. I rarely like to consider things as being my fault. I always liked to find blame with other people. I was a different man. I've been through a lot of experiences over the years as I met and married my incredible wife today, as I've become a father to three gorgeous children, as I started a company with friends that has now impacted thousands of lives and had hundreds of millions of dollars worth of impact on the economy. I've gone through a lot, and as I've grown, I've always known that service was important to experiencing joy and happiness. I've always thought of ways to serve others. I haven't always been good at focusing on a day-by-day basis on who I can serve next, but I've noticed at the times that I do, always being presently focused on finding opportunities to serve others, has created so much joy in my life that I almost always have a smile on my face.

This gentleman that I worked with many years before, the one that I sold shoes with, who's watched me on Facebook and who's connected with me there and watched my life change over the last eight or nine years. He messaged me one day and said, "Kevin, I have a question to ask you. I see your Facebook posts and I appreciate them. It seems like you always have something positive and motivational to say, and I'm thankful for that, and it inspires me," but he said, "Look, I've got a good job. I make good money. I have a car that I like. I have a house that I enjoy. I have a wife. I'm a dad, but I just don't smile, not nearly as much as I feel like I should. It seems like you smile a lot. Why do you smile?"

That had an emotional impact on me. I never considered that making small daily decisions day after day for years would have culminated in two men, both successful in their own right, both married, both with children, both with a house they love, both with a car they want to drive, both with a good income, but one finds it hard to smile. That was my friend.

I responded to him and I said, "There are just two things that I do all the time. One is I always look for the opportunity to serve every day. So, go find someone to serve today and you might find a smile break across your lips. The second," which actually is the next daily decision, is I told him to, "simply express gratitude for everything, no matter how bad, no matter how difficult, no matter how much of a hardship, no matter what, express gratitude for the life that is yours. Find the joy in the life that is yours and you will smile." In another book that I'm working on called, "Gratifuel," I talk a little bit about this concept of the gratitude solution. How one can flip the gratitude switch? There'll be more information on that at Gratifuel.com, if you're at all interested, but I said those two things. These are both simple daily decisions. Choose to serve someone today. It could be a client. It could be a new prospect.

There's a great program out there that I think is something to the effect of "Give Them a Pickle." It's this guy who talks about going the extra mile, to go out of your way to serve your customers. There's a great book called, "Hug Your Customers," a retail establishment, how they went out of their way to serve their customers understanding that through service they would, by providing more value, they would see more value in return and create success. But honestly, they were doing it with a spirit of service, being the heart of a servant. I happen to know that in this book there are some remarkable servants that also have chapters in this book. I think of two, Gary and Carolyn Norris, also known as the rebel entrepreneurs and these are individuals who absolutely have the heart of service that I've never seen them wake up a day in their life since I've known them and not make this a daily decision that they will find someone to serve. As a result, they have achieved unbelievable success in their industry. It's truly incredible to watch.

Make a choice every day to find someone to serve and please serve selflessly. It reminds me of another story that was viral on the Internet for a time. It was an individual, a young boy who worked at a grocery store and he was a bagger. The individual had Down Syndrome and wanted to have an impact on the world around him. Every night, he would go and find a motivational quote and he would cut out this little piece of paper of this motivational quote and he would drop it in the bags of the customers as they walked through the line and as he bagged their groceries. They would get home and they would find this motivational quote, and there's story after story of lives being touched and changed because a young man simply decided to do something so simple as serve as many people as he could with a very simple method. People began to go through that grocery store simply to receive that service, and as a result, more value was given, more value was created. The store had tremendous success because of a young man who simply had a desire to serve. Make the decision today you will go and serve someone.

I mentioned this already, but the next daily decision is this decision of gratitude. I mentioned the book "Gratifuel" and I mentioned Gratifuel. com. My friend, if you want to experience more happiness and more success in your business, choose to experience Gratitude. Let me give you an example of how this works. Our company was fortunate, and I repeat the word fortunate, to undergo a 14-month SEC investigation. This SEC investigation was very difficult. There were a few principals in our company that were named in this investigation and there were hundreds of allegations, were launched at us. The SEC will not disclose who they were launched by. We are operating under the belief that it was a difficult employee's client. Neither here nor there, they were launched. The SEC opened this investigation on our company, and for 14 months, they turned over every single rock and looked in every nook and cranny. What they found was not a single one of those allegations was proven to be right.

In our experience, when something like that happens and the SEC takes that amount of time, they will need to find something that they can use and they can take back to their supervisors, and at the end of the day, they took issue with how we valued the properties. I'm in the real estate industry. They took issue with the way we valued some properties and the way that we had offered the opportunity to raise money to buy these properties, and so they slapped us on the wrist and we paid the minimum fine.

We're not required to change our business model one bit. Not a single one of the allegations that were launched were ever found to be proven. They did not freeze our assets or close our company. We still function today as a much more successful company because we went through this 14-month SEC investigation. If we looked at that experience as a company and we did not choose to experience gratitude for it, what would happen as we would share it with other people is they would immediately want to engaged in doubt about our company, but we choose to view it as a badge of honor. We escaped the SEC without having to change the business model one bit, without having a single allegation found to be true.

Ladies and gentlemen, to me that is a huge blessing and something we experience a tremendous amount of gratitude for. If we choose to simply show up when something like that happens or when the question came out we tried to hide it or we didn't want to throw it out there and we were really, "Oh, I'm really scared to tell you this, but..." and if we were angry and experienced fear and frustration, we would not have the ability to have a successful company that is focused on providing value and serving other people. So, we choose to experience gratitude in everything, no matter how large, no matter how small, no matter how difficult the hardship may be, no matter how big the failure may seem.

If you can find the silver lining and choose to experience gratitude in it, you will create an unbelievable amount of success. Because we choose to experience gratitude, we have now helped thousands of clients, we've had a positive impact on the economy to the tune of hundreds of millions of dollars and we change people's lives every single day, because we choose to experience gratitude for the hardship that showed up in our life. There are only two daily decisions left, and then we'll wrap this up.

The next is health. I talked a little bit earlier about Jared, who made the daily decision that he would have a Subway sub. It's even more minute than a daily decision, right? It's these divine moments in time where we make small decisions, the decision to have the sandwich over the Big Mac. The same things needs to go with your health. For me, one of the things that's easy for me to make a daily decision on is to drink two liters of water. Now, I don't always like to drink a lot of water. I prefer diet soda, but I know that if I can at least drink two liters of water every day, that's a small decision that I can make day-after-day that will add to my health. It's just a simple decision for your health, whether that is you decide to limit your caloric intake and you only want to eat 1,500 calories, that's your decision that day—to eat 1,500 calories. Now, it's made up and comprises a number of divine moments of minute decisions to eat this food over this food, to grab the protein bar over the Twinkie, whatever the case may be. It's these tiny, tiny decisions that we make thousands of times a day, a week, a year that culminate in big results.

I want you to wake up every morning with the decision that today you will choose to do something for your physical body, you will choose to connect spiritually, you will choose to do something in your money life, you will choose to render service, you will choose to experience gratitude, you will choose to live a healthy lifestyle and the final daily decision is just that of success. Making a decision every day to engage success may seem simple, but it's not. There are millions of people that go through this life never feeling like they experienced success, because they choose to experience mediocrity. They choose to experience pain, whatever their decision is that they make, they choose to walk away from success. Make a decision to listen to a successful program, maybe that's a audio book, it's something on *YouTube*, it's a motivational talk, it's a motivational speech. It's reading a chapter that's motivating. It's listening to a program, watching a program. It's engaging in something that is dealing in the world of success, that will allow you to be more successful.

Friends, if you will simply wake up tomorrow or make the decision right now, this day, that you will begin doing these things I shared with you today, and you'll begin doing them today. As you do it day-after-day, time-after-time, you will create such unbelievable results in your life. You will look back and you may not even know how you got to where you are, but you'll go back and you'll break it down to these divine moments of minute decisions that you chose to make every single day. Maybe it was every minute of every day. You chose to make some decision. Maybe it was a decision about your physical body, about your spiritual life, about your money, about service, about gratitude, about experiencing a healthy lifestyle, about engaging success in some way, shape or form, whether that's a successful mindset or a successful audio program, a successful book, or you chose to show up and help someone else create by serving them and you can receive more success. Whatever it is, if you make a daily decision, these seven daily decisions, you will achieve such remarkable results and they will compound into something truly special.

The last bit that I wanted to share with you is that every single one of these daily decisions ought to be made in conjunction with those you love most. Make a decision to look good for your spouse and to physically do what it takes to make your spouse feel continually blessed that they are with you and not that you are letting yourself go and you do not care about their needs or desires. Make a decision to connect with your spouse and your children spiritually. Make that decision every day. Make the decision that you will have an open money conversation with your spouse, with your children, with your loved ones, with your family members, whoever that may be for you.

Family is the fundamental building block of a successful society. So, choose today to serve your family, your children, your spouse. Choose to experience gratitude. One of the things I've done in the past is I've kept a daily gratitude journal and I will write down a thing that I am thankful for, one for each of my children and one for my wife, something they did that day, some way that I wanted to express gratitude for them. I write that down so I become conscious to that gratitude.

Choose to be healthy for your spouse. Choose to be healthy with them. Choose to be healthy for your children and to teach them healthy habits. Choose to teach your loved ones how to be successful. Choose to show up as a successful individual, so they can learn from your example. Each of these daily decisions will impact your business life. They will impact your family life. They will culminate as you make them, day-after-day, into an incredible result. You will look back and you will look at your success, you will look at your accomplishments, you will look at your family, you will look at your wealth. You will look at everything you've accomplished and you will do nothing but experience gratitude knowing that you were the one who got you there, because of small, divine moments of minute decisions that you made every day in these seven categories.

Helen verDuin Palit, D.H.L.

Helen verDuin Palit is a Social Entrepreneur who has pioneered a perishable food recovery system that feeds one million people a day in 1,303 cities around the globe—providing over seven billion meals and counting since 1981. Launched with the creative use of a restaurant's surplus cooked potato insides, her first food harvesting program, sponsored by Yale University, grew to maturity in New York City where she founded the City Harvest program. This award-winning model was institutionalized and has been replicated in cities throughout the world while tailoring it to each city's ethos and spirit. As each program is conducted by—and for—the community, its successes are garnered with local civic and corporate support.

In each city, good, unserved perishable food (hot or cold, fresh or frozen) is collected from food companies, restaurants, caterers, and other sources, then delivered free and immediately to soup kitchens and emergency shelters to provide meals for homeless men, women, and children the same day.

This innovative system creates unique solutions while meeting diverse needs smartly and simply in a situation where everyone wins. The most rewarding part of this work is the way it empowers individuals of all walks of life to develop their own potential and then see their communities "harvest" the incredible results.

Helen verDuin Palit, D.H.L.
Contact: *hpalit@americaharvest.org*
Website*: www.americaharvest.org*
213.280.0585

Levi:

I am here with Helen verDuin Palit. Helen, you've been very successful in a unique, often misunderstood niche, which is the non-profit arena. It's very admirable. You've been able to use your entrepreneurial skills to improve society in a cause that you're passionate about. You've been called a social entrepreneur. I'd love for you to explain what it means to be a social entrepreneur.

Helen:

I'll begin by quoting from the website of Ashoka: Innovators for the Public, a global association that supports social entrepreneurship, "Over the past two decades, the citizen sector has discovered what the business sector learned long ago: There is nothing as powerful as a new idea in the hands of a first-class entrepreneur.

"Social entrepreneurs are individuals with innovative solutions to society's most pressing social problems. They are ambitious and persistent, tackling major social issues and offering new ideas for wide-scale change.

"Rather than leaving societal needs to the government or business sectors, social entrepreneurs find what is not working and solve the problem by changing the system, spreading the solution, and persuading entire societies to move in different directions.

"Social entrepreneurs often seem to be possessed by their ideas, committing their lives to changing the direction of their field. They are visionaries, but also realists, and are ultimately concerned with the practical implementation of their vision above all else.

"Social entrepreneurs present user-friendly, understandable, and ethical ideas that engage widespread support in order to maximize the number of citizens that will stand up, seize their idea, and implement it. Leading social entrepreneurs are mass recruiters of local changemakers—role models proving that citizens who channel their ideas into action can do almost anything." (https://www.ashoka.org/social_entrepreneur)

Being a social entrepreneur is taking all the professional skill sets that for-profit entrepreneurs use for their businesses to buy and sell products or services. Social entrepreneurs use exactly the same skills, but with a social perspective, helping humanity and/or the world. In my case, these include accounting, logistics, marketing, and transportation. It's just using these skills with a different end goal in mind. In the for-profit business, you design a beautiful dress and then the woman buys it. You design a one-on-one relationship. You made the dress, she gives you cash.

But in the non-profit arena, we don't have that one-on-one relationship between the product or service provider and the buyer. There are four players in the philanthropic relationship: our charity, our financial supporters, the shelter providing food, and the ultimate "customer," the hungry people. Our charity provides a service that is delivered (figuratively or literally) to another charity: a soup kitchen, food pantry, or emergency shelter that distributes our food on a plate or in a bag to the hungry and homeless men, women, and children. Then we report the successes and challenges of our service back to the foundations, corporations, government, and individuals giving us their money. We describe our service(s) (food distribution), our numbers (4,012 meals delivered today in Los Angeles, for instance), our successes (delivering Wolfgang Puck's food), our challenges (truck repair), and our efficiencies.

Levi:
Tell us a little bit more about what exactly you are doing professionally within the non-profit arena, which, by the way, I think is wonderful and actually very impressive, because you've taken a very unique approach to what you're doing. Why don't you go ahead and share what you're actually doing currently?

Helen:
My professional skills I developed while putting myself through college, working as a restaurant manager, truck driver, accountant, charity

director, and volunteering in various charities. The same logic, systems, and equipment I have learned to adapt and utilize in a different arena.

Levi:
You're basically taking traditional business skills and using them in a social arena. Why don't you talk to us a little bit about the social arena that you're operating in, because I think it's very exciting.

Helen:
Have you ever been to a catered event, maybe at somebody's wedding or at a corporate conference—possibly on the buffet line—where you wondered if some of the foods might be left over and possibly wasted? My Harvest charity in your city, at the request of the hotels, universities, caterers, and others, will pick up their donated food, weigh the food, issue a donation receipt, and immediately deliver the food to the local soup kitchens, food pantries, and emergency shelters for the hungry and homeless men, women, and children's next meal—respecting the religious and cultural restrictions of that charity's clients. We also buy insurance on the food, with the food companies' names listed on the account. The Bill Emerson Act protects anyone donating food in good faith from being sued. Our distribution system in the office is the logistics teams on phones to assist our uniformed staff commercial truck drivers, who are Health Department certified, driving spotless refrigerated trucks 24/7/365, thanks to Roger S. Penske, Jr. and Penske Truck Leasing. We operate like UPS, who is moving packages, while we are handling food.

Before you finish your dinner tonight, my independent Harvest teams in 1,303 cities of the world will pick up and deliver enough food for one million meals for hungry and homeless men, women, and children. This is the best food in each city. Seven billion meals and counting since 1981. Our total operating cost is 25 cents for each meal. For each dollar donated, 86 cents goes to our program costs (our charity service), including the drivers, trucks, Health Department classes, and insurance on the food, trucks, and food donors.

The various food industries and companies with food have always wanted to donate their good food, but they did not know how to or which charity to call. Their lawyers were concerned about some-one getting sick or dying and suing the company. Therefore I and all whom I advise when setting up a new program to first go to the Health Department, top lawyers, and insurance companies in that city to set up protections on all sides. Since 1981, when we started, no one has gotten sick, died, or sued any of our Harvests anywhere in the world.

Levi:
That's amazing.

Helen:
Thank you.

Levi:
That's really amazing. How did you get into this, Helen?

Helen:
I've been a volunteer since I was 6 years old when my mother said, "There's a really fun thing we're going to do." Just before Christmas, we gift-wrapped 3 cigarettes together for each mental patient at the state hospital—menthols with a green ribbon, regular cigarettes with red. We loaded them, all wrapped, into the car and drove through the deep Cleveland snow to deliver them to the hospital. Afterwards, the patients waved as we were leaving. It was really neat for a 6-year-old.

Since then, I have volunteered in each city I have lived in, doing all types of charity work—at a suicide hotline, library, youth hotline, drug crisis center, Planned Parenthood—and I started a homeless shelter, which became the first in Connecticut uniquely for both men and women. I met many of my best friends while volunteering—people who share their time to help others.

In New Haven, Connecticut, I had an opportunity to run a soup kitchen for Yale University. I thought, "Wow, this is pretty impressive—Yale's commitment to feed the hungry people." At that time, in 1981, all the soup kitchens and shelters of America could only afford to give the hungry or homeless people soup and bread. If Frank, one of my guests, liked my soup, he'd have 12 bowls of it, and he'd eat an entire loaf of bread because this was his only meal for the day.

After one particularly trying day at the soup kitchen—it must have been a full moon, because many of the guests were acting out—I needed to chill out. I went across the street to my favorite little restaurant and ordered a potato skin appetizer with my margarita. When the potato skins came, for some reason, I looked at them from a different point of view. I mean, I'd eaten them before, really enjoyed them, but all of a sudden I decided to ask the chef, "What do you do with the insides of these potatoes?" He replied, "You know, even though we sell mashed potatoes, potato soup, potato chowder every day, we still have 30 gallons of cooked potato insides left over every day that we can't do anything else with."

Now, if you visualize your refrigerator at home, including the metal and plastic parts, and all the space inside, double that: that's the volume of 30 gallons. I told the chef, "Our soup kitchen is right there across the street, 60 feet away. We could really use them." He replied, "Great. I'll see you tomorrow." The next day he came with the potato insides; then he brought them daily. Additionally, he brought other foods. One day there were perfect quiches—he had forgotten to put in the ham, and ham quiche was announced on the menu. My volunteers were intrigued: "How did all these other foods start showing up?" I told them about the insides of the potatoes that could feed the world. On their own, they went out to their favorite restaurants, caterers, retailers, wholesalers, and universities to ask them to donate food.

In three months, we had a gourmet soup kitchen. Now we had appetizers, we had salads, we had entrees, we had beef, pork, chicken, seafood, and lamb, which we could have never afforded to buy, and we even had desserts, which was really awesome.

In another three months, we had TOO MUCH FOOD, but by then, I had started two more soup kitchens: one on the north side of town and one on the east side of town, so I could direct food donations to the kitchens nearest the donors' locations.

As more and larger food donation calls kept coming, I would first ask them what part of town they were in, because I was now wearing my truck driver hat in the game of time, temperature, and distance logistics. When Lenders Bagels called with five 18-wheeler trailers full of frozen chopped vegetables, I realized this had become a larger adventure. I got the veggies stored free in cold storage, then mentally organized a larger food distribution system for a six-city area.

This became the New Haven Food Salvage Project, which was under Yale University's sponsorship. Not a great name, but operationally it worked perfectly. By our third month of operation, Helmer "Butch" Ekstrom, Associate Director of the New Haven Community Foundation, handed me a $25,000 check—a gold mine for an untested charity concept in 1981.

The New York Times called. They wanted to do a little story for their Connecticut edition. Great! What I like to do is thank the people who are contributing food by featuring them in publicity. Allen was running the 22 cafeterias for Yale University and donating from each of them. He agreed to be interviewed for the story. This news story went global in 1981. I had just moved to the Big Apple, and was starting to manage The Yorkville Common Pantry and Soup Kitchen in Manhattan.

At the time, when Mayor Koch was running New York City, he— like all government people—had his hunger person, his arts, medicine, music contacts in the city. He called Gretchen Buchenholz, the President of the Yorkville Common Pantry and his hunger person. He said, "I read a second story about this woman Helen Palit in today's New York Times. She's up there in Connecticut. We've got to get her down here to New York City. We need her food program in our city. Can you help me?" Gretchen said, "Hang on." I was literally sitting right there in her office. He asked what he could do so we could have my Harvest program in his city. I said, "A meeting with the Health Department would be great." He called back 20 minutes later and said, "Okay, 8:00 tomorrow morning."

I figured I would be meeting with one of the department's junior people for maybe 20 minutes and that would be it. I showed up and here's the commissioner, David Sencer, and four top aides. We brainstormed the moving of various food types, the time and temperatures involved. We played out various situations: "Okay, it's 99 degrees with matching humidity in New York City and there is some food to be donated over by JFK Airport," an hour or two east, depending on traffic, from Manhattan where the closest volunteer was. And we wanted to deliver the food up in the Bronx which is another hour and a half north. We're dealing with time, temperature, logistics. We played all these different kinds of games to figure out the challenges I would have to manage smartly to make sure all of the food could be moved safely and no one would get sick, or worse. At the end of four hours, they gave me their blessings, and since then they've always been there for us to brainstorm with to meet other challenges.

Next, I went to the best lawyers to learn about the New York City and New York State rules and regulations. Then to the insurance companies, "Teach me what we need to buy so there is never a problem."

With Mayor Koch's support, City Harvest began with volunteers in December 1982, serving all five boroughs of the Big Apple. From day one, the media loved it, and now there are over 1,000 of my Harvest programs in the world feeding the hungry.

I think this whole concept started years ago, when my mother told us kids, "Don't waste the food on your plate, because there are hungry children in various Third World countries in the world." We ate all of our food, yet that message hit home for me.

Levi:
That's amazing.

Helen:
What's really exciting for me is that we're enabling all of these corporations, schools, colleges, caterers, fishing companies, bakeries, and government agencies to donate these good foods that they can't sell yet are fresh and unserved as if they had never left their kitchen. Food is donated from U.S. Navy submarines in Pearl Harbor, hospitals in Montreal, cafes in Paris, the Oscars and Grammys in Los Angeles, wild geese hunters in Winnipeg, Queen Elizabeth's teas in Sydney, Oktoberfest in Berlin, the kibbutzes in Israel, tea houses in Kyoto, international car races in 42 cities, fishing boats in Halifax, and grocery stores in Wellington. In New York State, prison and jail inmates are growing organic gardens for their communities' charities, feeding the hungry men, women, and children.

Levi:

I have talked to a lot of aspiring entrepreneurs, people who want to do good in the world. They want to start something like you started. But they are hampered by the lack of resources available to them, and they often don't know where to start. You've definitely overcome the scalability issue, but where does somebody start when they're trying to do something like this?

Helen:

I started with a simple idea. I tossed the idea around with trusted colleagues and then asked who they knew who might be interested to brainstorm with me. Aspiring social entrepreneurs should think about who they know in specific fields (hospitality, legal, insurance, logistics, etc.) for their proposed business, maybe a teacher or a professor or family's friends or colleagues. They should also volunteer in the type of charity they might want to have.

For example, my friend Rachel studied and became qualified as a lawyer. She got her first job and after two years she was so unhappy. She quit, so then she went to another job and another. In four years, she went through six jobs. She was asking what she could do, and I just blurted out, "Do you like being a lawyer?" The expression on her face as her jaw dropped to the floor was rather revealing.

Of course she was still paying off her student loans. I could see all that going through her head, but she didn't like the tasks involved in being a lawyer. I suggested, "Go volunteer some place or at a corporation, become an intern even if you're fifty years young. Go be an intern for them and see if you like the type of business—do you like the people and the work?"

Levi:

They test the water, they jump in. What would you say to someone who says that non-profits are great but they'll never be as effective as a profit-seeking business?

Helen:

Non-profits measure their efficiency differently from the for-profit companies, and they are not listed on the Stock Exchange for their performance. There are many excellent charities and non-profits that surpass many for-profits' effectiveness. How does one measure saving a whale, or hundreds of whales? What about the impact of teaching people how to paint or grow a garden?

When he was Chairman of the Board for American Express, James D. Robinson III was very excited about our work in New York City. Each time he and I met, he had new questions of how X gets to Y. A week later he was at Buckingham Palace. Much of his conversation with Queen Elizabeth over dinner was about Helen Palit and City Harvest and the new Canadian Harvest charities in Montreal, Dartmouth, Kitchener, Ottawa, Edmonton, Toronto, Halifax, Winnipeg and Vancouver. The queen was very pleased that good food was not being wasted.

John Reed, the Chairman of the Board of Citibank N.A., jumped on board with City Harvest from the get go. One of his branch managers in Stuyvesant Town in Lower Manhattan had the idea to start a canned food drive with Citibank and the two other banks in the settlement within the first month of City Harvest's operation, in 1982. With Mr. Reed's continued support these year-round canned food drives have expanded throughout his bank's New York City system and beyond.

A shy former Fortune 100 Chairman of the Board, after reviewing my charity's numbers, was stunned to see that we were more cost effective than his global company. He offered me a high level job, though he knew I would turn it down because my passion is helping others. Yes, non-profits can be very cost effective and can use their assets, including their people, well.

The other concern for many people is their financial rewards. Generally, non-profits and charities pay less, but the personal rewards and benefits are being able to help people and the world.

Maybe they should sit down to have a long talk with themselves. What gives them pleasure and satisfaction? Do they like people, animals, nature, or art? Then go volunteer or intern to test the waters, honestly.

What are their areas of interest? Search the internet. There are all kinds of charities doing all kinds of work. Many in America and thousands around the world have amazing track records. It's just working in a different arena. They need to do their homework and go visit these programs and see if they like them.

Levi:
One of the things that I find fascinating about your journey is how effectively you have been able to run this organization from a cost management standpoint as well as a logistics standpoint. I think that's a factor that often gets left out when people are trying to do good in the world. I was wondering if you'd share a little bit about your process and your methodology in running a non-profit as a business.

Helen:
I've been an accountant for global oil corporations, the U.S. military, and private companies. I naturally have a head for numbers, logistics, and understanding systems. In our Harvest business, we get a lot of really great numbers we can work with to not only tell our story but also measure our effectiveness. All of my drivers, who are health department certified, are in green uniforms in really nice spotless trucks, because we have an amazing deal from Penske forever, which is really quite great. My drivers go pick up the food and weigh the food on the scales in the truck. They immediately give the tax-deductible receipt for the food to the donor. Then, using our agency paperwork, the drivers determine which of the nearby approved soup kitchens, pantries, or shelters can use that type of food. The drivers continue their pickups and deliveries for their route. In New York City, they can meet the next driver at a subway station—one jumps in and the other out—to continue the pickup and delivery system.

Next the driver will call ahead to an approved soup kitchen or shelter to see if they want, or, more important, have refrigeration or freezer space for, the food in his truck, which might be fresh brussels sprouts or chocolate ice cream. This saves fuel and time if the kitchen or shelter cannot store that food that day. They will get food another day, when they have the space, and the driver will look for another kitchen or shelter who can accept the food.

We also deliver the food to each charity based on the religious and ethnic choices of the people needing the food. Some groups choose to not eat pork, others eat Kosher. All these different things go into our system, which our drivers manage hour by hour, day by day. Many of our trucks in many cities of the world are running 24/7/365.

We measure our success by how many meals we pick up and deliver each day. Caterers tell us that one appetizer, salad, entrée with vegetables, and dessert weighs one pound. That makes it simple to report how many meals we distribute each day, month, and year. It's a great way to measure success.

On the other side of the equation, not only are our drivers paid well, but all of our staff are paid at for-profit rates with for-profit compensation packages. You get what you pay for. Plus everyone in my programs gets their birthdays off with full pay, like I saw in Europe when I worked there. It is THEIR day.

June, one of our drivers, is a big, burly strong guy, somewhat intimidating if you were walking down the street towards him at a late hour. He came into my office one day, almost shy. He reminded me that his birthday was next Wednesday and I was "not to worry." He had already prepared all of the paperwork and trained Bob, who would drive his route. Each of my staff in any city is so appreciative for Their Day. It is one the best investments we have ever made. The staff morale is amazing.

I am also blessed that Richard Norton, a retired senior partner at Ernst & Young continues to help me with the numbers, making sure I use them correctly. When I first met him, he and I just totally clicked as we talked about how we measure success. We tried different ways of using numbers to tell a story. A wholesaler donated five 18-wheelers full of canned tomato sauce in giant commercial size cans. I wanted our supporters to understand how big this donation was. With that idea, I went online to find out how many gallons of water it takes to fill an Olympic-sized swimming pool. From the tomato sauce can given to me by my driver, I recorded the number of ounces per can. I did the math and ran my calculations by Richard. I asked him, "Did they donate enough tomato sauce to fill an Olympic-sized swimming pool, yes or no?" He did the numbers and said, "Yep, and you're right."

It's just playing in a delightful way, but also a meaningful way, that people can understand—as I told you earlier about all those potato skins—because the average person doesn't know what a pound of food looks like. Therefore, we measure our success by the number of meals, not pounds, we deliver for the hungry people. For example: "Today our HARVEST commercial truck drivers picked up and delivered immediately enough food for another free 5,782 meals to the hungry men, women, and children in our city."

From the beginning the New York Times was 200% supportive of our work. Reporters from various departments told our story. Riding with volunteers for our early days, then on our trucks to meet the food donors and the charity directors plus the hungry women, men and kids eating their fresh foods.

Levi:
Sure. You basically break it down so that the average person can understand it so you can communicate your successes properly.

Helen:
Yes.

Levi:
You've talked a lot about the numbers and the efficiency, certainly about your passion for it and some of your stories. One question we get asked a lot is how technology impacts an individual's business. I'm just curious if technology has played a big role in your type of organization, or has it been pretty nominal?

Helen:
Well, we started City Harvest in the early 1980s and operated for several years before cell phones, faxes, and computers. For efficiency of communications, we would give our drivers rolls of quarters so they could call us from the local pay phones for route updates or new food pickups. Technology, as it became available, greatly helped our systems be more time and cost effective. Yes, it was a learning curve, but well worth it. And it really was a blessing for all of us.

Levi:
Why do you say that?

Helen:

With the cell phone, for instance, when there is a new food donation, we can call a driver who is close by the donor's location, so it saves time and fuel too. Like all smart delivery companies, we use technology to work closely and smartly with all customers in spite of weather, accidents, and the challenges of logistics.

Levi:

So technology has accelerated your communication and greatly increased, not diminished, your efficiency cost. Fuel and time are expensive not only in dollars but also in effectiveness and efficiency.

Helen:

While at City Harvest, I thought a connection with UPS would be beneficial. We're both in the distribution business, but their drivers are in brown and ours are in green. I told my Board of Directors that I would be reaching out to the top of UPS. One of my board members knew the Chairman and made the connection for us. UPS asked what I would like. I asked if they could meet with my in-house logistics team to see if there were other systems we should initiate since our logistics systems were expanding.

The next week, their top New York City technicians arrived to ascertain and teach my distribution people, headed by Dominic Percibelli, in the office, coordinating all the 24/7 routes and the food systems. After five hours, the UPS fellow supervisor came to us and said, "We can't teach your guys anything. In fact, they've taught us some things that we're going to use in our system now." Again, I knew we had the best people in the office, on the trucks, and in the system, and then, of course, on the Board of Directors, volunteer teams, and all the different teams we had assembled. They brought their skills and their knowledge base to the challenge.

Levi:

Absolutely. You've obviously been very successful at growing this. It's continuing to grow. What's next on your horizon? What are your goals for the future?

Helen:

There are 39,000 cities in the world that are not harvesting their food yet. Introducing Harvest programs in all of them is my long-term goal, because why shouldn't every city, town, and village have this?

I once lived in a small Texas village that had a 7-Eleven store, a gas station, and a post office for the 250 residents. Yet some of the people in the village were hungry. This was long before I got into my Harvesting program, but just using it as an example: That 7-Eleven had all these hot dogs they'd cooked up that they didn't sell that day. They could have been given to someone. A volunteer or the store manager could have quietly delivered those hotdogs, along with some unsold baked goods, and soon-to-expire dairy products, to a family who didn't have lunch that day or to the church.

There's food in every community. It's just a matter of getting the food to the people. It's a game of logistics, no matter how big or small, with transportation in a back pack or back seat of the car or a pickup.

Many years ago, a big shipment of rice was delivered by ocean freighter to a small African country. The tons and tons of rice were offloaded at the port. But the tires for the trucks, which were fully paid for and desperately needed to deliver the rice to the remote villages, did not come on that ship. The rice rotted in the hot sun while people were hungry—a game of failed logistics.

Levi:

A game of logistics—it makes perfect sense. In conclusion, if you could give just one piece of advice that you consider to be of the highest importance, if you had nothing else that you could say to someone, what would that last, most important piece of advice be to someone either considering making a difference or doing a non-profit and moving forward in the world?

Helen:

Two things. First: when I first envisioned my non-profit perishable food distribution system, many people said it could not be done. "Why?" I asked. "Because no one has done it," was their answer. But as a former restaurant manager and commercial truck driver, I thought I had good information.

As I researched my concept, which confirmed that no one had done it, I wondered why and what was I possibly missing. I met with the local Health Department, who gave me their approval, then with the lawyers for the permits and regulations, which I got, again with their blessings. Next, I met with the insurance companies for their wisdom and experience as they signed me up.

Today 1,013 cities of the world are harvesting with my proven system. Six billion meals delivered. No person has gotten sick, died, or sued any of the companies donating their good unserved perishable food since 1981.

When others ask why, I answer, "Why not?"

Second: Sit down and have a long talk with yourself. See what you really love doing. What is fascinating? What is fun? What is something that just gets you so excited? I mean, go out and do it.

Here are some additional thoughts in the form of questions and answers I've thought about as I've been on my journey:

1. *What does it take to be a leader?*
   Compassion, diligence, tenacity, and vision, with a great
   team at home and at work sharing your passion.
2. *When you get discouraged, what techniques do you use to pull yourself out?*
   Wherever I am at the time, I find a botanical garden or outdoor
   art, turn off my cell and computers, tell NO ONE where I am and
   when I am expected back, so I can relax, enjoy nature and the
   wonderful world Mother Nature gave us. I regroup and all is well.
3. *What advice and encouragement would you give to a budding entrepreneur?*
   Reach out to other entrepreneurs of any business. Ask for their
   wisdom and suggestions. CEO Space International has been a
   terrific resource for me, from their brilliant and compassionate
   faulty and management team to the other graduates and
   students. *Dave@globalceospace.com* is a great connection.
4. *What inspires you?*
   People who look beyond the status quo for a new future
   for everyone. They take action and go forth, sometimes at

great risk or peril for their loved ones. People like Mandela, Steve Jobs, Van Gogh, the astronauts going out into space, fire fighters, and peace keepers around the world.

5. *Why do you do what you do?*
My personal passion is traveling the world while being of service to others. I also enjoy solving all types logistical challenges. I love art, music, and especially getting to know and learn from people of all different cultures, religions, and professions. This work combines all of these loves.

6. *What do you like best about what you do?*
We connect people of all cultures, professions, faiths, cities, and countries together so that everyone wins. Each connection begins a new relationship that has neither boundaries nor ending dates.

7. *If you could share any advice with someone what would it be?*
Look into your life. What excites you? What challenges you? What do you wonder about? Why not explore it? Volunteer somewhere to try on your ideas? Why not?

8. *What type of legacy do you want to leave?*
Following the traditions of my ancestors from both my mother's and father's sides to give back to our community one way or another as a professional, volunteer, or as a friend, as a person. Inspiring others to look beyond the normal or traditional.

Levi:
I love it. I'm going to end the recording now. Thank you so much.

Jonathan Jaussi

Jonathan is a natural-born friend that loves helping people solve problems and find their path of truth. His career path has always been in service. He has lived his life by the motto that says, "Everyone that knows me has, at least, one friend."

He started out in social work and soon added law and business mentorship. He really enjoys meeting new people and is the type of person who knows everybody's name at the grocery store, bank, and school because he has talked with each of them and made a connection. He is a husband and proud father of four girls and one little boy.

He is unorthodox, yet resourceful and precise, these are the best ways to describe his methods of solving complex challenges that his clients face. He has helped manage matters from small amounts to 600 million and never forgets that the person always comes first. In business, Jonathan is fiercely loyal and is known for his candor and direct way of getting to the heart of the matter to find real solutions.

Levi:

Jonathan, you're in an area of business that is very unique, meaning that you're trying to do something that is new in the legal space, and you're tackling it from more of an emotion side, not, "How do I win this lawsuit?" But really, how do people survive legal issues and still come out on top? How do they survive mentally and emotionally? I'd like to know how you got into this market space.

Jonathan:

Well, I've been practicing for over 10 years now in the field of law, and I've worked on some very hotly litigated cases—cases where the outcome was going to make a big difference in somebody's life. As I have seen these processes go through, I've been watching the people involved because I am a people-watcher. I like to understand people. I like to understand their different backgrounds, and to see what makes them tick, i.e. what makes them feel like they were successful, and feel like they had a good outcome on a case. I not only watch the clients that are involved in legal situations, but I also watch the different styles of litigation as well as the emotional styles of the attorneys that are involved.

As I watched that over the last decade, I was watching the clients particularly, and I was noticing that no one was taking care of the clients' emotional needs. The clients didn't have the skills to deal with the stress and the impact of the lawsuit, i.e. the legal stress, or the legal situation. They just didn't know how to deal with it. A lot of times, they were suffering from the feeling that it was just not going to come out well. Sometimes, they didn't feel like they understood the legal processes. Other times, they had questions as to what their lawyer was doing or if their lawyer was loyal.

It basically came down to a feeling of being out of control. And, I saw that impact on their quality of life. I saw that impact on the quality of their relationships. So, it really got me thinking that I needed to try to put together something that would really focus on stress and strategy in legal situations. That is an interesting concept. As I've been trying to put form to what I've noticed, I really don't want to be somebody's lawyer. They already have a lawyer who's the technician, and who's dealing with the legal situation. What I wanted to do was to help people to understand how to work with their lawyer, as well as how to work with their situation, and how to deal with the emotional and financial stress. I also want them to know how to manage it all, and how to pick strategies that work right for them.

So many times, people that I've talked with and people who have been working with lawyers have ended up just following whatever strategy their attorney said. And, they didn't even feel like they could ask intelligent questions. They just didn't feel like they understood the situation well enough to even be part of the conversation. So, I want to help people with that. I want to help them to get in touch with what is a good outcome for them. I also want to teach them how to control the pieces of the situation that they can control, and teach them how to find peace with the parts that they cannot.

Levi:
Sure. Statistically, I think that most of us entrepreneurs know that being involved in a lawsuit is something that most of us will experience, or we already have experienced it, and perhaps we'll experience it again. There have been studies that have demonstrated the impact of happiness on your ability to perform. I've certainly witnessed it in my own experience as well as for clients that I help with the stress that you're talking about while going through a legal situation. Stress can often paralyze people, and it also can diminish that quality of life. I think that you used the term "quality of life." So, explain this term just a little bit for someone who is in that situation right now. And, let's just say that it's a lawsuit because that's the big one that normally comes to mind. What's somebody's first step? What do they need to do so that they don't get caught in this shell-shock state where they're immobilized?

Jonathan:
Well, that's such an important question, Levi, because it really is a shell-shock state. It takes not only money and time out of your schedule and out of your wallet, but it also takes productive energy away from you. I think that the most important thing when facing that is to realize that you are experiencing stress. Look for the signs. The signs

that you're simply just not being as productive in your free time, or in accomplishing your goals. You're feeling a sense of the problems that are closing in on you, or you're just feeling some general irritation.

Those negative emotions are highly correlated with business failure, and I think that you pointed that out already. That in order to succeed at business, we need to have a positive outlook, and we need to be able to see ourselves being successful. There are three top stressors that I see coming out of situations where people are working with an attorney regarding a legal issue. The number one comment that I hear over and over again is, "I'm not sure who my lawyer is working for." Now, they can be put into the category of Loyalty. People don't know if their lawyer is being loyal to them. That can be a very frustrating thing by itself. This is especially true when you're already in that stressful situation, and when you're already wondering if your lawyer is taking care of your interests, instead of just looking out for his or her self.

The second thing that I hear people say is, "I don't understand why it costs so much." They can be put under the category of Cost. These people really just don't understand what they're purchasing, they don't understand if they have to purchase it, and they don't understand price-scaling options that they could employ. Frankly, when someone ends up with a legal situation, they go out, and they start shopping for attorneys. And, the attorneys tell them what they should purchase. So, they generally rely on that information from the sellers to make a purchasing decision.

Unlike other purchasing decisions that we make, we generally don't do this frequently. So, we don't have a huge backdrop of hiring and firing lawyers. We're left basically trying to take a stab in the dark. I like helping people to see that there are a variety of ways and styles to engage a lawyer. One or more of those styles could work better for you, while someone else may be better off with another style.

The third thing that I hear people say when they come in is that they just don't understand the process. This is a really, really big frustration because what you'll find is that while they've had multiple conversations with their attorney, they still just don't understand the process. And, not wanting to feel stupid, they've stopped asking questions. Now, they feel like they're just a trailer being towed along behind the bus.

All three of these concerns lead people to a sense of powerlessness, which is very discouraging. I think that it runs very counter to the creativity and freedom that you need to have as an entrepreneur. As an entrepreneur, you're out there trying to create. You're trying to create new business, new opportunities, and new ideas. Those ideas and that process of creation really do require you to be free in order for it to work. If you're not free, then you feel clamped down, and you feel stuck. When people are stuck, they just don't perform well. So, those are the main areas that I like to emphasize when I help people. I like to make them feel like they can take control of their situation again so that they can be the stronger for it.

Levi:
Well, there definitely is a need in the market space. I agree with all of the points that you've gone through, including that sense of helplessness, and the desire to not want to ask questions, because of not wanting to feel stupid, or because each of those questions cost money.

Jonathan:
Right.

Levi:
In working with attorneys, you're right; most people don't understand what the costs are, and what the process is. We've talked about lawsuits, which are normally quite scary, but you actually broke it down even further. Legal issues can cause stressors even in the process of selling a business, buying a business, or even down to the levels of compliance or in succession planning. Talk to us a little bit about what you've seen and experienced in that space. And, perhaps, tell us about some of the solutions that you've been able to implement.

Jonathan:
Well, I think that one of the most important things is distinguishing what's a threat and what's really not. I have a friend who is a real estate professional, who runs a busy brokerage. I'm also acting as his attorney; I'm the general counsel for his firm. One of the most fright-

ening things that he goes through from day-to-day is trying to make sure that his agents don't make mistakes that will end up costing the firm a lot of money. In doing that, he experiences a considerable amount of stress. When I first met him, and I know that he wouldn't mind me telling you this, he was almost paralyzed with fear. Any time that anyone on the other side of a transaction would mention anything about illegality, or saying something to the effect of, "We've got to talk to the lawyers about this," he would almost wither. He would stay up at night stressing about the situation, and subsequently worry himself almost into a fit to where he couldn't sleep, which really impacted his productivity at work.

The first thing that I went to work on with him was perspective, i.e. understanding what really was a risk, and what's the outcome if something goes wrong. Sometimes, the impact of something is not anywhere near what we think it is. Therefore, we don't have to be afraid of it. The unfortunate reality is that so often people end up terrified of an outcome because they don't understand it because it's new or foreign. They group legal issues broadly into that category where, "Oh no, I'm in a legal situation, and that must mean that I'm going to lose everything." As a matter of fact, that's the chatter that my friend has heard in the real estate circles. According to commonly held opinion, you should avoid a lawsuit at all costs because nobody ever wins in a lawsuit. This is actually bad advice. I worked with him by helping him to get a better perspective on that. And, I helped him to see that business is about taking calculated risks, and then managing those risks once they've been taken.

If you are in a position where you become afraid of taking risks, and it becomes a consuming fear, then pretty soon you become risk-averse, which each of us knows is going to be really detrimental to being an entrepreneur. So, I help people to distinguish between the two, i.e. defining what's a real risk as opposed to what's not a risk. I give them the tools to evaluate risks effectively, and to make calculated risks, just as you do with investments.

Levi:
One thing that I think rarely, if ever, gets brought up, when it comes to dealing with attorneys or dealing with the law, in legal situations is the

return on investment. If I understand correctly, then what you're por-
traying, at least the strategic component, is that there is a ROI to it be-
cause you actually help people to not only go through a salvation pro-
cess, where they increase their productivity because they're no longer
stressed, but you also help them to save money because you give them
that insight into what is best for them from a legal standpoint. Those
people are asking the questions, "Should I hire this attorney? Should I
not?" as well as "Should I go through this process? Should I not?" So, I'd
love it if you'd expound a little bit further this ROI concept on both legal
coaching as well as on using attorneys in general.

Jonathan:
Yes. Well, ROI is interesting in the sense that it can be both experiential and speculative, but that's the nature of business. We do speculate
sometimes, both in the positive and in the negative. In the positive, we
speculate to the extent that we have some intelligence that says that
we can make money doing a certain activity, so we go out and do that.
To the extent that we think a certain behavior or process is going to
cost us money, we tend to speculate against it unless the amount of
money it's going to cost us is nominal. The return on investment from
a legal situation is something that almost nobody thinks about because
they're just looking at avoiding it at all costs, or sometimes they're
looking at it from an emotional perspective, e.g. where somebody has
wronged them, and they feel like they need to defend their honor.

Ultimately, we need to go back and figure, each one of us, "What is
the outcome that we want? How do we place a value on it? What is
the cost and benefit of the process?" This may seem over-simplistic,
but it's really not something that most attorneys talk about with their
clients because, ultimately, most clients don't feel like they have a
choice whether or not to engage in the process. Often, they do.

We might look at peace of mind for getting an existing legal situation or legal problem solved, and taken care of, or there might be
a competitive advantage in business. Another return on investment
might be the knowledge of having gone through the process, and that
you're now not scared of going through the process anymore because
you now have experience. As far as the costs that we have to evaluate

and decide, we need to ask the question, "Do we want to be involved in a legal process?" We look at the impact on us, emotionally and financially. And, I think that we also have to speculate on what is unknowable, i.e. if there is an increase in cost due to unknown circumstances that we can't control.

Levi:

Many times, in conversations with entrepreneurs, we talk about the importance of entrepreneurs, or of mentors, and the importance of making relationships with people who can really help you to understand. I know in my own business that I have sought out mentors and guidance from people that I trusted in the legal field. For yourself and also for those that are reading this book, where do you place the value on mentorship?

Jonathan:

I place the value on mentorship really at a premium. There really is something in the human nature that does not like to ask questions, and that wants to try to figure it out on their own. Not everybody is like this, but I think that most people have a modicum of pride, and they want to think sometimes that they have all of the answers. It took me some time to realize that I don't want to be right in the sense of my personal pride; it is more than I want to be successful. I really do want to be successful. As a result, I try to pick people that are ahead of me on the highway of life, if you will, and follow them to see where they're succeeding, and where they've failed. And, where they swerve to miss the proverbial pothole, I also swerve. I think that's an extremely valuable thing because out there in the experience of life there are always going to be people that are ahead of you, and there are always going to be people that are behind you. It's incumbent upon all of us if we want to be successful that we need to also give some of that mentoring back to others. I think that it's part of the process of growth and learning, and that it's a wonderful experience.

Levi:

Definitely, I absolutely agree. Another question that I always like to explore is that you've been in business for quite a while. You've experienced your ups and downs, and you're successful at what you're doing.

Just what advice would you give to an entrepreneur out there? And, your response doesn't necessarily have to be directed toward legal coaching. What advice do you think that everyone getting into entrepreneurship should know?

Jonathan:
I think that the first thing that I would tell somebody is to keep their eye on what they want to create, and not on what they're afraid of happening. This is such a simple piece of advice, but so often I meet with people and tell them this, and they'll say, "Yes, yes, I understand that," and then they'll continue on talking about things that they're most afraid of happening. This is something that we really need to put into practice. If we want to test the upper limits of our potential for success, then we need to keep our eye on the desired outcome, and on what we want to create, and then just go for it. Sure, concerns are going to come up, but if we see those as just hurdles that we need to overcome in this race towards our goal, rather than the key object of our focus, then we're more successful.

I've found in my experience in business that when I look at an obstacle, I spend too much time dwelling on it, rather than on the end goal of what I want to create. What happens is that I become disoriented. I lose the ability to focus on the goal, and instead I start focusing on the problem. And, before long, I'm not really even sure which direction I'm pointed in, and I've completely lost my lock on the goal. So, experience has taught me that if you want to build something, then you need to primarily focus on that. Sure, you should deal with the concerns as they come up, but you should never take your eye off the goal. And, that's step number one.

Step number two is to get the naysayers out of your world. There's always going to be people who say that you cannot build what you're trying to build, that your idea is stupid, and that nobody needs what you have. You do not want these people around you because they will absolutely act like vampires, sucking the life out of your dreams. If you have a dream to create something, then go do it. Find the people who can help. Find the mentors who can lift you. Find the people with the skills that you can build a team with, and make it happen. I have many times tried to build something, and as soon as somebody finds out about it, they begin attacking the idea and pulling me down. I've learned not to listen to those people because they are anti-creative. That is not something that anybody needs while they're trying to build something.

Levi:
This is all great advice, Jonathan. In conclusion, if you're going to be an entrepreneur, then you're going to deal with the law. You're going to deal with legal issues. There's a chance that you could get in a lawsuit, and what you're saying is, "It's not as scary as you think." Hopefully, it doesn't happen, but if it happens, then obviously you're going to want to know what you're doing. How can people get educated about your space, and then educated about what actions that they should take moving forward?

Jonathan:
Well, certainly I would advise anyone to read up on his or her situation. The Internet, in my opinion, is one of the greatest resources to come about in the last 100 years. It's a virtual library of Alexandria at our fingertips. We have the ability to read about almost any topic, as well as the ability to hear about other people's experiences, and the opportunity to have discussions with other people from all over the world that are going through similar situations.

So, my advice would be to reach out on the Internet, to know that you're not alone, and to soak up the experiences of other people who have gone through or who are currently going through what you're experiencing. Also, you should rely on your attorney if you've hired one. You should rely on your attorney to teach you and to train you. Finally, if you don't understand something, then you should know that you can always call somebody like myself who can help you to get a handle on the costs as well as the understanding that you need and the opportunities that you're looking for in your situation. You should always feel like you're in control.

Marci Lock

The Body-Mind Mentor
- TV and Radio Show Host

  Best Selling Author & Speaker
- Nutrition, Fitness Expert Life Transformation Coach & Trainer

Marci Lock is known for "Lockin' Down the Truth" weekly on TV and doing Radio programs, she is also known for inspiring others to Break Through the Barriers to get Break Through Results in your body as well as every aspect of life to truly Have it All. As a Nutrition and Fitness expert, she loves to teach how to "Rock out the Body" by turning your body into a Fat Burning Machine and your Ultimate Partner. She implements how to be super effective and get crazy fast results. However, she believes that no matter how much you know about food and fitness, it will never last unless you break through the BELIEFS and the ROOT Causes that are holding you back. Why do you continue to sabotage having a Body of Health and life you want? Why don't you have and keep the results you want? It's because we've been targeting the surface "symptom," which is the weight vs. the "root" cause which is what got you here. Losing weight is easy, so the question is why aren't you?

As the Creator of the *90 Day Mind-Body Break Through Program*, and the *Goddess Warrior Program* she teaches people how they can implement ALL of the components to unlock the door for lifetime success. You can get the results, and live in a healthy body that lasts. The Key Element that has been missing from everything else is what's going on inside you. She combines this with learning the Nutrition—Fitness—Mindset and Skillset to get the body and life you have always wanted.

Visit *MindBody90.com* to access a free video series training on how you can break through the lies and be liberated to have the body and life you want.

Listen in on Marci's *Warrior Woman Radio Show* every Wednesday and get access by downloading the WakeUpWarrior App on iTunes

Follow Marci Lock on Facebook as she Locks Down the Truth daily

Catch her on TV weekly on Abc4 or join her at one of her seminars, events, or retreats.

Levi:

We are locking down the truth with Marci Lock; she's known for being the Body-Mind Mentor, as well as, Nutrition, Fitness, Mindset Expert on TV and radio.

Marci, you were doing something really great in the world. I like to say that the best businesses are businesses that solve real-world problems. The real-world problem, especially here in America, which is not a secret, is that we have an obesity problem and a health problem. You're taking an approach that I think is very unique and quite fascinating which is finding that connection between the mind and the body, which is where most of us breakdown. I think what I would like to do first is just tell us how you got into this and how you developed this concept of this mind-body connection?

Marci:

Well, I actually started my focus on the body at age four being obsessed about my weight. That sounds crazy, I know.

People think, "What? At age four? How could you worry about your weight?" The TRUTH is that this very young age is when we start creating our belief systems and perceptions about the world, ourselves, and how LIFE really works. I'll give you a little story background about myself to see how this was true for me and it leads me on my journey and path. I have a memory at around age three of my mother being very upset. What she was upset about was gaining back 5 pounds after working so hard to diet and lose it.

I clearly remember her words, "I work so hard and then, I just gain it back again."

Now, if you could see my mother through my eyes in that moment you'd see that all I saw was my perfect Mom. All I felt for her was love. At a young age, your parents are your world and that's all you really know. All I knew is that my Mom was upset and I wanted to make her happy.

In my attempt to do so, I clearly remember saying to her, "Maybe God gave you back the five lbs because you needed it."

Obviously, I didn't completely understand the concept of weight but I did take on how important it was to my Mother and how much it affected her. I did, however, understand she was upset, didn't feel good enough about herself, and that it correlated to her body.

The next clear memory where this builds onto my perceptions of the body was at four years old when my Mom wanted to go walking outside for some exercise and of course, I wanted to go with her.

As we got onto the sidewalk, I went to hold her hand and she said, "I can't hold your hand, I've got to swing my arms to burn more calories." In that moment, I made a decision and belief about myself that would change the course of my life. The thought in my head from the evidence I had seen and was seeing now, was that your body is so important, that if I don't have a good body then I'm not good enough. The core belief—that I'm not good enough unless I show up a certain way—stems into a perfectionist identity to become what society says

you need to be in order to be accepted, validated, and loved. Now, what I want to point out is this was not a traumatic experience and it doesn't take a traumatic experience to make a decision or create a belief. My mother is amazing and she was never intentionally trying to hurt me or tell me that I wasn't good enough unless I had a "good body." She was just acting out the behaviors for her to be good enough based on what she took on and believed. Yes, her mother cared a lot about her weight as well. That meant my mother took on those perceptions from what she saw and so began to fight with the "body battle" to be good enough throughout her life.

It's a vicious cycle that consumes our life's energy, focus, and moments we can't get back. We should instead use the body for what it is intended for—to be our tool and vehicle to seize and experience life.

Why we are experiencing what we are with our bodies, money, our businesses, relationships, and spiritual connections all comes down to this. When we are born we have a clean slate with no idea, concept or frame around what life, our bodies, relationships, money experience or anything is supposed to look like. Each experience and how we perceive it gives us the opportunity to make a decision or belief based on that experience. I take responsibility for the beliefs I took on myself at the time that I had to have a good body to be loved and how it then played out in my life.

This is where it starts and why I began worrying about my body image at such an early age of four. Fast forward to how this played out and by age 14, I was anorexic and bulimic, doing diet after diet, working out for hours, one program to the next, next pill, next product and next everything as I was constantly striving to be good enough. At about age 21, I literally felt so overweight, fat, sluggish tired and depressed that I would wait to go to the grocery store late at night when no one was there because the only thing that fit was my sweats. I was so embarrassed and ashamed that I would walk with my head down, unable to even look anyone in the eyes. I felt so disgusted with myself because I was constantly up and down with my weight on the roller coaster and to me at that time based on my beliefs, which meant I was never good enough. I knew I had to change.

How did it change? I had to discover the missing component that had everything to do with the body. One day, I realized what I was doing was Insanity. I continued to do the same things over and over and it never changed. Everyone around me seemed to be doing the same things, struggling and fighting the body diet after diet, going to the gym, pills, and programs continually. I looked at the results we have as a nation and realized it wasn't working. I believe "Results Don't Lie" and they are pretty clear that we are obese as a society and nation. I asked myself "Well, if I've done everything and tried everything, what else can I try?" Literally, I heard divine inspiration whisper in my ear saying, "You've never tried education and the mind."

That struck me to the core and completely changed my path. I realized I had never actually learned how my body worked, what it needed or wanted to take care of it, function, thrive and for me to work with it. Instead, I was just always looking outside myself for the next quick fix instead of actually going internal and saying, "What's really going on here that keeps me in these patterns on a roller coaster, sabotaging and fighting my body? I dedicated my life from that moment on to understanding the body to be at peace with it, but I had no idea it would take me on a deep journey of the mind."

My journey began seeking to understand the behavioral side of the body and I discovered my body is actually already a natural Fat Burning Machine and my Ultimate Partner. What I didn't know, was that through this journey of discovering peace with my body, I would only get there by understanding the connection to the Mind.

I discovered that to live in the body and life you want, you get to first break through the BELIEFS behind the behaviors. These beliefs have created our identity patterns, perceptions and our entire life experience. Otherwise, you will continue to sabotage not only the body but the money freedom, relationships, connection, and entire life you want because deep down you don't believe you can have it, or have associations that scare you and keep you in your comfort zone based on what you believe. I wanted to share the freedom of how to work with all components to Lifetime Success which meant understanding the behaviors such as turning your body into a fat burning machine, the nutrition and fitness aspects to make it easy for life. This was never going to last though unless we targeted the missing component which is the Mindset and the Skill-set to continually break through to a more amazing body and life.

The point I want to share and get back to is that I realized the reason I never allowed myself to have the body when I obsessed about it my entire life and doing everything to focus on it behaviorally, was because my belief system internally was that "I'm not good enough." I had to prove this right. How this showed up was that every time I would get close to my goal weight or even have it for a little bit, of course it made me uncomfortable and anxious and so I'd sabotage. We find some way to prove ourselves right and sabotage to keep us in our comfort zone because that is what we believe we can have and deserve. How could I let myself have an awesome body or life if I believed deep down I wasn't good enough, worth it and therefore didn't deserve it because it conflicted with my core beliefs? I couldn't... we look for validations, excuses and reasons we can't have it to keep us in this safety net of our comfort zone and what we believe we can have.

Now, fast-forward to the process of discovering how to break through these roots and the tools and Skill-set to get a different experience. Now, I've lived in a lean-ripped body where I always have a 6 pack effortlessly and I've had it for 10 plus years. Understanding these tools, even after having children and having a 60 lb weight gain with my oldest, and a 70lb weight gain with my youngest, I was back to lean and shredded 90 days later. The reason I live in it so effortlessly however is because of the Mindset.

Levi:
Many have said your program is disguised as a Fitness and Nutrition or Body program on the surface, but underneath it is something different entirely. Will you explain that?

Marci:
Yes, it's true. Many people see me on TV, hear me on the radio, or see me as Nutrition, Fitness Expert that teaches how to Rock out the body and think it must be about the body. In many ways, I feel extremely blessed for this because on the surface of seeking validation, approval and love they want the body because they think it will lead them to happier, more confident and better life. All of this is TRUE as your BODY is your tool and vehicle that allows you to experience and create EVERYTHING else. I, 100% believe that if you are not in tune with your tool, then, you are operating out of less than 1/3 of your capacity and paying a cost in every realm of your life. However, I know the deeper step to ever getting the body and life has nothing to do with the behaviors.

I always say, "Losing weight is easy, the question is, why aren't you?"

Teaching the behaviors to work with your body as a fat burning machine is really super easy; it's the beliefs behind the behaviors that are stopping you.

The reason I am motivated to teach the truth is I know it is these deeper shifts that give a person the life and freedom they want. I saw how my life had played out from all my beliefs I had taken on.

My life experience wasn't hard just because the beliefs I took on about my body. I created the beliefs that life was hard, money was hard, the world was scary and unsafe, and love didn't last and was untrusting. Again, this showed up with experiences such as at age 11, having a Stalker, as well as several rape—and—kidnapping attempts through my teenage years. I believed the body was a struggle and didn't work because I'd seen so much sickness and dysfunction around the body with my relatives and my dad passing away from complications of a life long battle with diabetes when I was 15. So, all growing up I had ulcers, headaches, migraines, and body sickness and dysfunction to even having a heart attack at 19 and Breast Cancer at age 24. I then experienced a cheating husband and became a divorced single Mom at 28 again reflecting my beliefs on love and life. All of these things were part of my validation story, that I wasn't failing at the body because there always had to be trauma or something wrong with my body or hard things showing up that proved as a perfectionist I wasn't failing because the circumstances kept me from succeeding. It also kept me in my comfort zone and my identity of the victim who survived.

My True Passion and what inspires me is seeing people expand to greater heights by releasing themselves from the boxes, conditioning and prisons they've created. I love seeing them come alive, see and experience their potential through both the body showing up in health and Mind to give them the opportunity to truly HAVE IT ALL. To experience a PHENOMENAL LIFE in every aspect. I work with amazing individuals around the world that are extremely successful in their business but yet won't allow themselves to live in a rockin body of health or keep themselves from amazing relationships or one or more aspects of their lives is not amazing. All of these connect to our core beliefs, identity patterns, subconscious behaviors and the life experience we are living.

How can I not want to share this and be this tool in God's hand to give this gift and freedom to others? I know how horrible that prison feels and how amazing living in the paradise at peace & freedom with your body and life is when you break through. My journey has been for this purpose and giving others the path to have this freedom in every aspect of life.

Levi:

That very much validates a concept that I teach is if you change your process, you'll change your outcome. For you, you had followed the process.

You saw what was going on in your own life and then also the people around you and said, "Hey, something's not right here. I've got to change something."

It's very telling that you started educating. There are a lot of people out there as I know you know that have that limiting belief system. First of all, how do they even get the idea that they need to change something? Then, after that, where do they go for help? How do they get started?

Marci:

Great questions... the first step to change is awareness. We've been trained and conditioned in our society that when we see a problem or feel discomfort and pain, we run from the awareness that shows up to a subconscious pattern to feel comfort. This is why FOOD is so heavily a distraction of sabotage for many because of the associations of comfort we receive in our conditioning our entire lives around food. It usually changes for people only when they see enough PAIN in what they are experiencing and more PLEASURE in changing it, that they look at the results of their life they are in and realize they've got to make a change.

If you want different results, you've got to do something different. I want people to hear that when problems or pain shows up, it is really just a gift of awareness, a gift of feedback. Let's make it really simple. If you're having a negative emotion show up, a pattern, or behaviors that you realize is only sabotaging what you say you really want in your life, such as sabotaging with food, lashing out with relationships, or even, finding yourself distracted in your business and resisting doing the action that you know is going to get you the results you want—this is the gift in front of you of awareness and the first step to change it. This experience in this moment is a gift in front of you that if you become CONSCIOUS of it, then you can take action and do something about it to get different results.

As a society what I find is most people are aware. They're aware that they sabotage, they're aware that they're holding themselves back. They tell me I know I keep myself from this, I know I hide away from that, I know I don't do the things I know I should do to get those results... they're aware enough they are in a negative pattern or action but they don't know how to change it. The reason they don't know how to change it is because all they've ever known to do and be is the identity they've chosen, as well as the patterns and behaviors they chosen to protect themselves in staying in this belief system.

When problems shows up, it's just an action signal and gift saying "look here" to see what's really going on and why is this stopping you? This is where I teach a five step process to overcoming sabotage and get conscious of what's really going on so that you can then move through it and get what you want.

How people change is they become conscious of their own limiting story, perception, or belief they are in that is only going to keep them in the same experience. What we're used to doing is giving ourselves reasons, validations, and excuses as to why we can't have it. I'd like to remind people that whatever you are looking for you're going to find and so you will find those reasons and stay in the same results. In other words, what consumes your mind, controls your life. The question is do you want the reasons you are looking for that stop you, or do you want results?

If you're looking for all the excuses, all the reasons why you can't, all the validation stories, then you miss the solution to how you can. This doesn't mean they don't feel true to you, look true for you or haven't been a true and real experience for you. It comes down to are you looking for blame or for the solution?

Levi:
How do you define failure then?

250

Marci:

Giving up. There is no such thing as failure if you are failing forward. I believe you can only be failing if you decide to not move. If you fall and decide not to take any action, that is failure. As long as you are continuing to move, even if you think it's not good enough and looks like failure, it is failing forward. It is always teaching you something and it is always feedback and experience to learn from and take new action on. One of the greatest gifts we can give ourselves to get what we want is to see the problems that show up as a gift, see it through the eyes of gratitude. Look for the success in it, what it taught us & for the evidence that supports us in creating the life we want. When we can just look at it, we can move on to change it to what we do want to be experiencing.

If we even just ask ourselves one simple question in these moments such as my favorite, "What do I want?" what will follow is our mind seeking an answer. Now, what do I get to do to have a different experience? I can either stay in my story, perception & behaviors that aren't giving me what I want or I can now do something about it.

This is where I believe in coaches and mentors. I know I wouldn't be where I'm at if I didn't choose to have a coach or mentor that assisted me with the right knowledge and path to continue to grow and expand to greater and greater results. Most people look at change as a cost vs. the TRUTH is that it is an investment into them getting the life they want to experience. You are your greatest asset and without you nothing else is possible.

Instead, if we saw the TRUE COST we are paying in every aspect of our lives then we'd be willing to do anything to change. When you are not connected to your body as your tool, you are limited and unable to show up in your life. A Broken Body equates to a Broken Life. The Truth is this tool connected and clear is how you create in your business, feel confident, capable to fully show up in purpose, feel passion and energy to thrive in all relationship connections and experiences in life. I am passionate about the body because I know it is truly our vehicle to experience everything else. It is the gateway to your power.

The barrier for people is they look at change or the experience of a coach as a cost. Instead of seeing it as the investment in their life to

Be, Do and Have the life they want to be living. They are already paying a massive cost and missing out on the precious life experiences, moments and relationships they can never get back.

Levi:
What would you say then is the process you as a Coach take people through to get the results?

Marci:
There definitely is a system to success. Did you know that it's been proven that 19 out of 20 people fail at getting what they want? That means only 1 out of 20 knows how to be successful at getting what they actually want to experience.

What does this 1 out of 20 know? They follow a system to success which is getting the right knowledge, Right Plan of how to implement it, feedback and evaluating what barriers came up and what did or didn't work, and then, adjusting the plan to do it again. It's all feedback but our society usually sees this as failure because it hits those core root beliefs and then they run the stories of excuses and validations and never move onto getting it.

This quick fix mentality our society operates out of is what triggers us to see it as failure and give up. Just like trying a diet (which the long term success rate is less than 2% so, this is crazy, anyways...) but as soon as they don't see results right away, or they get triggered and sabotage, then they see it as failure, validate it or give up by saying I didn't want it anyways, now's not a good time, it wasn't that important, I can't right now because... you name it and we bail on what we really want.

We're focused on quick fixes instead of understanding when we plant a seed, then what comes next is we cultivate that seed to grow and expand with new patterns and new habits. We take daily action and these actions compound day after day to get the new results and experiences we want. Every day, if someone chooses to eat to support their body, exercise & live in the behaviors of health, then they will eventually get their results. They experience their body being a tool to THRIVE. Instead, most are looking through a foggy perception of I ate a salad today, so why don't I have my results? I guess I can't have it and so I'll find a way to give up on it. This just doesn't make sense but this is acting unconsciously.

This is why working with a coach or a mentor that has the result you want, can guide you through the blocks and barriers with the right knowledge, path and implementation and fill in those gaps you've been missing to get you to the desired results. This comes through learning to shift the daily behaviors, & mindset to implement the tools to get the results and keep them, as well as continue to get greater and greater results in life.

Levi:

I completely agree with you on the importance of finding people out there who have done what you want to do. It's been called the shortcut to success but it really is true. You have to go out and you have to find people. You have to provide something of value to them. I want to ask a question in a different way. When I was in high school, I was a high jumper. I remember I used to go into the gym and the coach made us do curls and bench press and all these other things. I remember asking, "If I am just running and jumping over a bar, why do I need to do these things?" "The thing that he taught me was, "You improve any part of your body, and it's going to improve your overall performance."

You've been very successful at taking people from where they're at, changing their bodies improving one area of their life, improving their mindset. How have you found that improving both mind and body, have converted to enter your entrepreneurial experience?

Marci:

Well, I'm so glad you asked that because this is the exact consciousness and perception shift I want to share. In society, we seem to have this fogged over misperception that our body is about how we look or it's the validation of who we are by expression of the image we portray. That is the biggest lie we've been telling ourselves. The truth is your body is simply your vehicle, vessel, and tool that you've been given to experience everything in every realm of your life. I know that if you're experiencing a Broken Body, then you are experiencing disconnect that affects every area of your life.

When you are disconnected from your body, you are disconnected from your life because you're showing up in less than 1/3 of your capacity. Literally, let's look at this. How easily can you create, connect and act when you are operating out of a fog? How do you fully show up when you're tired, sluggish, craving soda, candy or substances outside of yourself because your body can't function and has no energy?

Your body experience affects everything. It is your relationship connection, your spiritual alignment, and your ability to be clear, inspired and creative. When you are fit, you are focused, in clarity and on fire to live life full of passion and energy. After my morning workout and being connected to my tool I am focused and ready to create in my business, passion and purpose. This creates cash to live my life and as a tool of production. It creates connection in my relationships to be filled with energy to seize life instead of feeling irritated, and sluggish. When you are Fat you are frustrated and operating out of a fog. That is just what it comes down to.

I want you to think for a moment of the body like a garden hose. A garden hose is a great tool to water the grass or yard. What happens though if you kink the hose? Is it still the same tool? Yes, It's the same tool; it's just not as effective. The question we should ask ourselves then is if our tool affects every single realm of our life, why wouldn't we choose to live in health?

Our Society tends to twist this body perception into stories as to why we can't live in a rockin body of health. The most common is making it about the image that we have to look a certain way to be loved. The other common validation is to fight it by saying we are more than an image and so I'll just rebel and live in a body that is fat and frustrated. Either way is that story working for you or giving you the life experience you want? What I believe is that how your body is showing up externally is a reflection of your inner self worth. It's a reflection of what's going on internally for you. That is why I wouldn't allow myself to have the body when I didn't believe I was good enough, when I didn't believe I was worth it, and when I didn't love myself. If I believed the Truth, which is that I am worthy of living an amazing life and having it all. If I saw myself as the amazing daughter of God, that is a Divine Goddess and tool in God's hands that I am, then, of course, I would have nothing but an ultimate healthy body to experience life.

The crazy thought is that our life was meant to put all this unnecessary energy, time, effort and focus into what the body looks like instead of being at peace with this tool to simply be the vehicle to experience life.

You asked how this affects me as an Entrepreneur. It affects me in every single way. I know by me being in tune, I am inspired and clear to create. I believe that every thought that comes to me is really divine guidance and inspiration. I wake up every day and I'm so grateful for another amazing wonderful day that I get to be led and guided in all that I do, say, and create to bring value and transformation for others to experience freedom.

This clarity and connection is guidance and inspiration in those I coach, in the message that comes through me on TV, in my radio shows, or when I'm speaking at an event or seminar. This connection and guidance leads me down paths I would've never known if I wasn't in tune with my tool. 100% of the time it allows me to create in my business. It allows me to create the cash and financial business experience that I want as well as the spiritual connection that I want. It allows me to connect with my relationships. It is the connection piece to literally EVERYTHING else.

Levi:

You've talked about and I totally agree with you that you connect with your tool and the more connected we are, the more we can achieve in every area of our life which absolutely translates into our business. You're out there making a difference. You basically have taken your entrepreneurial skills and your personal skills and you're using them to improve the world around you in an area that you're passionate about. Tell us what's next on your horizon? What's your target goal that you're trying to achieve out there in the world?

Marci:

Well, my intention is to be a tool in God's hands to use my passion and purpose for good. I am guided constantly about where I get to grow, expand and share through many facets from my Mind-Body Break Through Transformation program, and now My Goddess Warrior Program, to retreats, seminars, TV, radio, my At Home Program and working with personal clients.

Right now I've had lots of inspirations and passion coming up that I feel more than ever called to lead women to step up more fully than they've ever stepped up before to fully show up in life. I now know my Truth of who I am and what I'm capable of as a Divine Daughter of God. I know I have a massive passion to share but I wouldn't be sharing it if I didn't break through the limitations that said what being a woman and a mother had to look like.

Six years ago, I found out I had a cheating husband, got divorced and became a single mom. My boys were just one and four and all of a sudden, it was like the responsibility of my little boys fell onto my shoulders. For me to discover myself and share my passion and purpose; I had to break through the beliefs that it had to look a certain way. I chose that it gets to look like whatever way I want it to look like and what is the best experience for me and my boys that serves us. I became empowered to live in and share my truth, and because of that my boys are so much more empowered then if I ever stayed in the limited mindset.

My little boys have seen me do many videos of messages as I share truths and principles.

My oldest will sometimes now just come to me and say, "Mom, I've got a message I feel inspired to share. "

This morning he did one talking about how kids at school told him that he talks too much and how, at first, he thought it made him a bad kid and that people didn't like him. We had to look at if that thought was even really true. Then, how he could shift the perception to see what was true. Does talking a lot as someone would put it mean that he's okay with speaking his message and having an opinion? It also can reflect that he's great with people, and makes friends easily. He can take the feedback as maybe he gets to allow other people to talk more but when people say something that's mean, it's usually because they're not happy with themselves and it's a mirror for them of what they don't like in themselves or want to be but won't allow themselves to be.

This just proves that what we choose to believe in a situation is what we create to be our experience and how it's going to affect our lives. He literally just pulled out the camera on my phone and taught this whole little message for kids to see themselves as perfect in who they are. I want women to stand in their power and know this truth for themselves. I believe that I'm now a way better mom, who is living authentically in my perfect process and empowered to teach my children to create the lives they want to experience. I feel more than ever called to inspire and lead women to recognize fully this power as I've seen most women have these limitations around what they can do as a woman in business and as a mother and why I've now started my Goddess Warrior program. In my own experience, from speaking events to business meetings, I'm usually surrounded by men. I've seen many women hold back their genius and gifts because they are afraid of being rejected by men or having their ego get offended. I, too, went through a stage where this was the case until I realized that if I had to limit my power and abilities, I was dealing with boys, not real men. I am so blessed to have warrior brothers and amazing friends that totally support me fully showing up in my power because they are confident in theirs. Men who are truly in tune with their power can stand without their ego affected by a female standing in her greatness. True men and women in power know that we all bring our own gifts of greatness and genius. Together, we can co-create something so much more powerful then we could alone.

Something else I've seen that is common among many women is choosing they can't do anything else because they think their role is only to be a mother, or it has to look a certain way to be accepted. I want to empower and inspire these women to know they get to share their genius, their passion, their gift, thrive and love life to realize that they can HAVE IT ALL. They can live in an amazing body as their tool, have amazing relationships with their spouse as co-creators, experience connected relationships with their kids, and be even more of a phenomenal mother by being filled up through sharing who they are.

Many women also live in the story that they come last and that is the exact thing they teach their kids. When we are filled up, we are overflowing with energy, love and passion. This gives us the ability to be a more effective mother, sister, friend, leader, and Goddess of Greatness to affect everyone around us.

Levi:

Marci, in conclusion, you're obviously extremely passionate and very inspiring. You're empowering people. If you could give just one call-to-action, just one singular thing that you want people that are reading this book to do, what is that one thing?

Marci:

The one call-to-action I would suggest is to look at the results in your life. If you aren't experiencing what you want, then ask yourself what do you get to do to start changing it and just moving towards it. Is what you are doing today going to get you closer to what you want tomorrow? If you want something, but aren't willing to take action on it now, then you are living in the stories, excuses and validations of "someday" that will never come.

We all can find validating reasons if we look for them. Reasons will never give us the results and so if I'm not living in a body of health, if I'm not experiencing amazing relationships, financially abundant or spiritually connected, and living a life of awesomeness and balance, then, what is the point to all of it?

My advice is to take a real honest look at yourself as to what you are experiencing and what do you now want to experience for the rest of your life? Your Tomorrow will only change if you take action Today. To sum it up, and Lock Down the Truth...

The Power of Choice is yours, Choose your Best Life!

You can access a free video series to get off the roller coaster and Liberate yourself from the Lies at *www.MindBody90.com*

Mykola Latansky

Mykola is a successful Ukrainian entrepreneur and thought leader. He is the world's first Russian-speaking motivational speaker as well as the #1 trainer and success coach for the Russian-speaking world. More than 85,000 people from 60 countries have chosen Mykola as their teacher. He has taught live in 20 countries on three continents.

Mykola is the founder of the *Academy of True Success*—the leading training company for the former USSR countries. In addition, he is the author of countless advanced techniques and methodologies for achieving success in life and business through uncovering people's natural genius.

Mykola belongs to the Million Dollar Speakers Club of the United States National Speakers Association. And, he is a member of the prestigious Global Millionaire Group—Maverick 1000.

Website: *www.latansky.com*

Levi:

Jack Canfield has often said that you're his biggest success story. You're also known as the number one success trainer and coach for the Russian-speaking world. Talk to us. What made you so successful and what is your secret recipe?

Mykola:

Someone once told me, "Your first two businesses most likely will be failures, but your third one must be a success!" This has been the case with me.

My first business was in the life insurance industry where I was building my MLM organization. That is where the transition from an employee's mentality to an entrepreneur's took place in me. I got a lot of business education there but not business success.

The second endeavor was my own engineering company designing automation projects for smart houses and intelligent buildings. I enjoyed significant success with that venture. But after several years, I realized it was not personally fulfilling.

My life was full of stress and meaningless day-to-day activities. I was starting to hate what I was doing and I knew for sure that I needed to reboot myself!

In late December 2006, I was sitting on a Red Sea beach in Egypt trying to relax with a big glass of the local gin and tonic. Back then I was drinking, smoking, and overeating a lot.

That day I had the book with me. Like all my trips in the previous two years, this book accompanied me everywhere but I never read it. I knew I had to read this book, but English—a foreign language to me—always stopped me. Not this time.

That book was *The Success Principles* by Jack Canfield.

Half drunk and tired of life, I opened the book and started reading it. Then, something miraculous happened. Nothing could stop me from reading it. I read all 440 pages in a matter of a few days.

The single question the book asked me again and again was, "What is it you really want to do in your life?"

I got goose bumps because I knew that I wanted to inspire and motivate other people by helping them to believe in themselves and their unlimited power, gifts, and talents through being who they truly are!

Six months later, I attended Jack Canfield's "Breakthrough to Success" workshop in Scottsdale, Arizona.

I wasn't considering a trainer's career yet and I didn't know anything about coaching. My only desire was to become a great motivational speaker because I wanted to inspire and motivate people.

Interestingly enough, in 2007 the professional speaker industry didn't exist in the countries of the former Soviet Union. Even today, it isn't well-developed. In the first eight months of my new business, I had not earned a dollar. I was close to quitting this new career, thinking to return to the engineering world.

Luckily, in one training, I learned what coaching is and soon started my coaching practice. Soon I added success seminars and found that I loved it. Within two years, I was earning six figures. The groups I lead have grown from 15 people to an average of 200 people and up to 700 people in my seminars.

As of this writing, I have taught live in 20 countries on three continents and my clientele comes from more than 60 countries.

For the last several years, I have been making more than a million dollars annually.

Levi:
You have found your passion, and you have found your voice. Now, it sounds like every day you're able to do what you enjoy doing.

Mykola:
Yes. Thanks to my reading *The Success Principles*, I realized that I was already doing what I wanted but without pay. I was inspiring and encouraging people every time I met someone who was doubting themselves. At that moment, I would stop whatever I was doing and devote myself completely to that person. Now, I do this consciously with thousands of people, and I'm enjoying great financial success.

Levi:
You've been doing this for a while now. What have you learned about success that you didn't know when you started?

Mykola:

What I learned was that achieving success in life, in business, in relationships, and in health is like opening a combination lock. If you know the code, the lock will open. The combination and its sequence is key to achieving any success you want.

Levi:

Oh, the code?

Mykola:

Yes, the code for the lock. There are many, many codes that you have to know; and, not only know, but apply to your situation. My own success became possible when I started to learn the laws of success—the codes—and apply them in my daily life.

Levi:

So, initially, when you started, you had read Jack's book, and you learned some of the important principles. But, it also sounds like you discovered that it's not enough to know the principles. You must apply the principles in the right order.

Mykola:

Some principles are primary and others secondary. For example, in my opinion, the major principle would be the principle of being 100 percent responsible for your outcomes. This means you, and only you, are creator of the results you get in your life. Your outcomes fully depend on the responses you choose in response to the events happening in your life.

Levi:

Ah, it makes perfect sense that if you're not taking action or ownership in the primary areas, the other areas aren't going to line up the way that you want them to.

Mykola:

Yes!

Levi:

Do you believe that with the right principles anybody can achieve anything?

Mykola:

I truly believe that everybody can achieve the life of their dreams if they follow their heart and do what they were meant to do. I completely disagree with the idea that the only way to be fulfilled is to run your own business.

Look, we all have our own purpose in life. Somebody is made to be the best taxi driver in the city. I know one guy who would drive the car 24/7 and be happy. He loves transporting people. There are people who are naturally born to be chefs, and others who are born to be pilots. There are people who are born to be journalists, and there are people who are made and born to be business owners and business managers.

People who want to be successful tend to look only at the big success stories in highly visible industries and, then, copy that. They erroneously assume that if that big success person has a happy family and leads a happy, fulfilled life, then it will work for them, too. This is one of the biggest, misleading ideas because we can only be successful doing what we were meant to do.

You will be unhappy and unsuccessful most of the time if you try to copy somebody else's success.

Levi:

I completely agree with you there. In fact, it's fascinating how this unfolds. We're in the middle of a technology revolution that is completely modifying the way that we interact with one another, including the rate and pace of business. I think that it's going to get to a point where we can't just rely on imitating someone else because what's going to happen is the game is going to change on us. The only way that we can truly succeed is by being true to what's unique about us. I absolutely agree with you on that principle.

Mykola:

I support this idea, and I have had firsthand experience with this phenomenon. There are people who are trying to copy my brand of success as trainer, coach, and speaker. I have found that some people have unsuccessfully copied some of my ideas, my training programs, sales pages or even the way I do my podcasting on YouTube.

By the way, I'm one of the most watched video podcasters for the Russian-speaking world in the personal development industry. Right now, I have more than four million views on YouTube.

In the last seven years of doing this business, I never did anything because somebody else was doing it. Instead, what I did was based on a gut feeling that now is the time to start doing this particular training, or recording this particular topic in a podcast.

To sum up, copying is a poor shortcut to success. To be successful, never copy someone. Sure, observe what other people do and, then, be the first to do what no one else is doing!

Levi:

Absolutely. What I believe that you're defining there is the difference. Actually, it's the difference in the definition of success, and it's also the difference in the concept of leadership. What you're describing is that in order to truly be successful, you have to be a leader in your own right. I'd love to have you explain even more. What does it take to be a leader? What does it take to be a pioneer?

Mykola:

To be a leader, especially an opinion leader, takes a lot of courage and understanding about people. Most of the time, especially at the beginning of your career, people won't understand what you're doing. People will laugh at what you're doing. People will disagree by putting you down for doing what nobody else is doing. In order to be a true leader the strength of your power must come from inside you.

I remember sitting in a huge gathering of the National Speakers Association Conference in Anaheim, California, a few years ago. Steve Siebold—one of my mentors—was on stage addressing 3,000+ professional speakers on behalf of the Million Dollar Speakers Club. That club is a group of professionals that earns more than one million dollars a year, a club I belong to now.

Steve said, "Yesterday, at our Million Dollar Speakers Club meeting, I was observing every single one of us looking for a single trait that unites us. There were only 36 people in the room each making more than a million dollars a year as professional speakers. I was curious, trying to figure out what distinguishes millionaire speakers from the other 10,000+ American professional speakers that are not that successful. I realized we—who earn most of the money in the industry—are the opinion leaders! We take risks, we say what others are afraid to say. Yes, we do make mistakes, but we are rewarded more than most. We do create the trends that the majority will follow.

Levi:
What you just shared is profound, not only in the speaking space, but that's true in the business space as well. It is the thought leaders, those that are willing to push the boundaries that are most successful. The ones willing to look at new spaces in the market and say, "You know what? There is a better way to do it, and this is how I think it should be done."

Mykola:
Yes.

Levi:
How do you define failure?

Mykola:
Failure, for me, is a unique way to learn what is not working for me personally or for my business. I mean the external world as well as my inner world.

Failure can show you that you are on the wrong path; that you need to pursue something different. Failure is a chance to course correct and change one's self. It is a chance to improve, eliminate, or replace what's not working.

Failure is a synonym to the word "feedback." Most people never associate those two words together. Very successful people know that most of the time failures are a great source for exceptional feedback. But you must be ready and willing to accept this form of feedback, regardless how painful it can be!

Levi:
For you, failure is not failure at all. It's data. It's merely information that you're getting that helps you to know how to move forward.

Mykola:
Exactly, Levi!

Another major law of success that I'm teaching is the "Law of Transparency." This means being true to who you are, accepting the truth about yourself including failures, mistakes, and drawbacks. This is instead of trying to impress other people by appearing "perfect."

When you are willing to accept yourself, then you are okay with failures. This is a form of feedback, too. Most importantly, you now can do something about it.

The reason most people don't want to admit failures is because they don't want to look bad in other people's eyes. It is more profound, more impactful, to share your failures. This creates trust and brings more success.

For example, because of my recent political involvement in the Russian-Ukrainian war, I lost 50-70 percent of my business volume. Most business owners would hide this sad truth from their clientele and their competition. Not me.

To recover my business, I knew I needed to apply another law of success—the "Law of Attraction." So I flew to Venice, Italy, for a vacation and chose to stay in the presidential suite of one of the best hotels there.

Immediately my vibrations change from scarcity to abundance. Soon, I am switching on my video camera and recording a lesson for my audience sharing what just happened to me.

I told my followers that my business was going down because of my political position. Then, I told why I chose to vacation in Venice and how it switched my internal vibrations to ones of abundance.

The moment that I started to share this message with my audience, I reconnected with myself, and I regained my power. I regained the control. Now I'm feeling great and starting to improve my financial situation, too.

It's not failure anymore. It's a learning curve. It's feedback and a good opportunity to change what I was doing and to do something else that I was not doing yet.

Levi:

One of the things that I often teach is that in order to create change, typically, you have to focus on behavior first. It doesn't matter whether or not it's your own behavior, or the behavior of those around you. You were willing to follow the Law of Transparency and to admit your own situation, not only to yourself, but to your audience. This impacted the way that you were behaving in reference to your audience. The moment that you were willing to accept the Law of Transparency, it changed the way that you started to behave towards your audience. If history holds true, then that switch in behavior will impact your business in a positive way.

Mykola:

Yes.

Levi:

At this point, obviously.

Mykola:

One more thing about hiding the truth. Whatever we choose to hide, we also choose to spend energy on hiding it. Consciously or unconsciously, we choose to lose energy. This reminds me of a ball someone is trying to hold under water. To keep it there, one has to spend energy. It's the same with our secrets. The more we hide, the less energy remains us to create the life of our dreams.

Levi:

At this point in your experience, obviously, there are many challenges. You're experiencing more change than most of us. You're in the middle of change due to the political climate of what's going on between Ukraine and Russia. How do you manage outside change when your marketplace is changing, when competitors come in, and when the government changes the rules of the game?

Mykola:

Believe it or not, I love crisis. The reason for this is simple—you cannot change the outside world. You can only change your inner world and your own behavior.

When change is happening, when crisis comes, the best rescue is to remember this: what used to work until now may no longer work!

People struggle in crisis because they try to do what they used to do but the rules of the game may have been changed.

One autumn day back in 2008, the Ukrainian currency hryvnia lost 40 percent of its value. People stopped paying. That same day I lost all my coaching clients.

The first two weeks of that crisis, I couldn't find anything better to do but be depressed. I wanted to coach people but they couldn't afford my services anymore. They had money but were afraid of spending it.

I asked myself, "Do I want to keep my prices up and be broke? Can I drop my prices and go back into business?" This was the pivotal point. I cut my prices three times! And guess what happened next? In less than three months, I was earning much more than before the crisis. I reinvented myself. I figured out what people needed and I played the numbers game—lower prices but wider clientele! My business started growing again.

My biggest learning out of that? When a crisis comes, say "Goodbye" to what you used to do. Change yourself. Be willing to reinvent every single thing that you used to do, understanding that what you have been doing may not work anymore.

Levi:

That is some of the best advice that I've ever heard in business and the technology climate right now. Honestly, it's so common to see individuals and businesses cling to what they used to do in the past and what used to work. Some kid in a college dorm room invents a technology that changes the game, and suddenly you can't play the game the way that it used to be played. I absolutely agree with you. That is honestly some of the best advice that I've ever heard.

Mykola:

Thank you, Levi! The good news is you don't need to wait for the crisis to come like the one we're having with Russia. Instead, keep up with new technologies that are coming into the market every day because if you don't, sooner or later you will be left behind. Continue to reinvent yourself everyday and you always will be the leader in your niche or industry.

My observations show me that, in highly competitive industries, businesses experience crisis on average every three months. Few are flexible enough to adapt to the continuously changing environment. Most will be bankrupt in less than three years from their creation date.

To be successful in business, you need to make it a habit to understand the variables that are involved. You must realize that you'll experience some form of hardship every few months. It is important to realize what is not working anymore, as well as the fact that you must continually reinvent yourself to succeed in business.

Levi:

That's awesome. So, in conclusion, for the entrepreneurs that you teach, your audience, and those that you hope to reach, what are the pieces of advice that every entrepreneur must know in order to be successful?

Mykola:

Through my experiences, I have found 12 key success factors responsible for extraordinary business success.

1st Key Success Factor: Decide to become the best of the best in your niche or industry.

When Jack Welch came to General Electric, he gathered his senior management team and set this goal: "In the next year, every single division of our business will be #1 or at least #2 in its industry. Everything that isn't we'll close down."

When I started my business, I decided to be the number one trainer, the number one coach, and the number one speaker in my industry. I truly believe in the value of how you refer to yourself, and if you work on achieving your goals, then that's what you'll become. If you decide to be the best of the best, then one day you will be the best of the best.

2nd Key Success Factor: Find the best of the best mentors. I only spend my time and my money to learn from the best of the best in their industries. Jack Canfield is one of them.

3rd Key Success Factor: Pursue the best education possible and never scrimp on it. Right now I am paying a $75,000 fee so my wife and I can meet Richard Branson next week on his private island in the British Virgin Islands. I invest in myself, and never scrimp on this. Investment in your own education is probably the best investment you can make. To date, I have invested more than $500,000 in my education.

4th Key Success Factor: Keep up with trends. Know what is going on in the technology world and how it applies to your business. Either you keep with technologies or you'll be left behind.

5th Key Success Factor: Big success is built by small steps. Most business owners dream about achieving huge overnight success. The truth is small steps will not always lead to huge success, but trying to achieve huge success from the beginning will lead to great failure and an irretrievable position. If people start thinking about helping people and serving people instead of making money, then money will always come.

Do we still have time, Levi?

Levi:
Yes, absolutely.

Mykola:
I want to share something with you.

A few weeks ago I was in Jamaica and had a conversation with an American billionaire. I have long been curious to learn firsthand the difference in the mindset of a billionaire and a millionaire. I asked him that question. The answer surprised me.

The billionaire told me, "Millionaires, from my experience, most of the time put the money first. However, we billionaires, think much less about money itself. What we think about is what great value we can create for a great number of people all over the nation or the whole world? Money is just a tool for creating something big and significant." He added, "Really, how much money do you need? You can only sleep on one bed a night. You can only eat a certain amount of food each day. You cannot wear all the clothes in the world or drive all the cars…"

This supports my **6th Key Success Factor: Serving people is the key to big money and big success.**

7th Key Success Factor: We talked about earlier today. **Be transparent, be real!** Do not pretend. Accept who you really are. If you don't like something about yourself, then accepting the truth is the first step to change whatever you don't like about yourself.

8th Key Success Factor: Commit to constant development and growth. We talked about this, too.

9th Key Success Factor: Love people and do what you love to do. Never work for money. Make money on what you love to do. Even without much money, you will become rich!

10th Key Success Factor: Be a good salesperson. Know how to sell and to promote. This one is obvious.

11th Key Success Factor: Develop your charisma to attract people like a magnet. Charisma is developed through connection to our true self. It is essential that we know what our values are, and that we actively demonstrate them by showing the world that we are true to our values.

12th Key Success Factor: Believe you are genius! Your genius will open up.

Levi:

All of this is wonderful advice. Honestly, again, this is some of the best advice that I've heard.

Mykola:

Thank you, Levi!

Levi:

I believe that, for any of us, regardless of whether or not we're an entrepreneur, or whether or not we're trying to accomplish something different in our personal life, that these principles, which you've encapsulated in advice, can serve to benefit all of us. That it's really a challenge, and that each of us should try to implement those steps in our lives. I appreciate very much your spending the time and sharing your knowledge and wisdom with us. On a final note, what's next on your horizon?

Mykola:

In the last three months, I've mostly thought about the political situation in my country. I want to contribute more to the success in Ukraine with the tools I already have: trainings, online programs, my YouTube channel, etc. I want to find ways to grow the consciousness of the people in my country. I want my country to succeed in the world arena. And I see an extraordinary opportunity for us to make a quantum leap as a country of 46 million people.

Also, I am writing a book, *The Power of Transparency.*

On the business side, we're opening up new markets in Azerbaijan, Armenia, Georgia, Latvia, Lithuania, Estonia, and Moldova, which are all former Soviet Union countries.

Levi:

That's wonderful, Mykola. Thank you very much!

Paul Novin

Paul W. Novin is provocative, decisive and challenging—but most importantly, he's effective. His advice to entrepreneurs has earned him the reputation as a "Visionary," "Millionaire Maker" and pioneer within the Lifestyle Business Industry. Every year, he and his business partners help thousands of business owners succeed all around the globe!

Contact: *IMGlobalTLC@gmail.com* • Skype: *paulnovin*
Mobile: 502-220-5241

Levi:
What age were you when you started your first business and what was it?

Paul:
I grew up in a single-parent, government-subsidized home and I was eating subsidized food in a rough part of town. I graduated High School as a C student, and I never went to college. So, when I am asked the question, "When did you learn that you were an entrepreneur?" two things come to mind. As a young child, I can remember taking a pad of paper on Saturday afternoons, after returning home from my youth bowling

league, and drawing 'layouts' for what would be my future bowling business 'when I grew up.' I also had a paper route as a teenager, but I guess that I started my first real or 'traditional business' when I was about 19 years old. It was called 'Paul's Auto Detail' and it was located in a two-car garage in Braintree, Massachusetts. I guess that is when I knew that I really enjoyed working and earning money for myself.

Levi:
What is the secret combination to finding success in your line of work?

Paul:
When I was first introduced to the 'home business industry' in 1993, I was taught the difference between 'Residual Income' and all other kinds of Income. And, I was taught what was called 'The 12 Success Factors.'

For anyone that is not familiar with the term 'Residual Income,' it is defined as, "an income that is received on a regular basis with little effort required to maintain it." The American Internal Revenue Service (IRS) categorizes income into three broad types: active income, passive income, and portfolio income. In plainspoken terms, I would define 'Residual Income' as, "an income that you receive over and over again for something that you did one time in the past."

Now, please allow me to list and share what these '12 Success Factors' are, and then please allow me to explain what each of these factors means:
- Company Track Record
- Financially Sound or Debt Free
- Strong Management
- Unique or Consumable Products
- Competitively Priced
- Low Personal Production
- High Retention
- Low Attrition
- Low Initial Investment
- Timing
- No Breakaways
- No Risk

With these '12 Success Factors' in place, anyone can be successful!

Anytime that I would evaluate a business that I was introduced to, or interested in enough to do some due diligence before getting involved with it, I would start by asking questions like…

What kind of a Company Track Record does the company have? How long have they been in business? What kind of industry are they in? What kind of products or services do they market?

Next, I look at the company's capitalization or funding to see if they are Financially Sound or Debt Free.

I would also do some background research or learn the history of the Management team to see if they have the experience or qualifications to run the company and to create a solid, viable future. It is important to ask, "What kind of character do these individuals have?" as well as "Do they have my best interest at heart?"

Then, I take into consideration the product or service lines that they offer to see if they are Unique or Consumable Products (and if the end consumer would purchase them even if there were not a 'profit motive' attached). Consumable products are those products that are used up and then need to be re-ordered on a consistent basis. This creates repeat business and residual income.

You also need to ask the question, "Are the products or services Competitively Priced?" It has been said that 'we get paid for bringing value to the marketplace.' If they are high priced products, then the masses most likely won't continue to purchase them month after month.

Next, you need to ask the question, "Does the company have a Low Personal-Production Requirement?" This means that you are NOT required to spend a fortune each month just to "qualify" to receive your commission pay. I call that my CODB, or 'Cost of Doing Business.'

Then, you need to ask, "Does the company experience a High Reorder Rate?" This means finding out about the percentage of repeat purchases. The company might experience a high reorder rate because they sell quality products, offer great value, or provide great customer service.

If a company has a Low Attrition rate, then that means that you don't have to spend a great deal of time 'replacing' the customers that are 'dropping out' of the program, which is exciting because that means that each month your efforts are in the 'growing of your business' and not in the 'replacing of your business'!

Also, you need to ask if there is a Low Initial Investment to get started with the business. Low barrier of entry allows the masses to come and join you! Too high a cost reduces the number of people that could or would join you.

You need to consider the Timing of the company, the market trends, the industry that they are in, and, of course, what is the timing in your life, i.e. what is going on personally that will allow you or disallow you to actively participate?

NO Breakaways means that you will not lose. Now, that could mean that you don't lose people, or that you don't lose income.

As an example, in the corporate or sales world, you could be responsible for building or growing a territory, only to be doing so well that the 'higher ups' take your territory and decide to split it with another salesperson.

That is an example of a Corporate Breakaway, where you lost sales and therefore income. In the home business industry, some companies have mechanisms called Breakaways, or these mechanisms could also be called Takeaways, within the compensation plan in order to benefit the company at the expense of the rep.

An example would be that you personally find a really motivated person that you take under your wing and mentor them in your business, and then that person takes off and goes on to have great success. Perhaps you are still working outside of your home, but the new person is able to work full time from home... An example of a Breakaway or Takeaway is when that person reaches the same rank, level, or status as you, and then the person above you in rank would now inherit that person as their own and you would perhaps just receive a small percentage of their sales volume or income rather than the larger part that you had previously earned! Not a very cool thing at all, either way!

And, lastly, you want to work with a company that offers an opportunity for everyone to make a Risk Free, or NO Risk decision! Some people have buyer's remorse, and other people realize that for them the product doesn't work, like if someone has a unique allergy to an ingredient. You always want the customer to have a pleasant experience and never at any time feel that they are at risk! A 30-day money back guarantee should be an automatic part of the company's philosophy for total customer satisfaction!

It has been said that most people 'plan more for a family vacation, than they plan for their life', so I encourage everyone to do their solid due diligence on a company, or any opportunity to earn income or change careers, BEFORE they jump!

Understand that this Lifestyle Business can start as a Part time gig, grow into a Full time business, and end up a highly compensated 'Lifetime Career of Freedom and Choice'!

That is why I would encourage anyone, or everyone, that is seriously considering starting their own Lifestyle Business, to determine that this is a potential 'career path' and worthy of a 3-5 year investment or commitment to learning, applying knowledge, OJT (on the job training), and consistent productive effort! Anything less than that is perhaps nothing more than 'taking on a new hobby'!

Perhaps this is why I have been able to pick the right companies to join, and why I have become a multi-million dollar producer in several different companies and have earned seven figures too!

Levi:
What do most people not know about your industry?

Paul:
The short answer is that most people don't know that this industry can be a part time, full time, or long time career!

It has been my personal experience that most people don't understand the principles and power of leverage. It is the only way (that I know of) to lengthen each day, and multiply your efforts and be paid handsomely.

Here is what I mean. There are only 168 hours in a week, right? That would be 7 days a week times 24 hours per day. Most people work 40 or so hours per week, and that is what they are paid for. Others may work overtime and get paid 1.5 times their normal hourly wage, etc...

Well, when you are growing your Lifestyle Business, you can actually have hundreds or even thousands of hours being invested into the growth of your business, even if you are only working 20 hours yourself. An example of this is if you enroll 10 new members personally, who in turn enroll five members each. If everyone invested just 10 hours per week into their personal business, then with just that many people (10+50 = 60) working part time would add up to over 600 hours PER WEEK in productive activity! And, yes, you would earn income from those 600 hours of productivity, even though you personally invested only 20 hours yourself!

J. Paul Getty once said, "I'd rather have 1% of the effort of 100 men than 100% of my own effort." He fully understood the truth and impact of leverage!

Enjoying a 'Lifestyle Business through Relationship Marketing' allows true accessibility for anyone, free from consideration as to one's race, religion, education, economic status, work history, country of origin, or gender. Everyone has a fair, accessible, and equitable opportunity to succeed. Most people don't realize that the Lifestyle Business industry is a multi-billion dollar industry, with decades of history along with a proven and successful track record.

It has been said that women start 73% of all Home businesses and when that business starts making noticeable money then the men or spouses want to get involved!

Also, most people don't know that of the women in America that earn over $100,000 per year in income, the large majority do so through the career or business decision of working or creating their 'Lifestyle Business' from home!

What makes a Lifestyle Business through Relationship Marketing so different is the No's!
- No large investment,
- No inventory,
- No need to deliver products,
- No repeat sales presentations,
- No pressuring customers to purchase,
- No billings or collections,
- No complicated paperwork, and
- NO risk!

Anyone can be successful!

Consider the alternatives: You can work the 47-47-47 PLAN, which is 47 hours per week, 47 Weeks per year, for 47 years, and then retire on a fraction of what you earned while you were employed in your career... OR... You can work the 40-40-40 PLAN, which is after you find a company that has met the 12 Success Factors, you share a 40 second message, with 40 people Daily, for 40 Days and you will have most likely laid the foundation to a solid Lifestyle Business that can pay you a solid residual income in the 5 figures, 6 figures, or even possibly 7 figures in annual RESIDUAL income!

Levi:
How has having a mentor helped you to be successful?

Paul:
By having an experienced and trustworthy person to work with, you gain so much, and yet avoid so much at the same time. What you have is a source of accountability, and a source of experiential knowledge instead of just 'head or book knowledge' to help guide you.

With a mentor, you are able to increase your knowledge in a much shorter period of time, while at the same time helping you to avoid the pitfalls that most mentors have already experienced. It was written a long time ago, "Where no counsel is the people fall, but in the multitude of counselors there is safety."

Here is a list of some things that a Mentor could tell the person he is working with... and would prove to the mentor that they are truly coachable and teachable:

10 Things that you MUST give up to Move Forward—by Marc
- Give up letting the opinions of others control your life.
- Give up the shame of past failures.
- Give up being indecisive about what you want.
- Give up procrastinating on the goals that matter to you.
- Give up choosing to do nothing.
- Give up your need to be right.
- Give up running from problems that could be fixed.
- Give up making excuses rather than decisions.

- Give up overlooking the positive points in your life.
- Give up not appreciating the present moment.

Every struggle in your life has shaped you into the person that you are today. Be thankful for the hard times; they have made you STRONGER and WISER—Lessons Learned in Life

I am grateful to have many mentors in my life, from my bowling days, to my many other sports activities, and now in my business endeavors!

Levi:

When someone is finding a mentor, what should they look for?

Paul:

The type of person that I personally have looked for and would advise others to look for in a mentor, is someone that has high integrity, strong character, and a proven track record of success! It doesn't matter if they are male or female, and they don't have to necessarily be in the same industry that you are pursuing. There are certain principles of success that 'cross-over' into different career fields or disciplines that can benefit you as well in your pursuit of your 'Lifestyle Business through Relationship Marketing.'

With that being said, It would be of supreme benefit if they did happen to be in the same profession, same company, and perhaps even within the same organization, especially if they have a proven system for marketing your business, and are willing to partner with you or are willing to match your productive effort with their own.

Consider this quote by Henry Ford:

"Coming together is a beginning... Keeping together is progress... Working together is success!"

Levi:

What advice and encouragement would you give to a budding entrepreneur?

Paul:

Be passionate! Go for it! I would highly encourage that each person do their due diligence, make educated decisions and not just emotional decisions, in order to minimize risks.

When you get all your answers, and have a comfort level to move forward (and I would recommend if married, talk with your spouse and seek their support, but even if they are not supportive be willing to move forward as long as it doesn't jeopardize your finances) and take all out MASSIVE ACTION for 30, 60 or even 90 days to develop your Success Story!

Creating your 'Success Story' may be the single most important thing to do when you first start building your Lifestyle Business through Relationship Marketing, because it is what you will tell your prospects, your team members, and the entire organization that you are growing for the rest of your career!

It is that story that will 'speak' to your people. It will resonate or they will identify with your decisions, your struggles, your fears, your obstacles, what you did to get started, what package you bought to get started, and ultimately what you earned in income your first 30-45 days that will be identifiable.

It is all of those things that will inspire them to take action and to become part of your team! And, although people may think that they have to be making BIG money in order to IMPRESS others, it has been my personal experience that this is not true. This is especially true because the average person can't picture what it is like to earn a 5 or 6 figure monthly income.

Keep in mind that only 13% of Individuals and 28% of Households (and by extension the majority of the world's nations as well) earn less than $75,000 per year in annual income. And, they do that by punching a clock, or by earning a miniscule amount of their Employer's total business through their salary or commissions, all the while answering to someone over them on a daily, weekly, monthly and yearly basis... So, by keeping it simple in sharing your 30, 60 or 90 day Success Story, you will be believable.

Zig Ziglar said it well, "If you can dream it, you can achieve it. You will get all you want in life if you help enough other people get what they want."

Levi:
What lessons have you learned from observing failure either in your own life, or the lives of others?

Paul:

The short answer that comes to mind is to NOT repeat what caused the failure! Learn from it, adjust or adapt where needed, and move forward.

The longer answer would be to evaluate whether the failure was something that you did, or didn't do, whichever would be the case. I always start with my own self-reflection or internal investigation. Then, I would look at the circumstances that led to the failures or disappointments and see if they were external, i.e. with the company or through things that were beyond your control, etc... The old adage of, "he who forgets history is doomed to repeat it," does have merit.

Levi:

What role has technology played in your business? (You can perhaps address the lifestyle topic here as well.)

Paul:

Technology has impacted every person's life worldwide, and I imagine that it has influenced how every single business conducts their business worldwide.

In our Lifestyle Business model, we have been able to leverage technology in order to 'collapse time frames', meaning that it takes far less time to achieve growth, numbers and therefore income goals as compared to the 'old methods' of marketing.

Allow me to explain.

In time past, before the advent of the desktop computer, or shipping systems and methods, including such visionaries in business like Fred Smith who started FedEx, or before UPS became a household name worldwide, people that participated in the Multi-Level Marketing (MLM) industry would literally have to be the 'middleman.'

These 'entrepreneurs' would have large investments in product until they got paid. They would have to inventory the products, and deliver orders to some people that couldn't make it to their 'garage' in order to move the product and 'get paid.' That is where the phrase, "Garage Qualified" came from. People would constantly have to make repeat sales presentations. Some people put tremendous pressure on friends or family members to purchase regularly, etc…

People were always doing 'in home' presentations, or having weekly, monthly or quarterly 'leadership' meetings or rallies. They would constantly be bombarded with the latest books or tapes 'to keep them motivated', etc… The majority of this business was face to face and it created some great relationships, but it also created a lot of stress from being away from home when a spouse had to work full time and then go 'show the plan' at night or on weekends! It put huge demands on one's time, and in a lot of cases it caused hurt feelings when someone decided to no longer participate, or if a spouse was gone all the time, they simply got tired of having to 'share their spouse with the business'!

Consider technology today, and what it has afforded the serious business-minded person by way of time savings, leveraged activities, and, as I said earlier, the opportunity to 'collapse time frames.'

We no longer have to leave the house and meet people at their homes, offices, or coffee shops in order to 'share the business' with someone. We can simply point them to a turnkey, 'done-for-you' marketing system, or website. Through technology, information is shared by doing the actual presentation for you 24/7/365, even while you are sound asleep or on vacation. This alone does 90% of the work. Therefore, we now are simply able to create more exposures to our business in far less time.

It use to average about 3-4 hours per appointment, including drive time, just to meet someone and 'show them your products or business model'… And, consider the worldwide 'Corporate' methods, including traveling domestically or internationally, living out of suitcases and eating at hotels. Not only is it expensive and time consuming, but after a while it can become a real burden. With technology, you can still have the same relationships worldwide without ever having to leave your home and you could even do your business in your sweat suit or pajamas… No kidding, I know many people that make millions and that is exactly how they choose to go about their daily routine, in their PJ's if they even choose to 'dress up'! Ties are optional!

The most common reasons or excuses that prospects use for not joining you are, "I have no time," "I have no money," or "I am not a salesperson." These are no longer valid reasons. We simply are paid for sharing information with those who will listen via social media, email, voice message, texting, blogging, or posting links, videos or information. From there, the system or technology will do the presenting and educating, and we simply help people to complete their self-registration with the company that we are working with.

Now, you can literally communicate with dozens of people in that same amount of time by phone calling, sending email, or even by using Skype or Google Hangouts to be face to face with your friend, contact, or business associate. And, I might add, you can do this just about anywhere in the world!

We are very much in the 'Relationship Marketing' business, but we now can conduct our business via our smart phone, iPad, handheld devices or our laptop without ever having to leave our house. Or, you can go with the other end of the spectrum by doing your business completely mobile from anywhere in the world that has an internet connection, and not only conduct 'business as usual' without missing a beat, but also, more importantly, you can be working and living your 'Lifestyle Business' from any place that you or your family choose, anywhere around the globe!

Levi:

We are in the midst of a technology revolution. How do you think that your business/home based businesses will be impacted as things continue to change?

Paul:

As technology continues to make advancements and impact our daily lives, the world is getting smaller! You are now able to meet people and build relationships not just within your neighborhood, city or town, state or even your country, but now you can meet and work together with people globally through the power of technology and 'Relationship Marketing'!

I have been able to meet and work with people in multiple countries, creating a solid international base of business in no small part due to technology, but also because people all over the world seek the same things, which are relationships with like-minded and caring people. My business is local, national and global now. It can be both stationary within my home, or it can be completely mobile anywhere in the world if I choose to live or travel abroad.

Technology has only enhanced the Lifestyle Business through Relationship Marketing model, not diminishing it one bit, and it will continue to be a positive influence and growth factor moving forward.

Levi:
Do you have any suggestions for staying ahead of the technology curve?

Paul:
Just like in any trade there are 'tools of that trade' that allow a person to do their job better, faster, or with less stress or hassle than working without them. The same applies with technology. Make sure to find and stay updated with technology by plugging in with others that are experts in that field.

Having a 'Mastermind Alliance' similar to what Andrew Carnegie had during the Industrial Age can work for us today in the Information or Technology Age. Surround yourself with those high quality people that are quite good at what they do, and keep in touch with them and allow them to share with you what is new or current, in order to see if there might be something that you can add to assist you and others in your Lifestyle Business.

Levi:
What do you believe the future will be like for home based businesses?

Paul:
It seems to me that all people want the same things, namely to provide a good quality of life for themselves or their families. They want to spend time with those they love, namely their family and friends. They want to feel appreciated and celebrated when they do a job that is well done! They appreciate the recognition that goes along with accomplishment, whether it be in the form of

financial benefit, a gift or plaque, or a time of acknowledgment among their peers!

More and more people want to work from home, spend more quality time with family, and make time to do the things that they enjoy! They are tired of fighting traffic, and living their life by a clock! There are many people that are willing to put in the work or do whatever it takes in order to see light at the end of the tunnel.

People get into debt in order to go to school only to NOT find a job in their area of degree. These are the same people that are putting off things like buying a car, buying a home, or even getting married due to being thousands of dollars in debt. With no savings or security in the workplace, older people are looking for ways to create supplemental or even retirement income. The term Middle class is almost extinct.

I am a firm believer that the Home or Lifestyle Business Industry can provide a vehicle to help anyone achieve their 'Why.' When you have determined your 'Why', the 'How' and 'What' will follow.

Start with your core purpose, cause, or belief, which is your 'Why.' When you have your Why, then there is nothing that can hold you back!

Levi:
Why do you do what you do?

Paul:

My short answer is, "To introduce, educate, train and engage the regular, common, ordinary person like myself, to become an Entrepreneur!" Why, because I truly believe that anyone can be successful. And just to be fair and transparent, I also work with many educated and already successful people too!

I could or would like to also add that I do what I do because I enjoy presenting, mentoring, and then watching others take full advantage of the opportunity to create an EXTRAORDINARY Lifestyle Business through developing new and exciting relationships! It changes others' lives, and my life, at the same time!

There is something special and quite fulfilling when I find that special person(s) that is willing to engage in their new endeavor, and have that 'I will NOT quit till I achieve the intended goal' type of attitude and determination... there is nothing quite like it!

That is why I do what I do, because I have experientially learned, and it is worth repeating, what the wonderful Zig Ziglar taught throughout his entire life, "If you can dream it, you can achieve it. You will get all you want in life if you help enough other people get what they want." Another saying has also proven true for me personally, "Choose a profession you love, and you will never have to work a day in your life."

And, then there is the topic of 'residual income' and the idea or opportunity to make more money than anyone else would be willing to pay you for your time or skill! The ability to receive compensation over and over, month after month, year after year, for something that you did one time in the past is totally awesome! Each month that you move forward always adding to what you have accomplished previously. It's just like compounding, or compound interest...

Here is a sophisticated or an 'educated person's' way to think about this business model... Here is the book definition, and then I'll massage it to fit the Lifestyle Business model.

Compound interest is... Interest calculated on the initial principal and also on the accumulated interest of previous periods of a deposit or loan.

Compound interest can be thought of as "interest on interest," and it will make a deposit or loan grow at a faster rate than simple interest... Let me simplify this... because I'm just a High School grad after all...

Allow me to say it this way: You alone start off as the 'initial principal.' However, for each person that joins you in your business and becomes a 'partner' that in turn grows your personal business. It's just like 'interest on interest.' And, for every person, someone other than yourself, that duplicates your efforts and results, they grow all the 'previous interests' at a faster rate than just the initial simple interest or 'initial principal'!

Another term that applies is "geometric progression," which is... "A series of numbers in which each number is multiplied by a particular quantity in order to get the next number, for example 1, 5, 25, 125, etc…" And, another term or phrase that applies here is "exponential growth," which is by definition, "an increase in number or size, at a constantly growing rate."

In your Lifestyle Business through Relationship Marketing, each time that you enroll a new person to join your team, it's like starting a little franchise, and you will receive financial benefit from each new person that you invest in.

It has been said that there are only two basic means to gain wealth, either to have money working for you or to have people working for you! I have found that in my career or business of Relationship Marketing that I have both, which gives the common, regular, ordinary person like me the opportunity to earn an EXTRA-ORDINARY income and to create an amazing lifestyle!

I choose to not only invest in monetary equity, but also people equity!

"One machine can do the work of 50 ordinary men. No machine can do the work of one EXTRAORDINARY man!" – Elbert Hubbard

Levi:
What do you like best about what you do?

Paul:
For me personally, I really appreciate the lifestyle that my business affords me, including being able to spend as much quality time with my family and friends as I choose, the time to take care of my physical wellbeing, and of course the financial security that comes with earning and growing a residual income!

However, one of the most dynamic and fantastic parts of my lifestyle business is meeting and working with like-minded people locally, nationally, and from all around the world, who are also self-motivated, dedicated to giving inspired effort, and who like working with people in a T.E.A.M. building model, as well as receiving recognition and financial compensation for individual productive efforts and accomplishments!

There is something to be said for a person, a group, a company, and a compensation and business model where each person can be generously compensated equal or even greatly ABOVE their productive efforts, perhaps for the first time in their life! Being paid what you are worth or far above what one would think is possible is an actual truism in my Lifestyle Business!

Levi:
If you could share any advice with someone, what would it be?

Paul:
To write out and define your ultimate "Why" for doing whatever you are looking to do. This will be the foundation that you will build your future on. Your "Why" will be what makes you get up and go when you feel like your get up has already went, or when the weather is challenging, or the finances are low, or the child is sick, or any other challenge (real or imagined) that seeks to take you away from pursuing or doing what you want to do!

Make sure to do your "due diligence," investigate "How" you can pursue, leverage, and market yourself, your time, or your business by taking advantage of technology, or systems that will create "Scalability." Here is what I mean by someone or something being scalable; by definition, "a characteristic of a system, model, or function that describes its capability to cope and perform under an increased or expanding workload. A system that scales well will be able to maintain or even increase its level of performance or efficiency when tested by larger operational (or business) demands."

I say it like this, invest a 'consistent' amount of hours into your business, train others to do what you do, and you will always have that balance in your business, as well as balance in your personal, family and spiritual life.

"Everything can be taken from a man but one thing, the last of the human freedoms—to choose one's attitude in any given set of circumstances, to choose one's own way." – Viktor E. Frankl

Levi:
What type of legacy do you want to leave?

Paul:
A legacy that inspired and impacted people's lives locally, nationally,

and globally through freedom, assurance, and abundance!

Regarding 'spiritual freedom' to seek and serve the 'Living God'....

Regarding 'financial freedom' by creating and experiencing 'residual income' month after month, and year after year creating assurance so that someone is then able to freely give of their resources (their time or money) to help others without reservation, as directed by God or opportunity. That to me is having abundance.

Regarding 'time freedom', achieving your S.M.A.R.T. goals, which stands for Specific, Measured, Attainable, Realistic, and Timed goals… that allows a person to choose to NOT have to work 'outside of the home', or 'Not have to work for others on their terms or for their pay scale'! To daily wake and have a clean slate to which you can daily write out what you want to do, rather than having others to tell you what you are doing. Having choices, in every aspect of one's life!

Regarding my family, to leave a 'Heritage' that serves God willfully in obedience to His Word, financially where there would be abundance for not only my children, but also my children's children, and to be remembered as a person that gave his all to help others to also leave a legacy for their families too.

"Let us hear the conclusion of the whole matter: Fear God, and keep His commandments: for this is the whole duty of man." – Ecclesiastes 12:13

Pertaining to Matthew 6:24-34 it is summarized in Matthew 6:33 "But seek ye first the kingdom of God, and His righteousness; and ALL these things shall be added unto you."

I believe in Total Life Changes, connect with me if you want, need, or have desire too!

My Final Thoughts… It has been my own personal experience that has sold me on the reality that anyone can start, grow, and build a Lifestyle Business through Relationship Marketing, no matter where they have been in life. It has been the absolute BEST business decision that I personally have ever made, but it does take courage, determination, some vision, and faith! It's not always easy, BUT just like anything in life that's valuable it IS worth it.

There are three simple rules in life! If you do not GO after what you want, then you'll never have it. If you do not ASK, then the answer will always be NO. If you do not step forward, then you'll always be in the same place.

It has been said of me that I dream too big, but I humbly say back to those people that they think too small.

In closing: Entrepreneurship is living a few years of your life like most people won't, so that you can spend the rest of your life like most people can't.

Start your Entrepreneurial journey with me TODAY!